THE RING OF FIRE

The Rape of Tahiti

THE RING OF FIRE

Volume IV

THE RAPE OF TAHITI

A Typical Nineteenth-Century Colonial Venture
Wherein several European Powers with their
Iron, Pox, Creed, Commerce and Cannon
Violate the Innocence of a Cluster of
Lovely Polynesian Islands in
The South Pacific Ocean

EDWARD DODD

DODD, MEAD & COMPANY · NEW YORK

1 2 3 4 5 6 7 8 9 10

Library of Congress Cataloging in Publication Data

Dodd, Edward H. (Edward Howard), date
The rape of Tahiti.

Bibliography: p.
Includes index.
1. Tahiti—History. I. Title.
DU870.D56 1983   996'.211   82–21997
ISBN 0–396–08114–2

For Camille
First and Last and Always

Contents

CONTENTS

Acknowledgments

A good many quotations, sometimes lengthy ones, have been used in this book. Almost all of them are from people who were in Tahiti at the time, on-the-scene observers or participants. Their passages appear throughout in *italics* rather than in the more conventional (but also more confusing) quotation marks, indentations or smaller-sized type.

I feel I owe much gratitude to these early writers and I owe their presence in a number of cases to Bengt Danielsson, who is a wizard at digging out obscure and almost lost commentators. Many of these I have translated from the French as they are quoted in Danielsson's *Mémorial Polynésienne,* a splendid six-volume work recently published in Tahiti.

I wish to give special thanks to Dr. Kenneth Emory for years of background experience and wisdom. The present-day author whom I have found most helpful is Peter Bellwood and his *Man's Conquest of the Pacific.* Of course the main collaborator, before she died, was, as she always has been, my wife, Camille.

PART ONE

PREHISTORY TO DISASTER

2000 B.C. to A.D. 1850

CHAPTER ONE

The Original Tahitian: Ancestral Traits

B.C.

L ife in Tahiti in the mid-eighteenth century was never the unso-
phisticated paradise of man and nature that it became in romantic European eyes after the raptures of Bougainville. It was instead a
far more developed and mature civilization than it has ever been given
credit for being. The illusion of primitive, uncorrupted Eden was understandably appealing to disenchanted Europeans in the throes of the
Seven Years' War, the conflict that Churchill later called the "real first
world war"; when England was throwing France out of America and
the struggles in Europe were sowing the seeds of the two great revolu-
tions, American then French, to be followed by the disastrous Napoleonic wars.

But Tahitians were not the children their "discoverers" so conde-
scendingly characterized them—and as we still are wont to do even
after two hundred years.

The arrival of the Polynesians themselves in Tahiti was never recorded in any way that our historians consider valid. It was never
incised on clay tablets or penned on scrolls. Instead, it was imprinted,
voluminously and meticulously, in the memorized annals of the chiefly
families and celebrated in the myths and legends of the race. Such
records are little respected, and usually they are even scorned, by our
present-day scientific historians. But it is undeniable that these Polyne-

3

sian people had (and in many ways still have) the most prodigious and detailed memories that are known to exist anywhere in the cultures of mankind. Their memories are their "documentations"; not only in their genealogies which correspond to our history books, but also in their precisely named starry skies (astronomical texts and navigational ephemerides) having individual names for over two hundred stars, and in their incredibly intimate knowledge of the whole scope of their physical surroundings: flowers, trees, rocks, fish, birds, insects, winds (texts of natural science which had, for instance, separate names for seventy different species of the coconut tree).

So although these people had no written records, their oral ones are marvelously convincing. And enough was written down by the early missionaries to give us firm though vague outlines of the original happenings and the ensuing events that led to the well-developed Stone Age culture that was thriving in the islands before the white man came to split it into pieces with the iron of his axe and the iron of his creed.

Most all other Stone Agers in all parts of the world had graduated slowly over hundreds or even thousands of years—through copper and bronze to iron. The Polynesian transition was a thunderclap of months and a handful of years.

We know now that the racial stocks of the Polynesians set out from Southeast Asia some 4000 or 5000 years ago. They migrated through the Indonesian archipelago, where one branch split off southwestward across the Indian Ocean to settle in Madagascar, as the predominant tribes of that fantastically polyglot land, and bestowed their original tongue as the *lingua franca* of the whole almost continental-size Malgash island. The main group continued to make its ways, gradually over centuries of time, past the unfriendly, already inhabited, and malarial-repulsive islands of Melanesia (some think north, some think south of New Guinea), to their first and westernmost island clusters of Fiji, Samoa, and Tonga. They have left along this trail the recently discovered shards of their own highly individualized Lapita pottery. They were quiet people, peaceable, horticultural, and above all maritime— settlers of the littoral; sailors of the high wide seas.

Here these oceanic islanders arrived on virgin land, regrouped, and multiplied. Here they developed their deep-sea sailing skills and evolved their great twin-hulled sailing vessels. Here they probably remained for a breathing spell of some five hundred years, while their ancestral Lapita pottery died out. (Gradually they ceased to boil their food in clay vessels and chose instead to bake it in earth ovens, as they still prefer to do today.) This gradual fading of Lapita pottery from intricate and highly distinctive decorative designs, to plainer and plainer surfaces, to no decoration at all, and then to no pottery at all—is an archaeological mystery. (They had no clay of course on the coral atolls, but it was always available on the volcanic islands.) Another mystery is the total absence of the wheel or even, apparently, a knowledge of its principle, not even in toys. They had a disc drill, but this was a reciprocating sort of flywheel, not a burden bearer. And of course they used rollers to move their great canoes ashore—sometimes indeed they were human bodies. The wheel must have been known in their Asiatic homelands so it too must have faded out like their pottery. But of course virtually all of their locomotion in the islands was by water. Everywhere they were seaside dwellers and when they made their brief excursions inland into the steep mountains, wheels would have been of little use to them.

After a half millenium in the three western Pacific island clusters, portions of these people set out to the east to discover new islands. We have radio-carbon dates and artifact sequences that place those migrations at around the time of the birth of Christ. Many modern scholars believe that it was in these three original island groups, and over this first millenium in the Pacific ocean, that they actually *became* Polynesian: a conglomerate racial mix, mostly mongoloid, but with some small percentage perhaps of caucasoid, and a dash-in-passing of australoid,* developed or evolved what we now recognize as a distinctive Polynesian culture.

As population pressures commenced to build up, the more adventur-

---

*Anthropologists are wary of dividing man up into races, but Carleton Coon's theory is simple and imaginative. There are five main races, he says: *caucasoid* or white from the areas embraced by the Black and Caspian seas; *mongoloid* or yellow from the heart of China and migrated via Bering Strait throughout the Americas; *australoid* or blue-black from the northern uplands of India pushed by Aryan caucasoid invasions into Papua-New Guinea, Australia and Tasmania; *negroid* or brown-black from equatorial Africa; *bushmanoid* or light brown from south Africa.

ous, or the exiled, or the deprived set sail in migratory waves—waves so small that they probably should be called ripples: eight, ten or a dozen canoe loads in a "fleet," at the most two hundred or three hundred men, women, children, with pigs, dogs, chickens and food plants. And at least one "useless" flower.

It is my personal belief that these adventurers knew where they were going, that advance scouting expeditions (of men only, in specially equipped expeditionary canoes) first explored different star-courses as far as what would have been their point of no return, until—probably after several disappointments—they spotted distant new islands. They then sailed back before the prevailing easterly winds to their home-lands. With the newly discovered star-courses implanted in the master navigator's brain, they then set about preparing their migratory groups —probably over at least one year, maybe two or even three—so that the star-course they had discovered and chosen could be taken up again, in the proper annual season, to lead them to a new homeland.

In such migrations they settled, first off, the central Polynesian islands, the Marquesan and Society groups, some two thousand miles to the east, to the windward of their home islands. Here again, as the archaeological datings tell us, they must have passed a few centuries before reaching the new population densities that would entice or urge or compel them to make exploratory voyages again. To the east they sailed—Easter Island. To the south—the Australs and Cooks. To the north—Hawaii. To the southwest—New Zealand. And in the mean-time some of them even sailed back to the original western homelands and beyond—the "Outliers."*

Thus, they distributed themselves over every inhabitable island in the vast Pacific several hundred years before the Europeans arrived to find them. They had fully populated an oceanic triangle five thousand miles on each side: 12 million square miles, an area larger than the whole of Africa, the most widespread single cohesive culture (although one of the smallest in numbers) anywhere on earth.

*The so-called Outliers are distinctly Polynesian islands embedded in Melanesian or Micronesian ocean areas: Kapingamerangi and Nukuoro to the north, Tikopia and Ontong Java to the west, and many others.

In so doing, they created—shortly before or after the birth of Christ —a separate civilization of their own, entirely isolated from, and entirely unknown to, the patchwork of civilizations on the other side of the world. After Polynesia reached its ultimate extent with the colonizations of Easter Island, Hawaii, and New Zealand, each of these two separate civilizations, dating back to the original birthplace in Fiji-Tonga-Samoa, had now been going its own way for at least three thousand years—as if both had been on different planets.

I have been playing a little geographical-ethnological game comparing events and developments within these two hemispheres, strangers to each other. One, we might call the "hemisphere of land" where men of different races marched or straggled to and fro mixing with each other, warring, trading, interbreeding; emerging as conquerors, subsiding as slaves. The other is the "hemisphere of water," almost equal in area, but minute in living space, where only one race proliferated to all the distant island outposts, retaining its unique homogeneity like a single closely related but widely scattered family. There was almost no intercourse between those outposts. They received variations of stimulus only from variations of ecology, and these, in the tropics, were changes of slight degree.

The comparative highlights of history of these two independent "hemispheres," are shown on the next two following pages. They parallel each other for the three thousand-odd years since their Original Split until the fateful engagement date of A.D. 1767, when the two worlds discovered each other.

Perhaps the best way to convey an impression of what Tahitian life was like in the latter half of the eighteenth century is to contrast some of the basic essentials with our own. Their physical conditions, housing, food, clothing, daily activities, and suchlike have all been detailed so often that they need no repetition here. Of course group comparisons —racial and social—tend to lead to treacherous generalizations, but if they are not used to upgrade or downgrade, they can be interesting to explore. A. G. Keller, disciple of the great William Graham Sumner, used to tell his students at Yale, myself among them, that the four

THE LAND WORLD

Year	ASIA & AMERICAS	EUROPE & ENGLAND	GREECE, ROME & MIDEAST	Year
1800	American Revolution	French Revolution / James Cook		1800
1700	Conquest of India			1700
1600	Taj Majal / Magellan	Louis XIV / Shakespeare		1600
1500	Columbus	Martin Luther / Gutenberg—*Printing*		1500
1400	Apex of the Inca	Henry the Navigator / The Black Death		1400
1300	Marco Polo	Chaucer	Ottoman Empire	1300
1200	Kublai Khan	Magna Carta		1200
1100	Sung Dynasty	Chartres Cathedral	The Eight Crusades	1100
1000	Gunpowder invented / Greenland visited	William the Conqueror		1000
900				900
800	Apex of the Maya	King Alfred		800
700	Great Buddha of Nara—*Japan*	Charlemagne	Fall of Rome	700
600	Tang Dynasty	Arthur's Round Table ·	First Popes	600
500	Sui Dynasty	Saxons invade England	Mohammed	500
400	Quipu Mnemonic Knots—*Peru*	Attila the Hun	Sack of Rome	400
300	Gupta in India	Romans leave Britain		300
200	Tea first drunk			200
100	Kanishka founds Kushana dynasty in India	St. Patrick in Ireland	Saint Paul	100
0	Magnetic Compass—*China*	Caesar invades Britain	Jesus born	0
100	Chin Dynasty		Carthage destroyed	100
200	Great Wall of China started		Aristotle	200
300	Alexander in India		Alexander the Great / Marathon	300
400	Buddha born		Coinage invented	400
500	Confuscius		Roman Republic	500
600	Upanishads / Lao Tse		Parthenon	600
700			Romulus & Remus	700
800			Homer	800
900	Chou Dynasty	Iron Age begins	Solomon	900
1000	Rigveda	Bronze Age ends	1st Phoenician Voyaging	1000
1100			Fail of Troy	1100
1200			Moses & the Exodus	1200
1300	Aryans invade India		Late Bronze Age	1300
1400	Shang Bronze Age		Alphabet invented	1400
1500			Iron Age begins	1500

	TONGA & SAMOA	MARQUESAS, TAHITI & EASTER	HAWAII, NEW ZEALAND, COOKS, ETC.	
1800	Tui Kanopuolu Dynasty continues to today	Mahaiatia Marae—T	Kamehameha—H	1800
1700		Statues toppled—E / Hane IV—M	Pas & tatooed heads—NZ / Lei niho palaoa—H	1700
1600	Tui Kanopuolu Dynasty—Tonga	Oponuhu–T	Greenstone—NZ	1600
1500	Tui Ha'a Dynasty—Tonga		Pu'uhonua site—H	1500
1400	Tui Mu'a Dynasty—Tonga	Orongo—E	Maori overpopulation, warfare & decline	1400
1300	Langi burial mounds—Tonga	Statue building—E	Moa extinction—NZ	1300
1200	Paepae o Telea—Tonga		Valley settlement—H	1200
1100		Hane III—M	Waiahukini site—H	1100
1000	Ha'amonga Trilithon	Hane II—M	New Zealand settled / Mangareva settled	1000
900		Maupiti burial—T	Rarotonga settled	900
800		Vinapu & Tahai—E	Halawa site—H / Tubuai settled	800
700		Vaitootai site—T		700
600	Mound Construction—Samoa	Great Ahu construction—E	Hawaii settled	600
500		Hane I—M		500
400	Kumara (sweet potato) introduced from S. America	Easter settled		400
300		Tahiti settled		300
200	Exploratory voyaging 1000-1400 miles to east	Marquesas settled		200
100	All pottery ceases			
0	Triangular adze crosses the Andesite Line			
100	Adze Kit III, Ovens begin			
200	Pottery loses decoration			
300	West Samoa settled			
400	Lapita losing decoration			
500	Adze Kit II			
600	Lapita starts fading			
700				
800	Voyaging, Navigation and Trade			
900	Lapita flourishes			
1000	Voyaging flourishes, Samoa settled; Adze Kit 1			
1100	Interisland Voyaging			
1200	Tonga settled			
1300	Interisland Voyaging starts			
1400	Fiji settled			
1500	Early Lapita in Eastern Melanesia / Migrations from Indonesia to Melanesia			

Since the Polynesians left no written records, we have only legendary accounts of their great heroes and events. These epics are copious and wonderful, but there is no way to date them. This WATER WORLD table, therefore, is taken only from hard archeological evidence. Lapita Pottery is our most significant clue to the earliest stages of the developing culture. The Adze Kits refer to distinct, datable refinements of tools, weapons, utensils, houses, canoes, arts and crafts in the parental or core island clusters of Fiji-Tonga-Samoa. The Hane series shows similar sequences in the Marquesas. Place names of fruitful "digs" indicate progressions in the other islands. Tahiti today has scarcely been scratched and the Cooks, Australs, Gambiers, etc. lay waiting to reveal their share of the mysteries that led all of these widely scattered islands to the high points of culture that were first discovered by us landlubbers just prior to 1800.

The LAND WORLD table shows a parallel set of familiar high-spot historical coincidences.

fundamental drives of man are Hunger, Love, Vanity, and Fear; in that order. Let me try to contrast those of the "prehistoric" Polynesian with our own, both contemporary and (since none of us has changed much) present day.

Hunger we can in this instance virtually dismiss, because it did not exist in Polynesia as a constantly motivating force. To be sure, there were times of sporadic, devastating dryness that caused widespread famine and even impelled migrations, but as we shall see later, methods of birth control, by abortion and infanticide, seem to have anticipated and ameliorated these aberrational shocks. It is hard for us bread-by-the-sweat-of-the-brow people to comprehend this, but everyone, almost all of the time, had plenty of food and experienced no trouble in getting it.

Love is perhaps the most intriguing of the other three drives. The contrasts in the realms of love are subtle and infinitely more complex than the popular assumption. Let us start at the beginning. (Conception? No, that belongs later on, in sex.) Birth. Many Polynesian infants never drew a first breath because they were strangled by their parents, usually their fathers, before they could take a first breath. In many respects, though not all, this was the main means of birth control. (Our corresponding one is abortion.) And birth control was even more important to them on their finite little islands—in an earlier stage of the evolution of their culture—than ours is now in an overpopulated, finite globe. We are only just beginning to realize the absolute necessity of abortion. You may cringe, as the missionaries did, at what they considered the unspeakable horror of infanticide, but if a fetus is to be curtailed, what really is the difference between three months and nine? Mind you, the importance to the Tahitian of a baby's first breath. If the mother wished to and was able to trick the fetus's father into going fishing or going into the mountains to fetch the orange-colored plantain, or going to carry a present to his sister on the other side of the island, or whatever, an hour before delivery, so that when he returned the infant was breathing, no power or spirit would make him go through with his obligation to snuff out the life. Because, with the first breath, life had begun, and no social law told him to be a murderer.

His duty to society, and also the mother's to social survival, was to abort the life before it started. So let that be the first contrast to our mores.

The next phase of the Love category is probably circumcision, though it may be menstruation. Circumcision was universal. Why this curious and useless operation was practiced throughout that independent oceanic offshoot of the human race is as old and unfathomable a riddle as any worldwide anthropological mystery. The Polynesian's way was a bit different from ours because the foreskin was split only along the top, not ringed round and removed. It was done with the razor-sharp edge of a split bamboo and I think with not much ritual, just a formal family occasion. But it was invariable and oceanwide.

Menstruation was more important—though less, or not at all, ceremonial. The unfortunate maiden was secluded as unclean, untouchable, even unseeable during her menstrual periods. Hers must have been a humiliating ordeal, and it might be said to have lasted a lifetime for a woman. In most ways she was distinctly inferior in Polynesian society. If you ate with a woman you became blind and crippled. The best foods—turtle, pig, and choice portions of others—were forbidden her. No woman was allowed on the community *marae,* the holy place of worship and sacrifice, although she could participate on the family *marae.* All of this must stem from the universal prejudice against menstrual blood: unclean. And yet, paradoxically, Polynesian society was in many ways matriarchal. Land was inherited from chiefesses and firstborn females. Lesser chiefs often became greater chiefs through their mother's or wife's lineage, when their father was not so high. The social fabric was shot through with Victorias, big and small. Ariitaimai tells us that *no where in the world was marriage a matter of more political and social consequence than in Tahiti.* (Ariitaimai will be a significant figure in this narrative. Her *Memoirs* recounted to Henry Adams toward the end of her life are a wealth of ancient Tahitian lore. We quote her here, long before she was born, because they retell the tales passed down to her through her ancestors, vividly depicting their customs and personalities, and recalling the legends of her race. She herself will be introduced later when, as a young maiden of high birth and dazzling charm, she enters upon her long and subtly influential role in Tahitian history.) *A powerful chiefess was free from her husband's control. She could have as many lovers as she wished but she could not rear a child of non-chiefly origin. He must be killed. There once was a chief of Papara, Ariifaataia, who wanted to marry Maheanu, chiefess of Vaiari and reigning beauty of the island. But she would have none of him. She thought him too ugly so she married a handsome lower born. Maheanu was not disposed to throw her beauty away merely for power.* Paradoxes, violent ones, are characteristic of this volatile race.

Once these rites or stages of puberty were passed, life was good for nubile Polynesians. They were not only permitted but expected to be promiscuous. Most of them were probably ready for sex before they were teenage, and "experimenting" usually lasted until the early twenties, a matter of eight or ten years. By then perhaps one would know pretty well whom one could marry with some expectation of duration. Captain Bligh enlightens us with a firsthand report:

The Women have too great an intercourse with different Men. ... [Yet] it is considered no infidelity, for I have known a Man to have done the Act in the presence of his own Wife, and it is a common thing for the Wife to assist the Husband in these Amours. But what is remarkable, it is not so among those who are not related to one another; it is then a violation if a married Couple err on either side, for if a Man finds another with his Wife he'll kill him if he can, and if the Woman discovers infidelity of the Husband she will certainly take revenge on the Woman.

Inclination seems to be the only binding law of Marriage in this Country, for a Woman will quit her husband if she pleases.

Once married, divorce was rare. Nonmarital sex was all right within reason and discretion, and illegitimate children were gladly adopted, but the family entity was very important, more sacred than personal infatuations or rivalries. After all, and above all, family meant land and inheritance. A man's land, or his wife's land, was his or her future on earth. They never conceived of a future in heaven or hell; just a flapping about of spirits for a while or the enduring virtues of a respected ancestor, represented by his skull stored in the rafters of the house. The constant, permanent symbol, the enduring entity of family was the *marae*, their open-air, rock-and-coral temple, their only structures of permanence. We must always keep in mind that these sacred stones were, for the Polynesian, what transcended and made lasting for generations his transient flesh. You might say their *maraes* were their counterparts of written histories. Ariitaimai says: *The marae represented more than all else, the family. Even the god was secondary. The family and the antiquity were alone seriously interesting. . . . Genealogy swallowed up history and made law a field of its own; it was the legal code.*

Let us assume that the next turn of Love is toward children. Here the Polynesian is characteristically more doting and indulgent than we are. A European's first reaction is that they spoil their babies inordinately. But they also scowl and slap and punish. After a while we realize that the essence of their treatment of children is perhaps more like a game; much play, some of it fun, some of it serious contention and training. Always there is a respect for the child as an equal entity as worthy to be fought with as to be loved. Remember that first breath and that succession on birth. These are embedded things, so long implanted as to become instinctual perhaps. But the enveloping element is attention and care. No Polynesian child is ever neglected.

Following these early-age contrasts between our Love lives and theirs, I would guess there is not much difference in our societal ways. Less divorce; more loyalty to and concern for the older generations, but that is to be expected in a smaller more familial group. Except of course the lifelong inferiority of the female. This is a notable present-day difference, but was it two hundred years ago? Women of Europe ate with their men, but the men owned and controlled property to a degree that never was obtained in Polynesia. In France even today the husband owns just about everything.

My great Yale sociologist's third fundamental drive, Vanity, can be very broadly defined to include such urgings or surgings as ambition, artistic attainment, supremacy in sports and war and oratory; heroism and grandeur as well as pride, shame and indulgence. And when so defined there is little basic difference between our social ways, except for the emphases placed on them. The Polynesian had no money and no interest in it and thus passed by one of our greatest vanities, wealth. But the ancient oriental element of "face" was decidedly more important to him than to a European. His highest art was the art of oratory. He revelled in the prowess of war, but his warfare was much more personal and formalized—more like our jousting of medieval knights. His devotion to sports was, as is ours, an obvious means of displaying personal vanities. But he far exceeded us in diversity. He played hundreds of games, from childhood up, and played them constantly; stilts, a sort of lob-in-the-air bowling, archery, kite flying, surfboarding, canoe racing of many sorts (first models, then kite sailing, plain sailing, paddling). Such as these were in addition to the usual combative and body-to-body contact or competitive sports like wrestling, racing afoot and in the water, boxing, etc. But it is notable that boxing was never bloody—body blows only, with the decision resting on a sort of mutual recognition of "points." And we must not forget the never-ceasing "sports" (which we might better call arts) of singing and dancing. Even eating became a refined form of vanity when they competed with each other in huge, recurrent, extravagant feasts.

The spectacular arts of the peripheral Polynesians obviously seem to have sprung from the vanities of their individual creators or their patrons, but these graphic or sculptural arts of the Tahitians are a puzzle, difficult to assess or to compare with those of their fellow Polynesians.

The Hawaiians have created the most stunning wooden statutes and the most brilliant use of color in featherwork; the Maori the most intricate and ingenious bas relief and screenic carvings; the Easter Islanders the most monumental stone sculpture and the smoothest, most meticulous wooden ancestral figures; the Cook and Austral Islanders exquisite pattern carving and god figures; the Marquesans the most versatile (in all respects) stone and wood carvings and tikis—and in graphics their labyrinthine tatu designs surpass all. Even the relatively stuffy ancestral folks, the Samoans, Tongans, and Fijiians, worked wonders with tapa, whale ivory, and shapely wooden tools and implements of war.

In contrast to all of these Polynesian cousins, the Tahitian appears a crude fellow. He has his inspirations. His fly-whisk handles are superb and mysterious, but they do seem frivolous objects on which to lavish one's subtlest craftsmanship. Some authorities think the finest of Tahitian carvings may have been burned in the great bonfires of Christian conversion. But I doubt it. Tahitian gods were sennit-woven bundles, receptacles for the spirits of their gods, never images of them. Their crude stone tikis seem more likely to have been ancestor figures—reminders rather than art.

No, the Tahitian's arts were the living ones: dance, drama, oratory, laughter and fresh-flower dress. In these (whether you call them exhibitionist vanities or performing arts) he rejoiced and excelled, but these arts left no tangible trace for us—only hearsay and echoes, which still reverberate today in the most joyous, playful, life-loving people of the ocean.

They had their skills, all right. Their superb canoes bear witness to that. These were unsurpassed in variety, size, craftsmanship, as well as the art with which they sailed them. And we should emphasize their songs. They were conceived and composed spontaneously, for almost any sort of occasion or occurrence: sad ones for partings, mournful ones for funerals, scornful ones for ridicule, joyous ones for any happy event, and most of all, perhaps, romantic ones for lovers lost or found, blessed or crossed.

Thus, in the realm of Vanity we might concede to the Tahitians the pleasures and exercises of the body and the senses, and reserve for our own vanities the exhilarations of the intellect and exercises of the brain.

So, for the enduring objects of art, one must look around the borders of Polynesia, not into the center. But for the transitory, lively arts one must turn from the relatively dour, pious, proper, savage, and warlike Hawaiians, Marquesans, Rapans, Rarotongans, Maori, Tongans, and Samoans to the gay, abandoned hedonists of the central core, our Tahitians.

Fear, the last of the four contrasting drives, is for us dominated by fear of loss—poverty, position, health, bodily injury, even loss of mind, insanity. But of course the most pervading and terrorizing of all our fears is death. In studying the Polynesian it has long seemed remarkable to me that of these primary fears of ours none was of much consequence to him. He seems in present reality as well as in historical and prehistorical retrospect to be almost immune to—and certainly casual about—them. One wonders whether instinct can account for this, as it seems persuasively to account for the Polynesian's almost total lack of fear of heights. (Like the American Indian, he can always get a highly paid job walking girders on skyscrapers and bridges.) Is it because he has scampered up coconut trees for untold generations—an acquired characteristic, anathema to geneticists—or was he born that way?

Where there is no pressure of money or lack of food there is obviously no fear of poverty. Position was foreordained by ancestral and parental rank, so there was no losing of it; nor much gaining either. As a race the Polynesians were extraordinarily healthy and had almost no diseases until the white man came: little to worry about on that score. (An exception was elephantiasis, but though sometimes hideously crippling, it was neither painful nor mortal.) About wounds, broken bones, even cracked skulls, the Polynesian seems to have been philosophical and capable of bearing what we would consider excruciating pain. But he knew he would heal quickly (if he didn't die quickly).

Let us set aside for a moment his psychological fears, to consider the Big Fear: death. Many a learned and experienced, sensitively intuitive writer has reported on the wondrous, calm resignation of the Polynesian confronted with his own death. Most striking are the many reliably recorded instances of people actually willing themselves to die. They made (and still make) a great fuss about another's death. Never has there been such wailing and lamentation, gashing of foreheads with shark's teeth to let the blood run, chopping off finger joints, setting out corpses to be mummified and watched over, polishing bones and skulls to be hidden away or revered as household companions. Yet, a personal, anticipatory fear of death seems not to have been a significant part of the Polynesian's emotional spectrum. He had no Heaven and no Hell, no afterlife in our sense of the concept (if there is any sense in it). He was fatalistic. He knew his time would come, and everyone who has lived with Polynesians knows that they have only the most casual, offhand sense of time.

But that, on our part, is perhaps a casual, offhand way of dismissing a very complex state of mind or emotion and it leads us back to the bypassed subject of imaginary fears. All people are haunted and harried by ghosts, witches, warlocks, trolls, elves, furies, banshees, and fairies —good and bad. I doubt, however, that they were as manifest and omnipresent or as terrifying in any culture as they were in the Polynesian.

The *oromatua* and *tu'paupau* were, and still are, everywhere. These were the ancestral spirits, almost invariably evil. One could hear them in the screech of the night birds, feel them in sudden gusts of wind round the corner, smell them in a crushed *tupa* crab, taste them in the brimstone of lightning. The only sense that failed one was sight. They were never to be seen, these evil spirits—even when they ate you or your child or your mother-in-law—remorselessly with long, sharpened teeth.

The Polynesian's fear of the spirits of the dead must be classified as psychotic I suppose, because we know it was an imagined fear, and that's the way we classify fears that are not real. But they were *real* to the Polynesian, not the unreal fears that we declare to be those of a sick man. If they were unreal to him, and therefore sick (and therefore curable by a good psychiatrist?), then the whole race was a society of sick men, for the *tu'paupau*s existed. Everybody knew they did. No one would ever say "Nonsense" or "That's your imagination." They would just hasten to make some magic to scare the evil one away, propitiate him/her, to hide or beg off till tomorrow's morning light.

So the Polynesian had his fears all right. It's just that they were different from ours. Might one say his were spiritual and ours are physical? What is Death, spiritual or physical?

I hope I have given the reader a glimmer at least of some of the basic contrasts between our separately evolved, ancestral social compositions. I am not advocating Hunger, Love, Vanity, and Fear as in any way being the *definitive* drives or norms or precepts. No doubt for the present-day social scientist they are now fifty years out of fashion. But this is not intended to be a comprehensive or scientific set of comparisons, merely a sampling. And my old social science teacher's Big Four are certainly with us still.

*   *   *

Two other elements of primary importance in contrasting our two cultures should be added to the Big Four, climate and religion.

Until you have lived for many years in these tropic salt-wind-swept, rain-cloud-drenched, sun-scorched, insect-munched islands, it is hard to realize how transient, how rapidly perishable is human flesh and all the fabrications contrived by it. Paintings, books, clothes, houses, even churches of coral blocks disintegrate and melt into the all-embracing compost of these tropics. They dissolve and give up their ghosts at a rate that is astonishing and despairing to those of us who have been building libraries, castles, galleries, cathedrals over the centuries. If, even in our benign temperate climates, our museums are desperately inventing and applying preservatives everywhere, for Florence, Venice, Easter Island and the dissolving Acropolis, how could the Polynesian preserve his precious works?

He didn't: he accepted. He built his house to last at most a generation. His roof he rethatched every four years if woven of *niau* coco fronds, seven years if of *fara* pandanus. His canoe hull, which took him two years to hew out, lasted perhaps seven years with constant care; its outrigger two or three years. Everything was contrived, used, discarded. Everything was as expendable, at their slower pace, as plastics, at our frantic pace, are to us today. Everything, that is, except the *marae*. Not only were its basalt boulders and coral slabs the Tahitian's concept of endurance, but the *mana*, the magic in them was longer lasting still. For when a clan set forth to found a new settlement on another island; or when a family left its ancestral *marae* for another shore; or when a son left his family temple to set up his own around the point, a special stone sacred to that clan, that family, that son, was always taken with them as the founding stone for the new *marae*, and the name of the ancestral *marae* was carried on as family names are perpetuated from generation to generation in the descendant *marae*

Except perhaps for a brief flirtation with disembodied spirits, I have not touched on the Tahitian's religion. Just where it belongs in those four big categories, I am not sure—perhaps partly in all of them;

perhaps mostly in Vanity and Fear. In any case, our religions were of
primary importance to both of us in the 1760s and they were different.
We will come to that dramatically and poignantly when we come to
consider the missionaries, later on. But here we should perhaps sketch
a brief outline of the nature of the Polynesian's religious belief. The
concept of creation is pithily expressed in the old chant to the originating god:

> *He was there Taaroa · was his name*
> *All about him was emptiness*
> *No where the land · No where the sky*
> *No where the sea · No where man*
> *Taaroa called out · No echo to answer*
>
> *Then in this solitude he became the world*
> *This knot of roots it is Taaroa*
> *The rocks are he again*
> *Taaroa · The song of the sea*
> *Taaroa · He named himself*
> *Taaroa · Transparence*
> *Taaroa · Eternity*
> *Taaroa · The Powerful*
>
> *Creator of the Universe which is but the shell of Taaroa*
> *Who bestows on it life in beautiful harmony*

It is a great pity the Polynesians never evolved a Homer, because
their chants and legends are wonderfully rich material, as distinctive as
Greek epics, Norse sagas, or Indian Vedas and Puranas. The creation
chants tell how Taaroa lay in the darkness of his shell for countless ages.
Nothing existed outside this shell—and even the nothingness is specified (no light, no noise, no sea, etc., etc.) at such lengths that the ages
do indeed seem boundless.

Eventually Taaroa himself becomes weary of inaction and begins to
stir. The shell cracks and, at length, he pushes it apart so that its upper
half becomes the dome of the sky. Then he converts the lower portion

into the Great Foundation Rock, Tumunui, which stands in utter darkness far down in a crevice of the extinct crater of the Temehani, by a great rushing stream of water called Vaitupo. Next, he commences the very long process of manufacturing the other gods; first, Tane (god of forests, rain, fertility); then, the other principals: Tu (stability), Atea (vast expanse),* Oro (war), etc. The list is bounteous and it is also confusing, because in the different island groups (such as the Tuamotus, Cooks, Australs, Hawaii, New Zealand) the various gods were given different attributes and different degrees of importance. (Even Tangaroa, the original, becomes only the god of the sea in Mangaia.) But it is a notable fact that in spite of superficial inconsistencies of function and rank, the same names are used throughout the distant island groups.

The secondary gods set about the housekeeping job of tidying up the universe. They prop up the heavens, create the stars, cover the earth with water, then pull up various islands with a fishing pole and magic hook. Most importantly, one or another of the gods fashions man and woman and sets them to propagating, while still others are clothing the mountains with forests, filling the seas with fish, calling forth all the various winds, and so on. Many of the final tasks, such as fetching fire and fishing up further islands, were left to demigods like Maui, for the members of the Polynesian pantheon, like those of their Greek contemporaries, did a good deal of consorting with humans—in the olden days, that is. There were many of these demigods: Hiro (patron of thieves) and another Hiro (the master canoe builder), Uahenga (*tatu* artist), Tafai (the overseas adventurer). But by far the most widely known and most popular of all was Maui, about whom, from the mythologist's point of view, perhaps the most remarkable thing was his ubiquity. Mauitikitiki was his full name, and he is found not only in the folklore of all the Polynesian islands; he was widely known in many areas of Micronesia and Melanesia as well. I believe he is the only hero of primitive religions who covers such distant territories.

Thus the Polynesian had a pantheon almost as populous as the

---

*Atea was usually female, and, fertilized by Taaroa, was the begetress of most of the other gods.

Greeks, but the most significant feature of it was that it was clearly *man* centered, rather than *god* centered. The gods were created for the benefit, though often the chastisement, of man. They had great powers for good and evil, but if one fishing god did not bring good luck or one war god bring victory, even after sacrifices, pleas, praises, and threats, he could be tossed aside and another one enlisted. Tane had been the paramount god for the Tahitians for many generations, but shortly before the white man's arrival (perhaps less than one hundred years before), Oro had come into fashion and power. Through his creation, the Arioi society, Oro's gospel was spreading from Raiatea throughout the islands, and he was certainly in the ascendant when Captain Wallis arrived in 1767 on Her Majesty's Ship *Dolphin*.

CHAPTER TWO

The Original Tahitian:
Human Nature

A.D.

O n Tahiti in the 1750s and 1760s there was clearly a hierarchical, feudal-like society: of high chiefs, the *arii,* who were very high indeed; of landowners or nobles, called the *raatira;* and of an ordinary lowborn class called *manahune* or *teuteu.* But unlike his European counterpart even the lowest could feed himself readily and build himself a shelter against the storms. While he lived as a servant-companion in his master's house or tilled his own "sharecropping" acre of his master's land, he still possessed a very important social right. If he deemed his *raatira* cruel or excessively demanding or unfair, he could pull up stakes and take his valuable labor to the land of another feudal lord, who would almost certainly welcome him. There were, significantly, no constraints upon this right except, importantly, the consent and sympathy of his fellow *manahune.*

The house of the highest chief was not much larger or more luxurious than anyone else's. There was no money, no gold, no jewels—and thus no riches piled up. Not even possessions such as mats or bark cloth, houses, or even canoes ever accumulated substantially as one man's property as contrasted with another's. To be sure the high chiefs gathered gifts or tribute in large quantities on occasions, but these were soon redistributed.

Nordoff and Hall have a nice way of explaining: *In these eastern*

22

*islands the humblest speaks to the most powerful without any title of
respect, with nothing corresponding to our "mister" or "sir." At first one
is inclined to believe that here is the beautiful and ideal democracy—
the realization of the communist's dream—and there are other things
which lead to the same conclusion. Servants, for one example, are treated
with extraordinary consideration and kindliness; when the feast is over
the mistress of the household is apt as not to dance with the man who
feeds her pigs, or the head of the family to take the arm of the girl who
has been waiting on his guests. The truth is that this impression of
equality is false; there are not many places in the world where a more
rigid social order exists—not of caste, but of classes. In the thousand or
fifteen hundred years that they have inhabited the islands the Polynesians have worked out a system of human relationships nearer the ultimate, perhaps, than our own idealists would have us believe. Wealth
counts for little, birth for everything; it is useless for an islander to think
of raising himself in a social way—where he is born he dies, and his
children after him. On the other hand, except for the abstract pleasure
of position, there is little to make the small man envious of the great;
he eats the same food, his dress is the same, he works as little or as much,
and the relations between the two are of the pleasantest. There is a really
charming lack of ostentation in these islands, where everything is known
about everyone, and it is useless to pretend to be what one is not. That
is at the root of it all—here is one place in the world, at least, where
every man is sure of himself.*

The one exception to this general state of relative equality of tangible
objects was, however, a very important one. It was land. Land was
inherited and land was bequeathed. Its possession was sacred and invio-
late to the bloodline of the family that owned it. Such ownership could
be enlarged or diminished only by marriage or by death. Even a victorious warrior could not take possession without marrying the widow or
sister or daughter of his slain foe; and even then it was not he who took
full title, but his progeny by the new wife. Peter Bellwood makes an
interesting comment: *There was no private ownership of land in the
English legal sense, although in practice a lineage or family had the right
to use its land in perpetuity.*

But though there were high chiefs in Tahiti, there was no king, no supreme monarch or Inca, Emperor, Maharaja or Mikado, as was to be found in virtually all other societies, primitive or sophisticated, all over the world. On this island and indeed on all other Pacific islands and groups of islands, all of them Polynesian, there were balanced clans with chiefs, some stronger or richer in land or prestige than others, but never a supreme chief. This is a curious societal phenomenon, and I believe you will find it rarely except in the Polynesian race. An American Indian anthropologist might cry, Exception! But the American tribes lived in widely separated, extensive territories, each one speaking its own language, while the Tahitian clans (not tribes) were crowded together on one small island group, with one language only. Each was, in effect, one large family.

Tahiti itself had many chiefs of its many districts. These areas were demarcated by the ridges of the many V-shaped valleys that radiate like jagged pieces of a pie from the central mountain peaks of the island. They vary greatly in size and shape of course, but their boundaries were as precisely known—to the inch—as were the complex kinships of aunts, uncles, cousins, children, and grandchildren of the fundamental owner, male or female. And there are valleys within valleys, which meant chiefs and subchiefs (or *raatira*) within chiefdoms. There are also islands and peninsulas and other natural divisions and subdivisions. The Polynesian was never a geometrical fellow as far as land was concerned, so in ancestral days there were never plots or blocks of land laid out in surveys as they are so meticulously delineated by the French today. The result was a multitude of landlords and properties that would be impossibly confusing, except to a Polynesian. Fortunately he had a memory and traditions as precise and reliable as a thousand books of affidavits and deeds.

An old-time tale is told of a chief in Raiatea who had a restless and ambitious younger son. Because his older brother was to inherit the land, the younger one set forth in a fine double canoe, well provisioned with fruits, animals, women, and male companions. Four generations later a descendant of his returned to the valley in Raiatea. There he learned that the original older brother's family had died out, so he claimed the ancient homeland. They asked him for proof of his rights and he recited without flaw the whole genealogy of the family, going back to the originating gods. This would have been a sacred family secret, so he was accepted immediately and granted the chieftainship of the land.

Just how so many ranks and files of blood relationships would balance out without a supreme authority is a puzzle to us. But for them it was resolved by a system (can one call such a tangle a "system"?) of clans and chiefs of clans. And in this way, broadly related blood genes took precedence over what might otherwise seem hopelessly scattered and complicated pieces of soil. There were, and had been since time immemorial, four or five or six dominant clans and for many generations preceding the fateful European arrival, these clans had always produced recognized senior, or paramount, chiefs or chiefesses. These were the governing body of the island.

An engaging insight into their personal relationships as well as into the vagaries of Tahitian love is given us by Ariitaimai.

About the year 1650, Tavi was chief of Tautira, and prided himself on being as generous as he was strong. All chiefs were obliged to be generous or they lost the respect and regard of their people; but Tavi was the most generous of all the chiefs of Tahiti. He had a wife, Taurua of Hitiaa, the most beautiful woman of her time.

The chief of Papara and head of the Tevas at that time was Tuiterai. Like many a vain chief in Tahiti, Tuiterai could not hear of a handsome woman without wanting her; but Tavi's wife was a person of too much consequence to be approached except in the forms of courtesy required between chiefs, and therefore Tuiterai sent his iotai or ambassador to Tavi to request the loan of his wife, with a formal pledge that she should be returned in seven days. In the Polynesian code of manners, such a request could not be refused without a quarrel. It could not even be evaded without creating ill-feeling that might end in trouble. Had Tuiterai asked for Tavi's child or anything else that he regarded as most precious, the gift would have to be made, subject of course to reciprocity, for every chief was bound to return as good a gift as he received. Tavi did not want to lend his wife, but his pride and perhaps his interest required the sacrifice, and with the best grace he could muster he sent her to Papara. Apparently she made no objection; if the husband was satisfied, the island code had nothing to say to the wife.

Taurua came to Papara, like a Polynesian queen of Sheba, and made her visit to Tuiterai, who immediately fell madly in love with her, showing it by some acts that were amusing, and by others that were too serious for us to laugh at even after eight generations. One of his amusing acts was to take the name Arorua (Aro, breast; rua, two) as a compliment to Taurua's charms and as Tuiterai arorua he is known to this day. The more serious act was that, at the end of the week's visit, he broke his pledge to Tavi, and refused to return Taurua to her husband. This was an outrage of the most grievous kind, such as he might perhaps have inflicted on a very low man—a man fit only for a human sacrifice —but not on a chief; least of all on a chief of equal rank with himself. It was a challenge of force; an act of war. Tuiterai did not attempt to excuse it except on the plea of his infatuation.

No sooner did Tuiterai's refusal reach Tautira than Tavi summoned his warriors and sent them against Papara with orders to destroy the land and to kill its chief. Papara had no walls like those of Troy to stand a siege, its forces were beaten in battle, Tuiterai was taken, and Taurua was recovered.

Among the score of wars fought in early societies about women, and then made the subjects of poetry or legend, the Tahitian variety has a charm of its own because its interest does not end as most of such stories end, with the revenge of the injured party. It should have ended in the usual way, and Tavi had intended to do what any Greek or Norse chief would have done: kill his rival and sack his villages; but the affair took another turn. Tuiterai was wounded, captured, and bound; but when his captors were about to kill him he remonstrated, not with any feeble appeal for mercy, but with the objection, much more forcible to a Polynesian, that a great chief like himself could not be put to death by an inferior. None but an equal could raise his hand against him. None but Tavi must kill Tuiterai.

Tavi's warriors, in spite of their orders, felt the force of the objection, which was, no doubt, in reality an appeal to religious fears, for Tuiterai as head-chief of the Tevas was a person of the most sacred character.

They carried him, bound and blindfolded along the shore, some thirty miles, to Tavi. The journey was long, and the wounded chief, feeling his strength fail, urged them on, and as they passed each stream he managed to dip his hand in the water to mark his progress, for he knew the touch of the water in every stream.

When Tavi learned that his warriors had brought Tuiterai alive, he reproached them for disobeying his orders. The pride of generosity had cost him his wife and a war; and still he must forfeit his character if he put Tuiterai to death with his own hand in his own house. The wars of Tahiti were as cruel and ferocious as the wars of any other early race, but such an act as this would have shocked Tahitian morality and decency. Tavi felt himself obliged to spare his rival's life, but between complete vengeance and complete mercy the law knew no interval. A chief spared was a guest and an equal. Tavi gave Tuiterai his life and his freedom and Taurua besides. The legend repeats his words in a song which is still sung as one of the best known Teva ballads:

TAVI AND TEURAITERAI

A mau ra i te vahine ai Taurua.
Tou hoa ite ee. e matatarai maua e.
Taurua horo poipoi oe iau nei.
To aiai no pohe mai nei au ite ono.
Nau hoi oe i teie nei ra.
A mau ra ia Taurua tou hoa ite ee.
Matatarai mauai maua e.

Take, then, your wife! Taurua! my friend! we are separated, she and I! Taurua, the morning star to me. For her beauty I would die. You were mine, but now—take, then Taurua! my friend! we are separated, she and I!

Nevertheless the overthrow of Papara was too serious a revolution not to affect the politics of the island. Tavi became by his triumph the most powerful chief in all Tahiti, and asserted his power by imposing a rahui. A rahui was a great exercise of authority, which might last a year or more, a sweeping order that everything produced during that time in the whole territory subject to the influence of the chief should be tabu. Not a pig should be killed; not a tapa cloth or fine mat should be made; "not a cock should crow."

The individual mid-eighteenth-century chiefs have come down to us in oral history, as recorded by the early discoverers and missionaries with reputations that can still thrill us today. Prowess in war or physical strength was respected and so was intellectual brilliance—even a master trickster or conniver or thief stood high in the esteem of the community. But the overriding, most worshipful quality of the great leaders was *mana:* a hard-to-define, commanding combination of wisdom, compassion, firmness, persuasiveness, and understanding—indeed the essence of what are generally recognized as the attributes of greatness in human beings anywhere, anytime.

Shortly before the commencement of this narrative, 1750 or so, one chief stood above all in respect, though not necessarily in power. Vehiatua, like Tavi, was the grand chief of the seaward Teva, the windward section of the most powerful and prestigious of the island's clans. (See map page 30.) Although Vehiatua was designated chief of the seaward Teva (as contrasted with the landward Teva) this was probably because his residence remained where he was born, in Taiarapu or "Little Tahiti," the peninsular island to the southeast. As their highest chief he was always recognized also by the landward Teva. It was they who owned and controlled the southern or landward districts of the island, Papara and Vaiari (now Papeari), the richest and most desirable lands of all.

During the years preceeding its "discovery" by Europe, there were on the island four main chiefs that concern us most. These chiefs were the *hui arii,* of which the high ones were *arii rahi* and the highest *arii tahi.* The whole concept of Tahitian hierarchy is complex, and interpretations of it differ depending on who is reporting it, a naval officer, a missionary, a merchant, a native Tahitian. The white man tends to simplify and twist into his own channels; this brown man tends to complicate—to a point of mystification.

The main thing to realize is that power (or persuasion or influence) is rooted in the land or title as well as in the person or in his or her bloodline. Power is also divided into two aspects: (1) spiritual power or hereditary prestige, and (2) political power or physical might. Complicate this further with male and female elements of both marriage and blood. Further still with the invariable inheritance of the firstborn son to the chief's title at the very moment of that son's birth, the chief then becoming regent. Multiply by five or six *hui arii* and their districts, intermarrying, interwarring, dying, and borning. And you have almost as many pieces and places to play with as you would in a chess game.

Another important thing to remember is the extraordinary rights and privileges of a high chief. All must defrock to the waist in his presence. He must be carried on a servant's shoulders everywhere, since whatever land or house or shore is touched by his foot becomes his property forever. He eats only the choicest foods and is usually fed by another. He alone can sit on his *marae* and wear his red or yellow feather girdle. He alone can command human sacrifice, and so on and on. *But* all of these sacred honors are strictly limited to his own land and district. The chief of Papara is powerless in Paea. He may not even be permitted to visit there without invitation. So in a way our "men" are as move-bound as chessmen.

Now, with these distinctions and particulars understood, let us return to the four most interesting chiefs in the Tahiti of the 1760s.

They were: (1) Vehiatua of Tautira, who was head of the seaward Teva and by seniority head of both Teva clans; but he was old and sickly and about to die. (2) Amo of Papara, head of the landward Teva and of the richest and most powerful districts of the island, for his authority extended over Vaiari and Mataeia as well—the whole southern section. But Amo was by this time only regent to his young son, Teriirere, seven years old in 1769, and his wife was the *femme fatale* Purea (more of her later). (3) Tuteha chief of the Atehuru, who reigned over the powerful western districts of Paea and Punaauia and was an uncle of the fourth, last, and most ambitious of the quartet. (4) Tu of Faaa. He was a relatively minor chief compared with the other three, but his clan was the Porionuu in the north, and to its Matavai Bay were about to come Wallis, Cook, Bligh, Vancouver, and the missionaries, bringing with them the powers of firearms and the concepts of kingship that

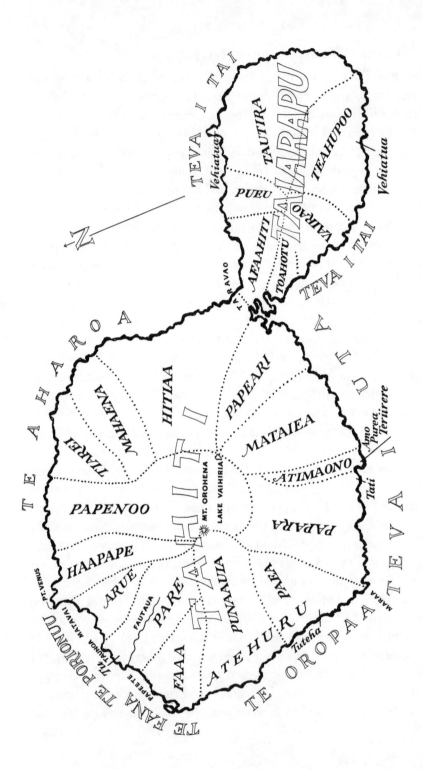

were revolutionary to the Tahitian structure of politics and prestige.

A few years before Wallis's arrival in the *Dolphin* in 1767, Purea, wife of Amo, had ordered the construction of the largest and most spectacular *marae* in Tahiti shortly after her first extant child was born, about 1762. According to Cook, who measured it carefully but not quite accurately, it was *a wonderful piece of Indian Architecture and far exceeds every thing of its kind upon the whole Island, it is a long square of stonework built Pyramidically, the base is 267 feet by 87, the breadth and length at top is 177 feet by 7, it riseth by large steps all round, like those leading up to a sundial, there are 11 of those each 4 feet high which makes the whole height 44 Feet.* Actually Cook's rough calculation must be wrong; it measures 267 by 377 feet, but according to Cook's great biographer, J. C. Beaglehole, it is *the greatest in Tahiti and indeed in all of Polynesia, and certainly one of the glories of "Indian Architecture."*

Purea's motives in launching this huge enterprise were perhaps to outshine her jealous sisters, to enhance the prestige of Papara, to demonstrate her own power. But mainly she wished to secure the future paramountcy of her son, Teriirere. There was also probably mixed into this an urge to rival or even to dominate her powerful husband Amo. Things evidently were not going well between them, for a few years later Amo found other vahines for his sleeping mat, and Purea was seen with other male companions. Teriirere was their only living child, although not the first conceived. They had both been Ariois of the highest order, so no doubt Purea had had a number of previous children that had been disposed of by the conventional infanticide. One suspects that she was anticipating a break with Amo and that this great *marae* was the best way to insure the future of her son. It was Teriirere's *marae;* not even his father, Amo, could sit in the place of honor. Sometime previously Terii had been invested with the sacred red feather girdle of Papara.

The story is an involved one. Purea was not the eldest, but she came from a sizable family of sons and daughters of a very high chief. The older sisters resented the arrogance and pride and ambition of the younger one. They were also no doubt jealous of her radiant charm, for

Purea was evidently blessed by the gods; she outshone even the great Amo. And she has always seemed to get her willful way—to wind up successfully in spite of her imperious airs.

But this time she went too far. One of her sisters-in-law was refused the hospitalities and rights due her rank. The child of another was insulted. A local war broke out. Mighty Papara was overwhelmed. Amo and Purea took to the mountains and another chiefly balance had been upset. All this had occurred before the coming of the white man, but by then the situation had been resolved. Purea was back to greet Wallis and enough in her old spirits so that he dubbed her queen of all Tahiti. But the upheaval had left an uncertainty in the air and enough disequilibrium among the older, higher chiefs so that a younger and lesser one could make progress—with European arms—a challenge that would never have been permitted had the old order been stable at the time.

Ariitaimai (our heroine Huruata Salmon) told Henry Adams, in her old age and looking back on those days of her native Papara's glory and disaster, that it was usually a female who wrecked a kingdom, and as long as her beloved Papara was fated to be humbled she was glad that at least her Great-Aunt Purea was a surpassingly beautiful woman.

Purea was the "Oberea" of Samuel Wallis, first European discoverer of Tahiti. In his eyes she was Queen of the island, a glamorous lady who arrived in a "royal barge," a large double canoe with a spacious deckhouse where she and her "ladies-in-waiting" disported themselves, feasted, and entertained. Ashore, he tells us, she had a house 327 feet long, 42 feet wide, and 30 feet high (but actually it was the district council house, not Oberea's private manse). Wallis apparently thought that she had fallen in love with him and one suspects that if he had not been so ill a royal romance of sorts might have come about. He was a prime novelty, the first great white chief, and besides, by this time Amo was casting elsewhere.

Purea's affair with the *Dolphin*'s captain, if you can call it that, was brief and fleeting; but she is for us a convenient transitional personage. She figures importantly just a few years later in Cook's introduction to "La Nouvelle Cythère."

CHAPTER THREE

First Encounter: The Explorers

1767 et seq.

Something very strange was brewing in Europe at this time. For centuries past there had been massive marchings of peoples in the hemisphere of land, unknown of course to the people of the ocean. Aryan hordes had poured from Persia to India between 2000 and 1200 B.C.*

Later Alexander had led the Greeks to India through Asia Minor. The Mongol hordes under Genghis Khan overran China. Greatest of all was the methodical Roman conquest of the Mediterranean basin, lasting some one thousand years until Attila the Hun and the Visigoth raiders toppled its tired, degenerate civilization. Then, after those vast continental upheavals, came the thousand-year Medieval slumber, during the same years when the Polynesians were regrouping and evolving themselves in the hemisphere of water on the western approaches to the Pacific.

The land masses of Eurasia and of Africa north of the Sahara were all spoken for now. In India and China, the two massive civilizations of Asia had long ago filled to overflowing their huge ecological niches. By the 1450s the restless and aggressive peoples of the European and Middle Eastern earth had reached the ultimate barriers of the world as they conceived its finite extent, a land mass encompassed by a mysterious infinite sea. Then Columbus found a new world and each

*Is it just possible that some of these filtered down over the subsequent centuries to supply the genes that were eventually to constitute a caucasoid component of Polynesian blood?

nation suddenly realized—as the Polynesians had before them on the other side of the globe—that the sea, instead of the fearsome barrier it had always been, was instead a highroad to new worlds to conquer. All that was needed were ships, and one by one the competitive states of Europe began to build them. Then the whole European subcontinent began to burst forth; not as a massive entity but in successive national pulsations. And these new ventures were selective invasions by sea in ships over the oceans, in place of the massive footslogging invasions of past history. Curiously enough this was roughly the same time when the Polynesians were reaching by sea their ultimate population limits on their most recently settled peripheral islands.

Of course ships had been known long since in Europe, but until Columbus, Europeans had never crossed the oceans. They had been coastal sailors only, not deep-water men. An exception was the Norsemen venturing to Greenland, island-hopping by way of the Shetlands, Faeroes, and Iceland, and even touching North America. But these open-water stretches were no more than three or four hundred miles. No one paid much attention to these Norsemen and purposely they did not spread the news of their sporadic feats. European maritime historians boast of the Phoenicians within the "vast" Mediterranean and of voyages out of the Strait of Gibraltar and along the Atlantic coasts to fetch lead and tin from Cornwall and Ireland. Arab dhows even sailed eastward to India, probably north-coasting the Arabian Sea. These were brave deeds, from Ulysses onward, but they were essentially coastal, rarely more than a few days out of sight of land. Even the Azores and Canaries were probably not discovered or at least not settled, until the twelfth or thirteenth century, more than one thousand years after the Polynesians were crossing the dark blue Pacific.

Only the ancestors of our Polynesians could claim true deep-sea voyaging before Columbus. And strangely enough, these illiterate "primitives" achieved not only that precedence but voyages of well over two thousand miles of open ocean. Nobody paid attention to them either. Indeed nobody in Europe even knew there was an ocean over there beyond the comfortable earthy borders of their nonglobular, flat, fearsomely water-surrounded world. The Polynesian concept was another story in another separate world; equally flat in projection, but a world of friendly water punctuated by rich little islands and similarly surrounded by the forbidding unknown.

Following the Portuguese pioneers, the Spaniards were of course the first conquistadores and they quickly gobbled up the enormous tropical areas of the new continents all the way from Florida to California southward to Peru. What a conquest! Larger than the whole of Europe and North Africa combined, indeed just about the same size as the whole of Europe's then known world except for hazy Asia, and the African deserts and jungles. No wonder such huge tracts made them greedy for more; and when the easy gold ran thin, no wonder they reached out over the barren North Pacific to the Philippines and the lands of spice. No wonder also that these Spaniards soon began to run thin themselves, and in time were the first to lose the only thing they ever really wanted: overseas gold.

Next came the Dutchmen to the East Indies and so entranced were they with the immediate riches of spices and trade that they ignored the austral continent which they had discovered and could have exploited for their exploding population. It was left then to the English and the French to conquer the rest of the world and we must give them some credit for they went out not exclusively to exploit but also to settle and, as they thought, to improve. Not *too* much credit, because they did some long-term exploiting also, especially in India, Egypt, Indochina, Algeria. Their Pacific settlements were dumpings, at first, of excess and unwanted growths in their own populations; criminals first, to empty their prisons into penal colonies; then nonconformists, religious fanatics, splinter sects—undesirables who were too respectable intellectually to be classed as lawbreakers, yet clearly citizens to be got rid of. Things at home were made difficult enough for these people so that most of them shipped themselves off to North America, Australia and New Zealand. Alas, they were self-righteous enough to decimate indigenous populations without a qualm: American Indians and Australian Aborigines, New Zealand Maori.

The English were a bit better at it than their rivals the French because, although the two countries whacked up the remaining world between them, the English bested the French in the long run because Englishmen came to stay, to work, to become Americans and Australians. Frenchmen came to suffer a necessary separation from La Belle France, always harboring within them a craving to return home again. They had not their hearts in it as did the English, and so, in time, they were thrown out, expelled militarily from America, thwarted in New Zealand, contained in the Middle East, excluded from India and southern Africa.

So the whole world was carved up as Europe helped herself while Russia slept and China's inner kingdom suffered humiliating intrusions even though she retained the basic integrity that she is at last asserting today. Japan fended off fiercely all attempts even of contact, but of course there was not much to conquer in those overpopulated, resource-poor islands. The rest of the world submitted, surly but subservient, as their peoples had always been, to remote masters. Whether the conquerors were white or black or yellow, Muslim, Christian, Buddhist, Confucian, or Hindu made little difference. Exploitation was the rule of the centuries. All stay-at-home peoples of the land half of the world were born and bred to it. A release from bondage was to come eventually in this twentieth century from their English masters, through the consciences and the weaknesses of their local governors powered by the gradual, oh-so-slow emergence of the concept of the equality of man. And the English example was, in time, to set that whole world tumultuously, bloodily, unpeacefully free.

But not the Pacific water world, not yet. And Tahiti? Here in microcosm was, and still is, a test-tube study of the evils and dubious blessings of the implacable Anglo-French drive to colonial conquest. North America had been staked out for the English when Wolfe defeated Montcalm at Quebec in 1759. And, oddly enough, three men participated in this critical battle who were later to loom large on Tahiti's horizon: Samuel Wallis, a midshipman transporting troops for Wolfe; Louis de Bougainville, then a soldier, aide-de-camp to Montcalm; and James Cook, a promising young marine surveyor in the Royal Navy who charted the river approaches for the British army landings.

The American Revolution had little direct effect on Tahiti except that it is interesting to note that Cook's voyages of exploration were protected from harassment by an understanding of mutual agreement between the British and their warring American colonies. In March 1779, Benjamin Franklin, then American ambassador to France, issued from his residence at Passy an open letter to all American shipmasters, bidding them aid Captain Cook's ships, despite their nationality, designating his mission *an undertaking truly laudable in itself, as the increase of geographical knowledge facilitates the communication between distant nations, in the exchange of useful products and manufactures, and the extension of arts, whereby the common enjoyments of human life are multiplied and augmented in general. . . .* A noble gesture even though the Congress failed to support it.

The French Revolution distracted both English and French from their colonizing ambitions for some decades while Nelson, heroically, and Napoleon, humiliatingly, were being disposed of. The British, having won the battle of Trafalgar in 1805, got a splendid head start at sea while the French were recovering from their gigantic European and domestic landward upheavals. The English secured the continent of Australia with ease, but they beat their rivals to the prize colonizing potential of New Zealand by only a few months. A French expedition under Lavaud, who was later to become the second governor of Tahiti, had set out to take over New Zealand early in 1840 and arrived at the Bay of Islands in May to find the British already in possession and to learn that the infamous Treaty of Waitangi had been signed only thirteen days before Lavaud had set sail from Brest. The French made a pass at the South Island, but after a bit of skirmishing, the local British commander was able to bluff them out of this alternative prize.

Now this digression to New Zealand may seem incidental to a history of Tahiti, but I feel it has a significant bearing because, as a result of their success in the western Pacific, the British were apparently willing to concede the Marquesas Islands and Tahiti to the French as consolation prizes. The scattered island world was there for the taking. As you read of protest and riposte, of give and take, of national prides inflamed and national tempers soothed in the minutes and demarches, the speeches and rhetoric that flew back and forth across the Channel from the British Foreign Office to the Ministry of State, even from the Chamber of Deputies to the House of Commons, you realize that a military and diplomatic game of chess was being played between these old rivals who at that time certainly considered themselves, and were indeed generally recognized as, the two great superpowers of the earth. A couple of pawns like Tahiti and the Marquesas could readily be sacrificed for a rook like New Zealand. And even a knight such as New Caledonia could be conceded for another pawn such as Norfolk while Fiji, the Solomons, the New Hebrides, and others awaited their turns. A concrete expression of this state of affairs appears in the instructions issued to Bougainville where Choiseul said that France would *spare no pains to gain a footing also, in whatever seas the English attempt to settle in;* she would *never consent to the formation by England of new colonies in any part of the world* unless she herself were free to form colonies in like manner. Of course an Englishman at the time would have discounted this as blustering French amour propre, but England was having trouble with her American colonies and did not want to add to her martial commitments for the sake of a few romantic islands.

This of course is to speak only of the Pacific: far-flung, small-fry compared to North Africa, where France was straining for Algeria and England for Egypt and both of them for the Middle East, India, Indochina, and such sub-Saharan lands as the Cape provinces and Madagascar.

But before the guns began to talk, the forces of the Gospels had begun to be deployed. The Spaniards had of course blazed the trails in reverse of the order to come, sending their priests into the wreckage left by their soldiers of the Aztec and Inca civilizations to consolidate their power so that their gold miners and merchants could reap the long-term rewards of conquest. The stakes were different in the Pacific: no gold mines or plantations, only islands—but such beautiful smiling islands with such peaceful smiling people on them. First off they seemed best for penal colonies, then for settlers, and always for strategic military bastions or supply depots on the great trade routes to China. Here again on the spiritual battlefield the British beat their rivals to the draw. The London Missionary Society sent out its first "troops" in 1797

and gained a foothold in Tahiti that makes Protestantism dominant to
this day in spite of official French Roman Catholic rule.

But we are getting ahead of ourselves. Before considering such post-
contact occurrences, let us review briefly the men and events that
brought the Europeans to Tahiti and in so doing revolutionized its way
of life and began the ravishment of its long-established culture. The
first to arrive was that same Samuel Wallis, midshipman, landing troops
on the Plains of Abraham. Now in 1767 he is a Lieutenant in the
British Navy in command of H.M.S. *Dolphin* on a voyage of exploration to find the fabulous southern continent that, as all the great
European geographers agreed, must be spread across the antipodes to
balance the known land masses of the Northern Hemisphere. Mind
you, the popular recognition of the roundness of the globe and especially the immensity of its size were relatively new concepts to the
European mind. Columbus's voyages had led to the discovery of the
two huge new continents. Magellan had spanned the North Pacific and
revealed its stunning extent. Surely, thought the sages of the Royal
Society and My Lords of the Admiralty, there must lie a vast new
continent in the vast new Southern Ocean. What an exciting idea and
nothing to gainsay it.

But Samuel Wallis did not find it. He was a poor choice for the job.
He arrived at Tahiti sick and discouraged after a fearful battle with the
elements to negotiate the Southern Straits. Tahiti's natives seemed
friendly at first, but they soon attacked with torrents of slingstones from
their canoes. Wallis retaliated with musket fire, grapeshot and cannon
ball, killing and wounding dozens of the astounded and helpless islanders. When they had fled to the hills, he sent his men ashore to destroy
wantonly their beached canoes—beautiful craft, the most precious fruit
of hundreds of man-years of patient Tahitian labor and skill. This was
to teach them a lesson. They learned it well, this first, swift, brutal
revelation of the cruel power and implacable nature of their white
visitors. After that there was no more lethal hostility, only the age-old
Polynesian games of thievery and seduction. To protect his men, Wallis
set a line of defense along the little river that ran between the mainland

and the point where his scurvy-ridden crew was recuperating. His armed patrols were effective enough in keeping the Tahitians safely to their side of the stream, but he had not reckoned on the beguiling wiles of the provocative vahines and soon found that most of his ailing invalids were crossing over to infiltrate the palms and bushes. Pursuits, threats, disciplines, rewards—no counter-measures that Wallis could muster were equal to the attractions of the wenches, so he soon pulled up anchor and, after only five weeks in port, almost all of which he himself spent on board ship, he sailed out of lovely Matavai Bay. The visit must have had a peculiar effect on his mind, for instead of heading south to pursue the designated purpose of his secret exploratory mission, he headed north and then west to encounter only a few tiny islands before engaging the conventional homeward route of the China trade.

Wallis himself kept a careful journal as he was required to do by Royal Navy orders. But it is dull reading and has never been published. His sailing master however, one George Robertson, has left us many, pithy human insights.

. . . The country hade the most Beautiful appearance its posable to Imagin, from the shore side, one two and three miles Back their is a fine Leavel country that appears to be all laid out in plantations, and the regular built Houses seems to be without number, all allong the Coast, they appeared lyke long Farmers Barns and seemed to be all very neatly thatched, with Great Numbers of Cocoa Nut Trees and several oyr trees that we could not know the name of all allong the shore—the Interior part of the country is very Mountaineous but their is beautiful valeys between the Mountains—from the foot of the Mountains half way up the Country appears to be all fine pasture land, except a few places which seemd to be plowed or dug up for planting or sowing some sort of seed-from that to the very topes of the Mountains is all full of tall trees but what sort they are I know not but the whole was Green. This appears to be the most populoss country I ever saw, the whole shore side was lined with men, women and children all the way we Saild along.

the natives . . . brought to the water side a good many fine young Girls down of different colours, some was a light coper collour oyrs a mullato and some almost if not altogether White—this new sight Attract our mens fance a good dale, and the natives observed it, and made the young girls play a great many droll wanting [wanton] tricks, and the men made signs of friendship to entice our people ashoar, but they prudently referd going ashore, untill we were better aquanted with the temper of this people.

Their love of Iron is so great that the women (or rather Girls, for they were very young and small) prostitute themselves to any of our People for a Nail, hardly looking upon Knives, Beads, or any toy. Yet I must say yt the Girls who were of the white sort would admit of any Freedom but the last . . . the Young Girls . . . had now rose their price . . . from a twenty to a thirty penny nail, to a forty penny nail, and some was so extravagant as to demand a Seven or nine inch Spick.

What must the Tahitian have thought of this sudden white-skinned, womanless arrival? He had known for generations a mythical tale of a white god arriving in a single-hull canoe—a vessel that would have been inconceivable to him except in a dream. Would he have accepted this miraculous presence from another world as Europe accepted the discovery of Columbus? Probably. No one there knew of the finite contours of our globe. No one had thought to sail out into ultra-oceanic space. For three thousand years these people had had their own self-contained world and one senses, perhaps irrationally but somehow intuitively, that they were getting tired of it. Ready to find something fresh and new and bigger, as we are today ready for the discovery of outer space.

As we look back on these islanders, they were wonderfully adaptable and long accustomed to change of all sorts. Our advent did not appear to shatter them, though actually it did. They had long been accustomed to changing names: important ones of high chiefs because of a sneeze in the night; of their staff of life, breadfruit, from *uru* to *maiore* because a bad chief chose to make his name Uru.

Captain Bligh obliges us again with an on-the-scene comment: *The People here as well as in England have several Names, and being differently used, it is frequently perplexing when the same person is spoke of, to know who is meant. Every Chief has perhaps a dozen Names in the course of 30 Years, so the Man or Woman that has been spoken of by one Navigator under a particular name, will not be known by another, unless other causes lead to a Discovery. . . . I now find that Otoo or more properly Tynah, for that is his name since the Sovereignty is devolved to his Son, is still the greatest personage on this part of the Island. I shall now therefore for the future call him Tynah, the name of Otoo or Too, as it is differently spoken, being now the name of his eldest Son who is between five and Six years Old, reigning under the direction of his Father, whose name always goes from him as soon as he has a Son. Under such circumstances that a Parent should lose his power and authority is a most extraordinary thing, but I believe it is not less true, than it is unnatural and absurd.*

Even changes of gods took place; such as the peaceful Tane of love and plenty to the warrior Oro, eater of men. Eventually they tossed aside their ancient religion and embraced the new one. It took some years and much agony to do so, but they had apparently reached a stage when the old religion was flagging. Perhaps they were bored with Oro and their many minor gods and ready for a fresh new world.

The next European to land on our island was Count Louis Antoine de Bougainville whom we first noted in the siege and capture of Quebec as an aide-de-camp of the glamorous French commander Montcalm. Bougainville had come a long way in the ensuing decade. An offspring of a middle-class but well-funded and influential family, he had soon shown an unusual intelligence and charm of personality. He had proved himself a bright and energetic aide to the general. His army was ready to send him swiftly upward, but he was evidently more interested in science, the arts, adventure, society, and diplomacy than in military tactics or strategy. He went to London to study and soon became a member of the Royal Society, a rare and distinguished compliment for a young French soldier-diplomat who was not of noble blood. Then somehow he made friends in Paris in the powerful Ministry of the Marine and became a sailor, later an admiral no less, and was now in charge of the first of a series of resplendent voyages of discovery to be sent out and welcomed back with all the trimmings by His Royal Majesty Louis XV, king of the French.

He had set sail from France in 1766 before Wallis had returned to Europe with the news of the discovery of Tahiti, so his own discovery in 1768 was a genuine one in the European, though not of course in the Polynesian, sense. He landed on the east coast of the island and nearly lost his two ships in a meager, exposed harbor, thereby showing he was not much of a sailor, for he could easily have coasted to protected harbors on the lee side. He was not much of an explorer either, in spite of the paeans of French historians, for he stayed only eight or nine days and walked hardly a mile from his ship. It would indeed seem to have been an uneventful and unimaginative visit, and yet it inspired the most romantic reaction of any discovery in history. Imagine yourself a European of those times. Columbus had only recently (two hundred fifty years was a short interval then) revealed the existence of two huge, utterly new continents. You had just begun to realize the immensity of the Pacific. Of course there must be a whole new continent to find and of course these new islands and new lands would be peopled with Jean-Jacques Rousseau's untouched, unspoiled children of nature—a living laboratory to make the dreams of the master philosopher and his thousands of cultists throughout Europe emerge from romantic idealism into suddenly confirming physical reality.

Bougainville named his island "La Nouvelle Cythère" after the legendary birthplace of Aphrodite and described its inhabitants as such happy children of a South Sea Eden that a whole newly strengthened mythology of the virtues of Man in Nature swept the cynical civilized world of the day. Indeed it still nourishes many a fond and foolish dreamer. Although Bougainville protested that his reports had been overblown, he did bring back with him a comely Tahitian lad who almost instantly took the fickle social world of Paris by storm. Ahutoru with his Polynesian smiles, courtesies and, perhaps, his Polynesian prowess in ladies' boudoirs, was Exhibit A in the flesh, the Man of Nature par excellence.

Bougainville also leaves us a telling insight into the intimate ways of Polynesian humanity and, coming from an intellectual Frenchman, it is naturally a bit more sophisticated, though perhaps no more intuitively unerring, than the perceptions of George Robertson.

Polygamy seems established amongst them; at least it is so amongst the chief people. As love is their only passion, the great number of women is the only luxury of the opulent. Their children are taken care of, both by their fathers and their mothers. It is not the custom at Tahiti, that the men occupied only with their fishery and their wars, leave to the weaker sex the toilsome works of husbandry and agriculture. Here a gentle indolence falls to the share of the women; and the endeavors to please are their most serious occupation. I cannot say whether their marriage is a civil contract, or whether it is consecrated by religion; whether it is indissoluble, or subject to the laws of divorce. Be this as it will, the wives owe their husbands a blind submission; they would wash with their blood any infidelity committed without their husband's consent. That, it is true, is easily obtained; and jealousy is so unknown a passion here, that the husband is commonly the first who persuades his wife to yield to another. An unmarried woman suffers no constraint on that account; every thing invited her to follow the inclination of her heart, or the instinct of her sensuality; and public applause honours her defeat: nor does it appear, that how great soever the number of her previous lovers may have been, it should prove an obstacle to her meeting with a husband afterwards. Then wherefore should she resist the influence of the climate, or the seduction of examples? The very air which people breathe, their songs, their dances, almost constantly attended with indecent postures, all conspire to call to mind the sweets of love, all engage to give themselves up to them. They dance to the sound of a kind of drum, and when they sing, they accompany their voices with a very soft kind of flute, with three or four holes, which, as I have observed above, they blow with their noses. They likewise practice a kind of wrestling; which, at the same time, is both exercise and play to them.

Thus accustomed to live continually immersed in pleasure the people of Tahiti have acquired a witty and humorous temper, which is the offspring of ease and Joy.

How did he learn so much in so short a time?

Another incident of Bougainville's brief dalliance is an amusing contrast to the two far-distant cultures. Philbert de Commerson, who was the surgeon and naturalist on Bougainville's companion ship, the *Etoile,* had brought with him a young valet to tend his personal needs and to help him with his collections, sketches, and records. When the valet first went ashore on an errand for his master, the Tahitians promptly laid hands on him and playfully stripped off his clothing; thereby revealing to his astonished shipmates an indubitable young maiden, one Jeanne Baret, who went on to become the first female of *Homo sapiens* (or perhaps any other species) to circumnavigate the globe.

Next of course and by far the most importantly comes our final member of the trio of Quebec, James Cook, to observe the transit of Venus in 1769 and on his second voyage in 1772–75 to zigzag through the southern reaches of the ocean and prove at last that there was no such thing as a great earth-balancing southern continent. His accomplishments as an explorer are too well known to need review here and he was not a particularly sensitive observer and recorder of Polynesian life, but there are a couple of entries in his journal that reintroduce to us Ariitaimai's Great-Aunt Purea, the one who had caused such trouble in Papara. She was in her forties now, well past her prime. In the words of Cook's young astronomer William Wales, *an old demi-rep of quality.*

Tuesday June 20th, 1769. Last night Obarea [Purea] *made us a Viset who we have not seen for some time: we were told of her coming and that she would bring with her some of the Stolen things, which we gave credit to because we knew several of them were in her possession, but we were surprised to find this woman put her self wholy in our power and not bring with her one article of what we had lost. The excuse she made was that her gallant, a Man that used to be along with her, did steal them and she had beat him and turn'd him away; but she was so sensible of her own guilt that she was ready to drop down through fear —and yet she had resolution enough to insist upon sleeping in Mr Bank's Tent all night and was with difficulty prevaild upon to go to her Canoe altho no one took the least notice of her. In the Morning she brought her Canoe with every thing she had to the Gate of the Fort, after which we could not help admireing her for her Courage and the confidence she seem'd to place in us and thought that we could do no less than to receive her into favour and accept the presents she had brought*

*us which Consisted of a Hog a Dog Some Bread fruit & Plantains. We
refused to except of the Dog as being an animal we had no use for, at
which she seem'd a little surprized and told us that it was very good
eating and we very soon had an oppertunity to find that it was so, for
Mr. Banks having bought a basket of fruit in which happened to be the
thigh of a Dog dress'd, of this several of us taisted and found that it was
meat not to be despise'd and therefore took Obarea's dog and had him
immidiatly dress'd by some of the Natives in the following manner. They
first made a fire, and heated some small Stones, while this was doing the
Dog was Strangle'd and the hair got off by laying him frequently upon
the fire, and as clean as if it had been scalded off with hot water, his
entrails were taken out and the whole washed clean, and as soon as the
stones and hole was sufficiently heated, the fire was put out, and part of
the Stones were left in the bottom of the hole, upon these stones were
laid Green leaves and upon them the Dog together with the entrails.
These were likewise cover'd with leaves and over them hot stones, and
then the whole was close cover'd with mould: after he had laid there
about 4 hours, the Oven (for so I must call it) was open'd and the Dog
taken out whole and well done, and it was the opinion of every one who
taisted of it that they Never eat sweeter meat, we therefore resolved for
the future not to despise Dog flesh. It is in this manner that the Natives
dress, or Bake all their Victuals that require it, Flesh, Fish and fruit.*

*Wednesday 21st. This morning a Chief whose name is Oamo [Amo]
and one we had not seen before, came to the Fort, there came with him
a Boy about 7 years of Age and a young Woman about 18 or 20; at the
time of their coming Obarea and several others were in the Fort, they
went out to meet them, having first uncover'd their heads and bodies as
low as their waists and the same thing was done by all those that were
on the out side of the Fort; as we looked upon this as a ceremonial
Respect and had not seen it paid to any one before we thought that this
Oamo must be some extraordinary person, and wonder'd to see so little
notice taken of him after the Ceremony was over. The young Woman
that came along with him Could not be prevail'd upon to come into the
Fort and the Boy was carried upon a Mans Back, altho he was as able
to walk as the Man who carried him. This lead us to inquire who they*

*were and we was inform'd that the Boy was Heir apparent to the Sove-
reignty of the Island and the young woman was his sister and as such
the respect was paid them, which was due to no one else except the
Areedehi which was not Tootaha from what we could learn, but some
other person who we had not seen, or like to do, for they say that he is
no friend of ours and therefore will not come near us. The young Boy
above mentioned is Son to Oamo by Obarea, but Oamo and Obarea did
not at this time live together as man and wife he not being able to endure
with her troublesome disposission, I mention this because it shews that
separation in the Marriage state is not unknown to this people.*

But Cook's significance to future internal events in the island lay not
in his splendid explorations and discoveries, but in his fixation on
Matavai Bay as the best of anchorages and his bequest of it to future
English mariners. He thus inadvertently allied European power with
the weaker, traditionally inferior chiefs of the north and opened the
way for the overthrow of the political equilibrium of the ancient Tahitian culture.

Other explorers to these islands and the Marquesas followed: the
cautious and methodical Vancouver, the Russians Lisiansky and Kotze-
bue, the Americans Porter and Ingraham. More were to follow at
intervals well into the 1800s. But the most notable reporter of our chief
interest here, the human natures of the island people, was Cook's
sailing master on his third and final voyage, William Bligh. Bligh is of
course best known for the mutiny, for its complex initial causes, for
Bligh's heroic escape, and for the dramatic fate of the mutineers on
Pitcairn Island. Little notice has been taken, however, of the serious
effects on the Tahitians caused by the presence of the desperadoes who
remained on the island for nearly two turbulent and corrupting years
before their recapture by the British authorities (but more of that later).
And Bligh should be given credit for being one of the keenest observers
of the idiosyncracies of these strangely individualistic beings, whom he
so acutely perceived as humans while most other of Her Majesty's
officers were looking down their noses at them as heathens, savages, or
at best children. I have sprinkled his comments through the text and
will sum up with: *I was under the necessity this afternoon to punish*

Alexn. Smith with 12 lashes for suffering the Gudgeon of the large Cutter to be drawn out without knowing it. Several Chiefs were on board at the time, and with their Wives interceded for the Man, but seeing it had no effect they retired, and the Women in general showed every degree of Sympathy which marked them to be the most humane and affectionate creatures in the World.

After the early explorers come the first of the aforementioned missionaries in the good ship *Duff* in 1797. Then the infiltrators—deserters, traders, beachcombers, merchants. After them the whalers, having pretty much fished out the Atlantic, break into our ocean and, finding Tahiti the best place to rest and refresh and regale themselves, bring as many as seventy or eighty ships a year into Papeete in the late 1830s. Their apostle is Herman Melville in 1843, but again we are getting ahead of our story.

CHAPTER FOUR

Penetration: The Missionaries
1797

T he missionaries were a curious breed. The London Missionary Society was founded in 1795, its moving and guiding spirit a Reverend Thomas Haweis. The founders and directors were a group of middle-class zealots apparently quite different from the aristocrats of the Church of England. They came from a variety of sects: Methodists, Baptists, Calvinists, Wesleyans, Presbyterians; rebels one might say, or escapists from the Established Anglican Church. Many such religious renegades had been migrating to the American colonies starting, of course, with the *Mayflower*. There they had continued their boisterous rebelliousness among themselves, Roger Williams splintering off to Rhode Island, a mass exodus to New Jersey, Cotton Mather and Jonathan Edwards fulminating from their pulpits, Salem burning its witches and so on for nearly a century. But now, after the revolution, America was no longer a brace of colonies, so where could the English nonconformist go? Fortunately new worlds had just been found by the explorers and they were filled with savages who had never heard of the True God and were reveling in heathen orgies that were pouring vast quantities of souls into Satan's lap as he sat smiling in Hell. These misguided children of nature knew nothing, alas, of their original sin. No one had told them about Adam and Eve and the Apple. So the confident saviors of London banded together, raised money from pious widows and alms-begging children; raised recruits partly from their own ordained brethren, but mostly from artisans, mechanics, carpenters, shipbuilders and the like, whose skills would teach the heathens to give up their idle, pleasure-loving ways and earn their bread by the sweat of their brows instead of plucking it slothfully from tree and vine. They would of course also build churches and structures to keep their teacher-saviors well housed and fed.

The potential evangelists exhorted each other in fiery meetings to go forth into strange lands and bring the holy light to shine in the dark corners of the earth. They were given detailed *Counsels and Instructions* for *I, Personal Conduct and Spirit, II, Internal Order Administration and Instruction, III, Regulations on the Voyage, IV, Concerning the Mode of Settlement in the Islands, V, Manner of Life in Society, Domestic Economy, and Employment of Time.* Here is a sampling from twenty odd pages of them.

Avoid as much as possible all occasions of temptation. Let no man be permitted, without leave of the community, to be absent at night from the common dormitory. In every journey, walk, occupation, let two or more brethren always be together.

Should any native women seek instruction in private, let one of our women sisters be their teachers. In public, all who please, and are silent, may attend our worship and instruction.

Every day the morning should open and the evening close with a chapter, prayer, a psalm or hymn; a short exposition may be given the one evening, and a short sermon the following evening, all through the week. Every man's gifts may thus be tried and brought forward; and let no man despise his brother, but encourage the feebleminded, and be patient towards all.

The assurance of an attainment of a happy and glorious eternity in a better world will afford a field of delightful instruction.

In all attempts to convince the natives of their sins, we should particularly select those instances of depravity which are most frequently striking, viz, the shocking crime of shedding human blood; the horrid murder of children; the abominable public prostitutions, and such other enormities as carry upon the face of them something revolting even to humanity. Avoid attacking their established customs of a more indifferent nature, such as their dress, amusements, however indecent the one may appear, or in their consequences apparently dangerous the other.

On shore, probably, the settlement itself should be formed, with some view of situation, easy of defence, and difficult of access, and the houses so situated, as to be surrounded with a ditch and pallisadoes, which, if no other purpose was answered, would render all nocturnal depredations from the natives more difficult; make it secure as the situation will admit, without appearing to erect a fortress, or to defend it by arms, which might alarm the jealousy and alienate the affection of the Chiefs. Our own peaceable and unassuming behaviour will soon convince them, that they have nothing to apprehend from us of danger, and every thing to expect of kindness and assistance.

On the very eve of departure a CHARGE was addressed to them by the Reverend Edward Williams, D.D.

Who can tell, but millions in succeeding ages may be everlasting benefited. The influence of a parent on his posterity may be great; the influence of a magistrate on the circle of his jurisdiction greater; the influence of a chief governor on his extensive dominions still greater; but a minister of God has an influence, good or bad, on the minds of men, still greater than them all, as he officially prepares, or neglects to prepare them for happiness in a never-ending state of existence. . . .

In all your traffic and covenants, in all your intercourse and public deportment, among the untaught natives of the South-Sea Islands be this your unvaried, inflexible aim—Their salvation. . . .

Evangelical truths are the weapons of your warfare, let them not be covered with unsightly rust, nor blunted by too much polish—mind chiefly the edge. Remember also, that the word is a two-edged sword, the law and the gospel—the one, to strike conviction into the consciences of sinners; and the other, to cut off sin from the believer in Jesus, as well as to lop off and consign to destruction all apostates. . . . *

Brethren, there are different sorts of trials—there are trials and snares even from prosperity: Prosperity! say you, (shaking your heads, and your hearts trembling with the expectation of the reverse) Who of us can expect prosperity? But are you not going to Otaheite? for the sake of

*See Heb. 2:1–3 and 4:11–12.

returning to which island of sensual delights a ship's crew mutinied? Ah, remember the history of the antidiluvian church; ye "sons of God," beware of the "daughters of men." Do not mistake me, I would not dissuade any from forming an honourable and godly connection; but see first that it be honourable and godly. Let not the Christian Missionary —the Christian mechanic—be dazzled with the prospect of alliance with the noblest families of the land, with the presumptuous hopes of making them afterwards Christians. Are you wiser than Solomon? I repeat the question, are you wiser than Solomon?—Oh cry to God all-sufficient for he alone can help you in so great a temptation, that the daughters of the land do not bear away your hearts, until they are made the daughters of God. Oh that none of you may be led in triumph by them, until they are led in triumph by divine grace!

They must have been brave young men indeed to venture into new lives with such heavy spiritual burdens. So heavy and so holy that it might be well to include a brief hint of other, more worldly motivations that had been slyly suggested by one John Callander in his three-volume history *Terra Australis Cognita* some thirty years previous to our heroes' departure in the good ship *Duff.*

Let us not forget here, that these distant regions are peopled with myriads of our fellow creatures, to whom our holy religion is utterly unknown. And what must his praise be, who shall prove an happy instrument in the hands of the Divine Providence to carry into those unknown regions the pure and unadulterated truths of Christianity, unmixed with Popish superstitions. . . . Surely this important considera- tion is enough to awake and inspirit us in the attempt; but when to this is joined the attractive charm of present gain [i.e., good business deals] *we must acknowledge, that we have here united the two strongest mo- tives that can prompt man to action.*

They seem to have been a mixed lot, these evangelists; many of them selfless, dedicated people; many of them seeking mostly adventure or change from the humdrum; most of them with little education and none of them with the slightest notion of the places where they were going or what it would be like once they got there. As we now look back on them out there on the islands, they were highly individualistic and seemed to dispute endlessly among themselves. With their elected, rotating committees and officers, they appeared to have been going in many directions at once with little defined purpose and very little discipline. A number of them deserted in each batch sent out. But there were always a few dedicated, stalwart men and, most importantly, stalwart wives who stuck it out in bad times and who reaped the glorious rewards of conversions when the tide turned. There were eighteen in all from the *Duff*, of which five were married. When wives died or bachelors became desperate, little groups of "pious maidens" were thoughtfully selected by the Directors and sent out. Marriages seemed to take place almost automatically and there are no reports of unhappy wedlock. But of course they were all so absorbed in their work for their True God that interpersonal love was perhaps of little consequence. Still, they had children.

It is difficult to form impressions of these men as individual human beings. They were very careful not to criticize each other in writing. For in the records the missionaries and their work must be blameless. All things good were exaggerated. All things bad were suppressed or glossed over. To be sure, if one of the brethren fell from grace and took to drink or to native women, he was promptly expelled and no more is heard of him. Brother Jefferson, who emerges as the most equal of the equals and who was most frequently elected their leader, enters in his diary: *Dec. 25, 1799. We took notice of our having passed the Church censure of Excommunication upon Mr. Thos Lewis for his connecting himself with an heathen woman.* This unfortunate was later murdered, probably by a jealous Tahitian *tane*.

It is evident that some were cantankerous, obstinate noncooperators. There was much talk in endless discussion groups, but very little of it was recorded. William Henry of the original group from the *Duff* in 1796 seems always to have been liked and respected. He spent more than forty years in Tahiti. Henry Nott, translator of the Bible, was another. John Davies was primarily a teacher. It was he who wrote the history of the mission and then refused to send it to London for fear the Directors would edit all the frankness and fact out of it. So it went to Sydney in manuscript and was not published until 1961. There were

at least two of the early ones who saw fit to preach and teach in their
own ways. James Elder was a constant problem because he would not
conform. Time and time again his peers would argue with him and
deplore his stubborn nature, but they never specify the manner of his
errings and they put up with him despite their disapproval. Another
one, William Read, went just too far, though what he did is a mystery.
He was expelled and shipped back to England.

The early years were discouraging ones. At first the natives seemed
curious; wanting to know what this new religion was all about. To them
it must have been a weird, and in many ways wondrous, Arabian Nights
tale. But once they had heard all the stories and learned of the mighty
heroes and villains of the Holy Scripture, they just got bored with the
repetitious preaching-praying-preaching and went back to their familiar
gods with their songs and dances.

Again William Bligh casts some on-the-spot light upon the situation:
*This brought on a religious conversation, and having told me their Great
God was called Oro and that they had many others of less consequence,
they asked me if I had any God. Having replied of course in the Affirma-
tive, I was asked if he had a Son and who his Wife was. I told them
he had a Son but no Wife. Who was his Father and Mother then? was
the next question. I said he never had either a Father or Mother. At this
they laughed exceedingly. You have a God then who never had a Father
or Mother had has a Child without a Wife, Aymah timoradei huheine
arrami no Mydiddee, i.e. did he not lie with a Woman to get him? I said
no. Who was then before Your God and where is he? Is he in the Winds
or in the Sun? Many other like questions were put to me concerning the
Divine Omnipotence, & I answered them in an as explanatory a manner
as the little knowledge I have of the language would allow me, but it
was too scanty to enable me to enter a discussion of their tenets.*

An interesting article has recently been published by an anthropologist named Christa Bausch. It is a study of the Polynesian concept of
light and darkness, *ao* and *po,* in contrast with the European or Western interpretation of those conditions. It is also a very shrewd percep-
tion of the missionary predicament.

It can be summarized, she writes, *by the slogan,* From Darkness to

Light, *which was the title of a book by one of the most prominent nineteenth-century missionaries in Polynesia, the Reverend W. Wyatt Gill. The concepts of "dark" and "light" underlay all the beliefs and actions of the missionaries whose goal it was to lead the natives from the "darkness" of heathenism to the "light" of Christianity.*

But of course to the Polynesian, po *or darkness had from their time immemorial meant the realm of sacred things, the spirit land of the souls of their ancestors and the birthplace and dwelling place of their gods.* Ao *or light on the other hand was the region of the every day life of man.*

Anthropologist Bausch traces the various aspects thoroughly and ingeniously from cosmology or creation, starting from nothingness, *po.* First the primal god Taaroa creates himself, impregnates the earth mother *papa* and generates the other gods who in turn are of the sky and light, *ao.* They then fish up islands from the primordial sea and make land. They clothe the islands with vegetation, fish, birds and animals, who occupy the new world. Last of all comes man born of the gods and forever linked with their holy forebears. The gods abide in the sacred *po* with the ancestral spirits; man lives fleetingly and happily in the secular land of light, *ao.*

From cosmology to religion po *and* ao *were more than concepts. They were religious realities, the supernatural roots of the world.*

The Polynesian was, and still is, a nocturnal creature. His chief activity, fishing, takes place by torchlight in the night and he sleeps away the sun-scorched, fly-buzzed day. Christa Bausch even points out, *In Polynesia there is no seasonal cycle: the sun is not revivifying as in European thought,* [or American Indian, for instance] *because on sandy islands it brings drought rather than life and the life giver was water, not the sun.* She adds sex to the po-ao symbolisms. *The dark womb is identified with* po *and seen as a space serving as a location for creation.* The souls of the dead are haere po, gone to night.

To reverse these anciently imbedded credos is to reverse the roles of God and the Devil. It could not be done. And the persistent stubbornness of the missionaries reveals flagrantly their inability to understand or their stupidity or their just plain implacable enmity.

From an intellectual viewpoint the po-system *was an achievement of highest quality . . . it was more comforting and enjoyable than the Genesis with its traumatic fall of Adam, punishment for sin and dismissal from paradise. The po-system was a continuum without an abrupt change or sharp contrasts; the sacred persisted into the present and was still available to man, not cut off as in the Genesis. I think the po-system is unique among all the cultures of the world. It is a beautiful symphony composed of space-light categories. . . . I believe that in the long run it was Christianity which was defeated in Polynesia, not the Polynesian religion as the missionaries thought.*

The lady makes a very convincing case though she does carry it to emotional, even passionate conclusions that almost equate our good Brethren with the Devil and the Polynesian with God Himself. She does not leave us with the impression that she is a coldly objective scientist, but lovers of the ocean-island race will clap their hands.

One of the most exasperating aspects of missionary life was the lack of communication from home and neglect on the part of their superiors in London. For a space of six whole years they received not a single letter or directive in response to their constant writings and implorings. Moreover, they soon ran out of goods to trade and none of the supplies promised them ever came. Of course they were totally dependent on nails, trinkets, woven cloth, tools. For although the natives were generous, they expected, as was the ancient Polynesian custom, generosity in return. Money was of no value whatsoever and words soon wore out their welcome.

Meanwhile ships of war stopped by, at first with nails and hoops of iron, but later with muskets and tools. Ships of trade en route to and from China stopped with cloth and with liquor. At first the missionaries vigorously forbade all trade in arms and alcohol, but they soon found that their righteous indignations and interferences were not only unenforceable but were being resented to the point of endangering their own personal safety. They had to back down, and in some cases, usually while acting as interpreters, they actually found themselves facilitating the dangerous trades. What a moral dilemma this was for them! And meanwhile as firearms and firewater filtered in, tribal rivalries mounted and exploded. At last in 1810, nearly fifteen years after their initial landing, after all their trial and hardship, their position became untenable. They moved to Moorea and Huahine and then all but two of them joined what they desperately called the "Exodus," to New South Wales.

Miraculously over the next couple of years the tide suddenly turned and the brethren came back from Australia. But although it was miraculous to some, it was quite evidently ironic to many; at least it is plainly so to us today. For the turn of this "tide" was the conversion of Pomare II to Christianity, a result of many past years of persuasion. But the basic, cynical motive of this conversion was the power he gained from the Europeans—military, commercial, religious alike—to defeat his rivals in bloody warfare and establish his tyrannical and corrupt supremacy over the whole troubled island. The converts following his example were baptized by the hundreds, souls were recorded as saved, ticked off and reckoned up, day by day, month by month, and the tallies reported joyously to London. Whereupon more missionaries were sent out and more funds raised in England and the True God prospered indeed.

In the years 1816–1819, three missionaries came out who were to dominate the evangelistic scene. William Ellis who arrived in 1816 spent only five or six years in the islands but returned to write his best-selling book, *Polynesian Researches*, and through it to tell the civilized world how interesting and glamorous the Polynesians were. He also made quite clear to his European audience how naturally depraved they were and how desperately in need of the ministrations of such enlightened fellows as himself and his brethren.

Their humour and their jests were, however, but rarely what might be termed innocent sallies of wit; they were in general low and immoral to a disgusting degree. Their common conversation, when engaged in their ordinary avocations, was often such as the ear could not listen to without pollution, presenting images, and conveying sentiments, whose most fleeting passage through the mind left contamination. Awfully dark, indeed, was their moral character, and notwithstanding the apparent mildness of their disposition, and the cheerful vivacity of their conversa-

*tion no portion of the human race was ever perhaps sunk lower in brutal
licentiousness and moral degradation, than this isolated people. . . . The
veil of oblivion must be spread over this part of their character.*

He also found them ingenuous.

Their ideas of the nature of these valuable articles [nails] *were very
singular. Perceiving, in their shape and colour, a resemblance to the
young shoots or scions that grow from the roots of the bread-fruit trees,
they imagined that they were a hard kind of plant, and procured in the
same way. Anxious to secure a more abundant supply, they divided the
first parcel of nails ever received, carried part to the temple, and depos-
ited them on the altar; the rest they actually planted in their gardens,
and awaited their growth with the highest anticipation.*

His observant eye is still appreciated by anthropologists today.

*The te-a, or archery, was also a sacred game, more so, perhaps, than
any other. . . . This was a sport in the highest esteem, the kings and chiefs
usually attending to witness the exercise. As soon as the game was
finished, the bow, with the quiver of arrows, was delivered to the charge
of a proper person: the archers repaired to the marae, and were obliged
to exchange their dress, and bathe their persons, before they could take
refreshment, or enter their dwellings. . . . The bow and arrow were never
used by the Society Islanders excepting in their amusements; hence,
perhaps, their arrows, though pointed, were not barbed, and they did not
shoot at a mark.*

*The most ancient, but certainly not the most innocent game among
the Tahitians, was the faatitoraamoa, literally, the causing fighting
among fowls, or cock-fighting. . . . The Tahitians do not appear to have
staked any property, or laid any bets, on their favourite birds, but to have
trained and fought them for the sake of the gratification they derived
from beholding them destroy each other. Long before the first foreign
vessel was seen off their shores, they were accustomed to train and to
fight their birds. The fowls designed for fighting were fed with great care;
a finely carved fatapua, or stand, was made as a perch for the birds. This
was planted in the house, and the bird fastened to it by a piece of cinet,
braided flat that it might not injure the leg. No other substance would
have been secure against the attacks of his beak. Their food was chiefly*

poe, or bruised breadfruit, rolled up in the hand like paste, and given in small pieces. The fowl was taught to open his mouth to receive his food and water, which was poured from his master's hand. It was also customary to sprinkle water over these birds to refresh them. The natives were universally addicted to this sport. The inhabitants of one district often matched their birds against those of another, or those of one division of a district against those of another. . . . More than two were seldom engaged at once, and so soon as one bird avoided the other, he was considered as vi, or beaten. Victory was declared in favour of his opponent, and they were immediately parted. This amusement was sometimes continued for several days successively, and, as well as the other recreations, was patronized by their idols. Ruaifaatoa, the god of cockfighters, appears among the earliest of their inferior divinities.

His list of sports is a long one and he sums it up contentedly.

These are only some of the principal games or amusements of the natives; others might be added, but these are sufficient to shew that they were not destitued of sources of entertainment, either in their juvenile or more advanced periods of life. With the exception of one or two, they have all, however, been discontinued, especially among the adults; and the number of those followed by the children is greatly diminished. That is, on no account, matter of regret. Many were in themselves repulsive to every feeling of common decency, and all were intimately connected with practices inimical to individual chastity, domestic peace, and public virtue. . . . In the Society Islands game playing is now altogether laid aside, in consequence of its connexion with their former idolatry. I do not think the Missionaries ever inculcated its discontinuance, but the adults do not appear to have thought of following this, or any other game, since Christianity has been introduced among them.

So be it, Brother Ellis, but we must note in passing that cock fighting today has resurged and is a tremendously popular and serious "sport," always involving heavy betting.

By this time in Europe the islanders were beginning to lose some of their Bougainvillian luster. Romantic myths are bound to require a bit of refurbishing after a while and Ellis's book did this most effectively. He was undoubtedly interested primarily in the glory of the God that he and his companions had transported to the Pacific. But he might also be called the first Pacific anthropologist. Not a very scientific one by our present-day standards, but a perceptive and appreciative first-hand observer. He made the people and their customs and their environment come alive. He wrote well; his enthusiasm was contagious, and his missionary work was widely applauded.

At the same time another anthropologically minded missionary was also busy in Tahiti collecting and recording even more valuable data and doing it even more exhaustively. This was John Muggeridge Orsmond. We know more about him personally because he was a controversial figure and after he was dismissed from the London Missionary Society, he could be openly criticized. He was born in a country town in England about 1784. He trained for the ministry and, as soon as he was ordained, decided he wanted to be a missionary. He was readily accepted by the L.M.S. and naturally he chose Tahiti. With a newly acquired wife, he set sail on a convict ship for Australia. It was an exciting voyage; first off a brush with Algerian pirates, a fire on board, and a mutiny of the convicts before they reached Sydney in 1817. Meanwhile during the long days at sea, the Reverend Orsmond devoted his considerable energies and good sense to the learning of the Tahitian language from several natives who were fellow passengers or sailors. By the time he reached Moorea in April, he could converse well and soon mastered the language. This fluency was of course of primary importance. It is an objective that seems obvious enough in these days of the field anthropologist, but in early times the chief concern of most settlers was to make *them* learn *our* language. But the missionaries had to preach in Tahitian in order to spread their Gospel. They also had to translate the Bible into Tahitian as a text to teach their parish children the mystic arts of reading and writing. The first Tahitian Bible was printed in London in 1840; truly a magnificent feat, for it remains today the fundament of Protestantism in the Society Islands. Catholic converts of course listen to incomprehensible Vulgate Latin, but fortunately for Polynesian students the Protestants greatly outnumber them. For the beauty of its ancient Tahitian language the London Missionary

Society recalls in our society the King James version, but, ironically, it remained until very recently the sole printed text by which little Tahitians could learn to read and write their own language. It is still the most important text by far. Since the spoken language has changed radically, they can scarcely understand a word of what they are reading and writing. So they are taught in French instead. Today the French have established an efficient, compulsory school system housed in modern, well-appointed, glass-louvered buildings, staffed with teachers from France on three-year tours of duty, in which hour after hour, day after day, only the French language is spoken or written. Moreover, it is taught from reading and spelling books that take little Polynesians down elevators to the supermarket and the hairdressers, or perhaps to the opera or the zoo.

Fortunately for us, the Reverend Orsmond had a strain of the cultural anthropologist in him. His primary enthusiasm and duty, like his fellows, was to convert the heathen, save souls and reveal the True God, but he also took patient care to record their own gospels: their chants, legends, myths, and genealogies. He learned them from all ranks of society, taking them down in writing as they spoke, recording them endlessly in their many variations. He often referred to the richness and poetical quality of the Polynesian tongue, showing an appreciation that was rare, perhaps unique, in those days.

He contributed significantly to the rendering of the Bible and also worked on the dictionary that the missionaries were preparing for publication by the Society in London. Indeed the late J. Frank Stimson, one of the most knowledgeable of our contemporary Polynesian linguists, felt that Orsmond was the chief architect of that invaluable work. When it was published, after many long delays, in 1851, it was attributed to the Reverend John Davies "with the assistance of D. Darling." But by that time Orsmond had been expelled because he had advocated submission to French and (as the brethren saw it) Roman Catholic rule. Actually he had the good sense to foresee the inevitable and to discard the myth of British intervention. So he decided to work with the French rather than against them and was branded a traitor. He continued to teach, probably just as effectively as ever because, of all the missionaries, he was the most respected by the Tahitians. Later the French put him in charge of their Protestant mission. But, most important to posterity, he continued the recording of native lore. Our most vivid report of Orsmond comes from a Frenchman. Let us go on a visit to Bora Bora in 1823 in the company of doctor/naturalist René Primavère Lesson of the corvette *La Coquille*.

May 26 The captain and his staff went ashore to make a formal visit to the missionary Orsmond who had embarked with us at Tahiti and whom we had taken to his island. We could not help but be astonished when reaching the waterside in our large canoe to encounter a jetty 140 meters long built of huge blocks of coral that Mr. Orsmond by his forceful tenacity had constrained the natives to transport and lay up. In this massive structure all fashioned by hand they had built open spaces filled by the sea where they kept fish from an overflowing catch and in some of the square ones they nourished and raised up young marine turtles. The end of the jetty gave into an avenue that led directly to the church: it was there that the missionary first directed our steps and although there was nothing remarkable about the exterior, we could not again help but be astonished at the satisfying aspect of the interior. The church is vast and divided into three parts each one having its own entry and lattice work partitions. The room to the right is reserved for the assembly of chiefs, for the ministry and courtroom; it is furnished only with a huge table surrounded by benches. The central section of the church occupies about half the edifice; serried tiers of seats are placed around the walls and surround the pulpit. Men, women and children occupy separate and distinct areas. The missionary took the greatest satisfaction in showing us a work in which he had good right to glorify himself, for the cut and polish of the benches and pulpit were truly worthy of the reputation of a master carpenter of England; and this was indeed the former profession of Mr. Orsmond in London, and I must declare that this manual labor, teaching the islanders a useful art, seemed to me quite properly to do honor to Mr. Orsmond as a true missionary. All the same I could only groan in thinking of the multitude of breadfruit trees that had to be cut down for that profusion of wood-work, and I imagined that famines might be in store for the future. This wood, from the most nourishing of trees, is of a fine reddish color; it is easily worked and its surface can acquire a remarkable luster; but this precious tree that they have cut down so nonchalantly is also desperately slow growing. One is tempted to blame the thoughtlessness of the missionaries, who facilitate the growth of the population, for removing the means of a sure nourishment. A false principle must also have motivated Mr. Orsmond because he told us: "It is not bad for these natives to be deprived of nourishment, because its abundance leads to their laziness, and idleness discourages their conversion."

Upon our leaving the church, the minister led us to his own house where we found Mistress Orsmond engaged in the saintly occupation of teaching several women who surrounded her to read; this pious lady's face showed a touching resignation and, like all of the missionary wives whom I have seen, one that seems to me most happily organized to convert souls to her belief. Mr. Orsmond as a proprietor who has a mania for construction and who loves to show off his projects, led us to a new house that he was building behind the one he occupied which he found too small. It was a vast affair built of wood plastered with lime in the European fashion: already the library had been transported to the minister's study and a curious piece of furniture there caught my eye: it was a Chinese winged armchair in bamboo, adjustable to all positions of the body, a fauteuil more suitable for a siesta than for composing a sermon. Behind the house they have laid out a vast area for a kitchen garden and an avenue of orange trees runs from this house to the church. One lone tree struck me as a stranger amongst all this oceanic vegetation; it was a fine tamarind from the Indies. To this sort of comfort so esteemed by the English, it joined numerous domestics of both sexes. Tefara and Mai the two kings [of Bora Bora] are really only the henchmen of the veritable autocrat who reigns on this island. This explains to me moreover how many men who have had in their own country only a lowly position should find themselves happy in a material sense in the supremacy they enjoy in faraway fertile abundant isles in the midst of a race so easy to manage.

All along, while this energetic missionary was recording the traditional material of the old Tahitian culture, he was also editing and preparing it for publication. Finally in 1848 he delivered his manuscript to the local French authorities headed by Commandant Lavaud, who in turn dispatched it to the Ministère des Colonies in Paris. And there it disappeared—forever. Oh that he had had a Xerox.

Many a search has been made for it subsequently by scholars and officials, but not a trace of it has ever been found. In his book on Polynesian migrations, published in 1866, Quartrefages, states that he examined some of the Reverend Orsmond's material in conducting his research in Paris, manuscripts in the Reverend's own handwriting, but he says the bulk of it had been lost. A Bishop Museum authority says it was probably burned, among other public documents circa 1848, during the advent of the Second Republic. At any rate, the Reverend Orsmond died in 1856 without learning anything of its fate. How heartbreaking for a lifetime's work and dedication.

Fortunately for us today, there is a not-unhappy sequel to this tale. The Reverend Orsmond lost his first wife, Mary, and their infant child only a few years after their marriage. By his second wife, Isabella, he had a daughter who married the son of his fellow missionary, William Henry, who was one of the originals on the *Duff*. These two, in turn, had a daughter whom they named Teuira; and Miss Henry, as she remained all her life, evidently discovered in herself a compulsive strain of her grandfather. She became a schoolteacher in Papeete. She inherited all of her grandfather's massive hoard of papers, the original notes, observations, and recordings upon which his book had been based. She trained herself to become an accomplished linguist. This is of the greatest importance, because all of the Reverend Orsmond's most valuable material was in archaic Tahitian, a language that had already been largely lost by the time Teuira took her task in hand and has now disappeared to such a degree that it is virtually impossible to correct or elaborate upon Teuira's text. And this is a pity because her published work, splendid as it is, could most probably be rendered much richer and more poetic if someone, Polynesian or expert linguist, could exhume it. Dr. Craighill Handy and Dr. Kenneth Emory, who are the only two men who have the qualifications to come close to such a challenge, declare that they are certain there are many possible meanings in addition to, and in elaboration of, the ones Teuira has chosen, but they know no way to find them.

Lest these final comments seem to cast a shadow on Teuira's book, it must be understood that, as I have said elsewhere, only a Polynesian Homer could have sung the true song. Moreover, the unhappy fact that Teuira died before her work was completed prevented her from reviewing, revising, polishing, and even from correcting obvious typographical errors. So, we can only be thankful, very thankful, for the unique and bountiful wealth of her *Ancient Tahiti.*

John Williams who had also arrived in 1817 was the third of the great missionary trio. His published account of his experiences is a valuable one, but he was such a traveler about the various, scattered islands of the great ocean that he has not much to add to our knowledge of Tahiti. He, more than any, wanted to spread the Gospel far and wide. He had a missionary ship built and spent most of his time establishing missionary outposts rather than cultivating a parish of his own. Indeed he was so zealous and so certain that he was a heaven-sent, always-welcome messenger from on high that he apparently paid little attention to the different temperaments of the various ocean peoples. Relying on the usual mild, friendly nature of the Polynesians whom he had come to know first, he ventured into Melanesia, jumped confidently out of his rowboat to walk ashore in Erromanga and welcome to Salvation the large, cheering crowd on the beach only to have them descend upon him with sticks and stones and club him to death.

In sum, the missionary life was rarely a happy one. There were patches of simple human satisfaction, of touching family life, and even of humor, but mostly these resident Brethren seem to fade sadly away and to leave few personal traces behind them. What they did leave, surprisingly, was their Protestant faith, which for nearly two hundred years now has withstood those "Popish superstitions" of historian Callander and stands firmly today as the religion of the great majority of Tahitians.

CHAPTER FIVE

Turmoil: The Old Order Changes
1815

Meanwhile the social structure of Tahiti was changing considerably. The traditional order of four or five more-or-less equal high chiefs had been upset by European monarchical tradition, by European arms and by the driving ambitions of one relatively low-ranking but ruthless line of chiefs who saw and seized their chance to become English-type "kings" with the help of muskets from English explorers and traders and even from English missionaries needing to protect themselves. A chief of Tuamotuan ancestry named Tu, who later renamed himself Pomare (and still later his son, Pomare II) became for the first time in its history the supreme chief of all Tahiti, introducing dictatorship to what had been an essentially democratic society.

The Pomares' ancestral lands were the low-lying coral atolls to the northeast. They are a huge archipelago some six hundred miles from end to end composed of nearly a hundred scattered islands, the remnants of what must have been a huge mountain range many, many millions of years ago. The tectonic plate on which these volcanoes rested had long since subsided into the Pacific floor, leaving rings of coral on the surface that had grown upward with the sun as their foundations sank. They were inhabited by a fierce branch of Polynesian warriors who were feared and despised by their neighbors to the northeast in the high, mountainous Marquesas Islands and their opposite neighbors to the southwest in the Society Islands. The Tuamotuans

66

were a hardy, aggressive race, perhaps because living was so precarious on those low, desolate coral rings where drinking water came only from coconuts and where fish and shellfish were the only protein and where none of the high-island vegetables would grow. The first Pomare gained a toe-hold in Tahiti by marrying the heiress of a small but independent district in the north of the island. Then, by persuading Cook and his successors (who had made Matavai Bay in the north their headquarters) that he was the king or at least the potential king, he waged war against the traditional chiefs. This was a long drawn-out process and one in which Tu himself did little fighting. The effectiveness of his power was owing almost entirely to the remnants of the *Bounty*, the nine mutineers and seven so-called innocents—sailors who had not joined the mutiny but whose skills were so valuable that Christian, leader of the rebels, had forced them to come with him.

The details of that phase of the famous mutiny (referred to above as little known but as of fateful consequence to the internal affairs of Tahiti) was virtually ignored until the publication of James Morrison's *Journal* in 1939. Morrison was Bligh's boatswain, a member of the "innocents" and an exceptionally articulate recorder of the events of approximately two years between the casting-off of Bligh and the imprisonment aboard H.M.S. *Pandora* of those left on Tahiti. The two *Bounty* mutineers who acted virtually as mercenary officers in Tu's "army" were the notorious Churchill and Thompson, who had secured a good supply of muskets from the *Bounty*'s store and whose professional training as Royal Marines rendered the forces of the old chiefs of the Atehuru and the Teva almost helpless. They were attacked separately and set against each other until by the end of a year or more of fighting, Tu was able to make a grand tour around the whole island with feasts and *marae* ceremonies featuring human sacrifices that terrified the populace and compelled obeisance from all the chiefs to his son. Everywhere the young Tu, later to become Pomare II, was invested with the *maro ura* or red girdle, this time fashioned not of the customary sacred red feathers but of the royal red ensign left behind by Wallis. Ironically it thus became a symbol of English support and of brutality.

By 1791 Tu's sway was virtually undisputed—in the strong-arm or military sense, but never in the old hereditary social sense. Although he was merely an upstart to the legendary chiefs, Pomare was a tremendous man in physical stature, over six feet in height and weighing three hundred pounds, a powerful and terrifying figure in his heyday, but a dissolute, cruel, and self-serving ruler.

Then one morning in the year 1803 he set out in his canoe in the harbor of Matavai to visit a British warship at anchor off shore. As he approached the ship he stood up to hail them, suddenly clutched his back, and fell precipitately into the canoe with his arms dangling lifeless over the sides. No one knew what caused this sudden death, but it was assumed that some internal convulsion, possibly kidney failure, had seized him.

He was succeeded by an even more power-hungry son, who named himself Pomare II in the European royal tradition at the age of about twenty-nine. Of course the new "king" was challenged and his fight for supremacy see-sawed over the next decade. He lost one critical battle and had to flee to Moorea for a year or more. But he shrewdly allowed himself to be converted to Christianity and thus won the support and (because of their fear of his opponents) sometimes the firearms of the missionaries. In a crucial battle with Tati, he defeated the great Teva clan in the south and then, instead of massacring them as was the old-time custom, he pardoned them and magnanimously clinched his supremacy. It was a calculated hypocrisy, and it worked. Although he had professed conversion for at least two years, the missionaries had been distrustful of his ruthless character and were wary. They kept postponing action, but this unprecedented gesture of what they chose to see as Christian mercy won their consent. He was officially accepted into the church: all the sacred (and ethnologically priceless) idols were burned in great bonfires. The ancient religion was joyously obliterated or at least driven underground. At the height of his power in 1819 he promulgated the "Code of Pomare," transforming the sectarian life of the island to English law, as he had the spiritual life to English religion. He then proceeded to drink himself to death in a gargantuan alcoholic binge that lasted for two years.

Pomare was forty-odd years old at the time. He had first married a chiefess named Tetua who died in 1806 aged twenty-five of "voluntary abortion" (mishandled infanticide perhaps? Pomare was an Arioi). Next he married Teriitaria, oldest daughter of Tamatoa IV, high chief of Raiatea. This was a stratagem for which the Pomares became notorious, because the high chiefs of Raiatea, the motherland of Tahiti and Holy Land of all central Polynesia, were the highest chiefs of all. However, he soon left Teriitaria for her younger sister, Teremoemoe, and of this union was born Aimata, who was eventually to become Tahiti's famous queen.

She was born in 1803 and considered "adulterine" by the missionaries. Not surprisingly the records, or interpretations of them, are confusing. Pomare may have had two wives (nothing unusual for a chief in pre-Christian times). In any case two sons were born later to the older sister and were recognized without hesitation as the regal heirs. The first of these died in infancy. The second, upon his father's death in 1821, became king of Tahiti in all his infant splendor at the age of eleven months.

Pomare III (Teriitaria) grew to be a handsome child with an alert, quick mind. He was the cherished hope of the missionaries who concentrated their ambitions for their own future influence on this successor to the dynasty that they had brought to power in the island. To be sure the first two Pomares, grandfather and father of this child, had been dynamic, ambitious, effective individuals. Even though it was imposed against the grain of traditional Tahitian society, the dynasty was now firmly established. Pomare I had bought his power from the explorers with pigs, scurvy-saving vegetables, and vahines. Pomare II had bought his from the missionaries by scuttling his ancient gods and converting himself and his subjects to Christianity. Of course there were some vahines thrown in too, and the *Bounty* "mercenaries" had perhaps been decisive. These then were the bare, brutal facts. The wise old traditional chiefs—Paofai, Tati, Hitoti and Utami—reluctantly recognized them and held themselves aloof. One cannot help but suspect that the people at large recognized them also. But what to do? And besides, by the time of Pomare II's death in 1821, they were becoming accustomed to their general situation. The internecine wars had ceased and, admire them or not, the Pomares had brought a stable peace to the land. Perhaps more important still the people had come to respect and even to love the individual missionaries who had lived with them so many years now and who had taught them the exciting new miracle of reading and writing. Although one must be cynical about how this dynasty came about, one must at the same time recognize that it had its benefits.

The coronation of Pomare III was planned to the last detail. The throne was to be set upon a two-tiered dais. A half-mile avenue led up to it strewn with flowers. First came the wives and children of the missionaries. Then the high chief Mahine, clasping a large Bible to his bosom, flanked by the senior missionaries and followed by the rest of the brethren. Then Utami, flanked by two other high chiefs. Then three more chiefs with Tati in the center bearing the crown. Next the boy king (about four years old) on the throne carried by four chief's sons; his mother and sister to his right; aunts to the left, followed by the brother-in-law of the old king, Tapoa, chief of Bora Bora, and others of the royal family. Judges, magistrates, songs, prayers, pledges, oaths and more songs and prayers. It was a ceremony far more of the church than of the *marae*.

So—with the bright young Pomare male successor in prospect, the missionaries were now writing the laws and directing the polity as well as guiding the religion. They were indeed the main stabilizing influence in the island. With their large civilian body of new converts and with their hopes bright for the future with a boy king who was completely under their influence, no other force in the island could challenge them. It was too late to reassert old family blood lines and traditional prestige. When the old gods were burned in deference to Jesus and failed to revenge themselves or to bring on catastrophes or even to put on a display of thunder and lightning, the *mana* of the ancient Tahitian religion lost its power forever. For the moment, the outlook for Tahiti was as relatively untroubled as could be hoped for.

In other lands too the "civilized" nations of Europe went right on subduing and converting to Jehovah's blessed, lovely ways the savage hordes all over the world. Little did the Polynesians realize that the shock troops of religion had plowed and sown the fields for the military harvest to come.

The death of Pomare II at the relatively young age of forty-two had been a strain on the whole society, the effects of which reverberated through the island for some years ahead. It was a great relief to some, especially to many of the powerful chiefs who had resented, even detested, his power and arrogance, and to the missionaries who were appalled by his debauchery. In his later years he had taken openly to such a depraved way of life that he could not be consulted on affairs of state without the presence, interference, and maudlin advice of one homosexual favorite or another—pitiful creatures whose only interests were more money, more whiskey, and more favors for themselves and for His Royal Highness. And yet the Brethren were now inevitably obligated to this second Pomare for his almost single-handed conversion of the majority of the populace.

But upon his death in 1821 preparations had been made swiftly to pick up the royal succession. We learn from the missionaries that little Teriitaria was a handsome boy and under their hopeful and assiduous tutelage he was soon recognized as the brightest in his class in the select mission school at Afareaitu on Moorea. One is inclined to suspect that the churchmen were perhaps patting themselves on their backs because here was their prize opportunity to mold a new ruler in their ideal image after more than twenty years of fervent, holy labor that had had no success in making Christian monarchs of the first two island "kings." But whether they were defending themselves or not, they are specific about the boy's earlier-than-average ability to read, his disposition as sunny as his royal skies, even his quickness at sports. For a good five years they watched him grow, green and tall as the ebullient vegetation all about him.

During the first year of his "reign" Tahiti adopted a national flag. Flags were becoming important those days as different ones fluttered and streamed from the sterns of square-riggers of many a distant king-

dom when the ships sailed (or were more often towed) through the pass
into the most welcome harbor of the Pacific. They must have made a
fine show of colors and symbols, crests and crowns. So naturally the
king of Tahiti must have one too, even though he was certainly not old
enough to know what was going on. The flag adopted was a missionarily
modest one—a red stripe at top and bottom, a broad horizontal band
of white between. All the clothing those days was striped yardage from
English cotton mills in pale blues, greens and pinks, a somber contrast
indeed to the present-day, crimson-flowered pareus. (Depraved French
influence no doubt, but beloved by the Polynesians.)

That plain flag was later briefly decorated with some compromising
stars and later still was to be troubled by a rash of royal embellishment.
But it quickly returned to its original simplicity and so it remains today,
vying (sometimes timidly, sometimes bravely) with its master the
French tricolor.

In the third year of this eventful reign the arrival of the controversial
missionary George Pritchard took place. In the fourth year the young
monarch wrote a letter, King-to-King, to George IV of England implor-
ing his protection from greedy foreigners—the first official premonition
of the brewing menace.

Tahiti Matorai
5 October 1825

O King George the Fourth,
*Peace to you from Jehovah and our Lord Jesus Christ. May your reign
be still prosperous and for ever. May it be agreeable to you, O king, to
listen to this petition. We wish you to be our friend and for you to protect
us. Let not our land be molested by British subjects now or at any future
time; and should we be invaded by any others, do you then defend us.
Should it be agreeable to you to grant this petition we then wish to use
the English flag. We are afraid on account of what we have heard from
Port Jackson. If we hoist the British Flag we are in fear, and if we hoist
our own flag we are also in fear lest we should be invaded by some other
country. Another petition also is, that you will never abandon us, but
regard us with kindness forever.*

*If agreeable to you, write us a letter that we may know our petition
is granted by you or even if it is otherwise.*

Peace be to you and to all your family.

(signed) Pomare

To the King of Britain & Ireland George the Fourth
The above is an accurate translation of the original letter enclosed.

Henry Nott
Wm. Ellis

King George never bothered to answer. The next year a treaty was
made with the young American republic assuring (as far as John Quincy
Adams could) the independent sovereignty of Tahiti.

Then one fateful day in 1827 Teriitaria was coming back from
Moorea where the mission had its school for little royal Tahitians, for
their own missionary children, and for those of favored foreign settlers.
His canoe ran into a sudden deluge, biting cold as they sometimes can
be. A cold or croup, dysentery or pneumonia, and he was dead.

Sad was the land. Not only the stricken missionaries but the high
chiefs also had made their peace over the prospects of this young boy.

Who was to succeed? Put yourself in their places. Let us think first
of the chiefs. They had always lived by old successional blood lines that
had been disrupted by the gunpowder intrusion of the Pomares. The
ancient fabric had been torn asunder. But now according to their
ancient custom the next, and only, in line of succession was the daughter of Queen Teriitaria's younger sister. The chiefs began to think over
again their doubts about the Pomare dynasty.

The missionaries had no doubts at all. Aimata was her name, which
means "Eater of Eyes." This may seem gruesome to us, but to a
Polynesian of those days it meant royalty or chieftanship, for the eye
of a sacrificial victim was always offered first to the highest chief
present. Presumably he ate it in the ancient cannibalistic days, but for
many generations now it had been merely a symbolic gesture. Aimata
was both illegitimate and a female. Not only a female but a flagrantly
pagan one. Aged fourteen, she was all that the missionaries particularly
deplored and she seemed of a pattern too set to convert and mold to

their beliefs. They had paid no attention to her as they concentrated on her promising young half brother. So first they looked about and naturally landed upon Tati, paramount chief of the most powerful clan, the Teva, whose commanding personality outshone all others.

Perhaps one of the chief causes of the growing uneasiness between the chiefs of the traditional clans and the missionary-sponsored Pomare dynasty was a newly arrived missionary named George Pritchard who came in 1824. He evidently had a quick and industrious mind for he soon became fluent in Tahitian. He settled in Papeete with his family and built himself a comfortable house on the Broom Road toward the western border of the town. Thus when six-and-a-half-year-old Pomare III died in 1827 Pritchard was well situated to take on the job of taming and converting the wild, new Queen.

Yes, sorry choice though she was to every one excepting her own immediate family, Aimata was made queen. Tati declined the missionaries' offer. Perhaps he sensed the troubles ahead and did not wish the responsibiltiy of dealing with the foreigners: the French and English military men, the troublesome missionaries, the still more troublesome traders, merchants, whalers, renegades and beachcombers. Perhaps also he felt, as did some of the other chiefs, that old Tahitian blood lines were the best law of succession even if they were the relatively low Pomares. Illegitimacy made no difference. Adopted children or extra-marital children were all the same in old Tahiti. They still are today. And in Tahitian eyes Aimata was an engaging personality. Pretty, flirtatious, lively and gay. Wanton? Well yes perhaps, but she was only fourteen years old. She had been three years married to Tapoa, future high chief of Bora Bora, but it had been a parental arrangement. He was several years younger than she and they were soon to be divorced.

After all the past bloodshed, corruption, and uncertainty why not a Pomare? When all the rights were reviewed and the wrongs weighed, the basic chiefs of the basic districts held firm against the missionaries. For the rest of her life Aimata never acted without a convocation of them and a consensus of their judgment. Perhaps supernal Polynesian blood was beginning to flow in her veins, perhaps her mother's.

Pritchard must have been skillful, for in a few years Pomare IV began to give up her wanton heathen ways and gradually to become a pious Christian. Indeed as her troubles commenced to build up, and as she was torn between military pressures from the French and missionary pressures from the English, her new religion and her new mentor became a refuge for her. She could not read or write, spoke very little English and no French. So of course she needed an interpreter and some one who could write messages, draft laws, send pleas to Queen Victoria, answer ultimatums from French admirals. Indeed she needed someone to attend to all court business and, as was to be expected, this naturally included advice and guidance. Every king and queen everywhere has had one, so Pomare had her Pritchard. And every counselor of the crown everywhere has had his political ambitions. So it is not surprising that George Pritchard developed his.

As this relationship ripened and became more and more apparent, the Mission brethren became uneasy. Politics and religion, Church and State, were not supposed to mix. But Pritchard seemed just as keen to have England take over Tahiti in order to fend off the threatening French as he was to have his true God take over the ancient idolatry and prevent the hated Catholics from moving in. There loomed always the specter of "infidel France."

When Pritchard applied to Lord Aberdeen, the foreign secretary, for the post of English consul in Tahiti, his colleagues were alarmed and insisted that he revoke or resign his religious status. There was a good deal of pulling and hauling both in Tahiti and in London. But when Pritchard was at last officially appointed consul, he agreed to surrender his position and functions in the Mission.

This seemed to clear the air a bit, but Pritchard had a gadfly. Five years after Pritchard had arrived in Tahiti a young Belgian merchant had come named Jacques Antoine Moerenhout. He was, of course, a Catholic and except for a technicality of birth (his natal town was just over the Belgian border) he was French. It was he in 1836 who welcomed the two French priests who came illicitly from Mangareva and whose ejection gave the French admiral later on his excuse to precipitate his crisis with Queen Pomare.

It is a strange tale, seemingly innocuous enough at first but building quickly into high drama involving a number of surprisingly fiery personalities. The two little priests, Caret and Laval, had been in Mangareva, where the first successful Catholic mission had been established. When they arrived at Tahiti, they were put ashore clandestinely on the southern part of the island from a small schooner. They expected the schooner would sail right on to her destination, Valparaiso, and they would thus be stranded on Tahiti, at least until another vessel arrived. They knew of course that their presence was illegal. The English Protestants had long since persuaded Pomare to prohibit the teaching or even the presence of teachers of any other religion. The priests therefore made their way secretly to Papeete, where they were immediately welcomed by Moerenhout.

Since this clever man was a merchant who befriended and supplied whalers and since the whalers were mostly American, he had somehow got himself appointed American consul to the Tahitian government and thus his premises enjoyed diplomatic immunity. Whether this was all a carefully planned plot, as Pritchard declared, or whether Moerenhout's protection was spontaneous is still moot. But there is no question that the priests were deliberately challenging the London missionaries and their policy of maintaining Tahiti as exclusive territory for the Protestant religion. It seems not unlikely that they were sent out from France by their Sacred Heart order for this precise purpose. When they were refused admission by order of the queen, Moerenhout locked them into his bamboo guest house to see that they were not molested. There the little priests knelt in prayer while appeals went forward on the part of the French residents in town and also on the part of some chiefs and other settlers, such as the esteemed Dr. Johnstone, who felt that religious discrimination was wrong.

Just how it was arranged, no one knows for sure. Moerenhout of course felt that the villain Pritchard was the instigator. At any rate, the schooner appeared unexpectedly in Papeete. Her captain said she had need of repairs before she could set out on the long ocean voyage. Toward midnight a group of husky Tahitians lifted off a portion of the coconut-frond roof of Moerenhout's guest house. You can see the two padres kneeling beside a flickering candle, reciting their prayers, probably in Vulgate Latin in this heathen land. To the Tahitians they were of course praying to Satan, far more dangerous than prayers to the old Tahitian gods, Oro, Taaroa, Rongo and the rest. So they dragged the priests from their trembling knees, two or three of them carrying each of the squirming little fellows by arms, legs and bodies; handed them out through the guest house roof and down to the beach, where a longboat was summoned from the schooner to come fetch its illegal popish cargo. This was all done as quickly as possible, but evidently there was enough of a scuffle so that Moerenhout came out in his nightshirt with a lantern to join the fray. But he was a small man and there were plenty of very large Tahitians about, ready to carry out the orders of their queen (or perhaps of her chief advisor). The priests were bundled into the longboat, but as soon as they were rowed a few yards out, they jumped into the shoal lagoon water and made their way back toward shore. There they were met by their abductors and put in the boat again. The captain of the schooner soon realized, however, that he must obey port regulations or his future trading rights would be in trouble. So they wound up on board well before dawn and eventually were sailed to Valparaiso. As we shall see, they were to return, but not for a number of years.

Meanwhile Queen Pomare was beginning to have trouble with some of the old-time chiefs of the powerful, rich districts on the west side of the island and on the peninsula. They had recognized defeat under Pomare II and accepted obeisance to his infant successor, but in spite of their initial concurrence they were not too happy with this upstart queen. There was no question of her succession: that was old Polynesian custom. But the blatant ascendancy of these inferior Pomares and especially the idea of an all-island queen must have rankled in many breasts. They were not as blissfully Christianized as the musket-powered Pomares.

Another most important development was beginning to cast its shadows before. For years the Pomares had been pinning their hopes for a degree of independence on English intervention. France was

beginning to threaten. All but Pomare herself and her closest followers
—such as Tapoa of Bora Bora, Tamatoa of Raiatea and Ariipaea of
Huahine (all of them relations of hers)—had begun to be convinced
that England was politely and diplomatically deferring to France. The
old chiefs were realizing that the time to choose sides was approaching
ominously.

CHAPTER SIX

Shock: The Impetuous Commodore
1838

I t was two years after the affair of the expulsion of the little Catholic
priests that Dupetit Thouars first arrived in 1838. Many years later
Pritchard's son William was to publish a vivid boyhood recollection of
the dramatic arrival and its subsequent events. Whether his account
is strictly reliable as history one might question, since this was the
beginning of the decisive struggle for the control of the island between
the various forces involved: the Protestants versus the Catholics, the
French military versus the British diplomatic, but most importantly,
the Tahitians for their own survival. Since William's father, George
Pritchard, was the "Generalissimo" on the British-Protestant side, and,
as he thought, the Tahitian forces contending with the French-Cath-
olic ones, young William would naturally be biased. But he is worth
reviewing because he gives the opposite view to the one which the
French have so assiduously presented to the world both officially and
through their presuming-to-be-dispassionate historians. They too would
naturally be biased. Another valuable contribution of young Pritchard
is his revealing of the actual documents that are either singularly lacking in the French accounts or, when quoted, are singularly different.
Of course one must allow for confusions or prejudices of translation.
There are three languages to consider, Tahitian, French, and English.
All of young Pritchard's are of course in English. There is also a very
real element of downright falsehood to be recognized here and there.

But it does seem interesting, whether it is strictly fair or not, to have a look at both British-missionary and French-military sides. Alas, the Tahitians, having no written language, can speak only through either one of the main contenders. The English military were taking instruction from their discreet diplomatic superiors. The French Catholics too were being wisely quiet, recognizing their great initial disadvantage and pinning their hopes largely on the latent powers of their Pope and their God, with some faint expectations perhaps of their French King, Emperor, or whatever might be in the changing governments in Paris during these times.

Capitaine de vaisseau Abel Dupetit Thouars was a fiery, ambitious young naval officer in a French navy that had recently been defeated and was now packed tight with glorious admirals who had nothing to do except keep themselves in office. His rank was Commodore at the time, halfway between captain and admiral. His only chance to break through the log jam was to do something spectacular in the field (or, in naval parlance, on the high seas). Whether his plans were laid before his arrival in Tahiti we do not know. It is almost certain that he had no instructions from headquarters to authorize his action. Guizot, the powerful Minister of Marine at that time, later repudiated what he considered Thouars's insubordination and was going to demote him upon his return to France until a sudden uprising in the streets of a glory-starved, victory-hungry populace made an on-the-spot hero of him and the chagrined Guizot had to dub him an admiral instead.

According to young Pritchard (whose account I shall summarize and occasionally quote), Dupetit immediately upon his arrival in the frigate *Venus* had a consultation lasting several hours with Moerenhout. This slippery fellow had recently been deprived of his American consulship so he, as well as Thouars, had strong motives to hatch a plot. Dupetit drew up an ultimatum. Not long after, Moerenhout was appointed consul of France, later on to be ratified by King Louis Philippe.

On the morning after that consultation, the following note was handed to Queen Pomare:

On board the French frigate, "Venus"
Papeete, 30th August, 10 a.m. 1838

To the Queen of Tahiti
  Madam,

The King of the French and his Government, justly irritated by the
outrages offered to the nation by the bad and cruel treatment which some
of his members who came to Tahiti have suffered, and especially Messrs.
Laval and Carret [sic], Apostolic Missionaries, who called at this island
in 1836, has sent me to reclaim, and enforce, if necessary, the immediate
reparation due to a great Power and a valiant nation, gravely insulted
without provocation. The King and his Government demand—

1st. That the Queen of Tahiti write to the King of the French to
excuse for the violence and other insults offered to the Frenchmen,
whose honourable conduct did not deserve such treatment. The letter of
the Queen will be written in the Tahitian and the French language, and
both will be signed by the Queen. The said letter of reparation will be
sent officially to the Commander of the Frigate "Venus," within twenty-
four hours after the present notification.

2nd. That the sum of two thousand Spanish dollars be paid within
twenty-four hours after the present notification into the cashier of the
Frigate "Venus," as an indemnification for Messrs. Laval and Carret
[sic], for the loss occasioned to them by the bad treatment they received
at Tahiti.

3rd. That after having complied with these two first obligations, the
French flag shall be hoisted the first day of September on the island of
Motu-uta, and shall be saluted by the Tahitian Government with twenty-
one guns.

I declare to your Majesty, that if the reparation demanded be not
subscribed within the specified time, I shall see myself under the obligation to declare war, and to commence hostilities immediately against all
the places of your Majesty's dominions, and which shall be continued
by all the French vessels of war which shall successively call here, and
shall continue to the time when France shall have obtained satisfaction.

I am, of your Majesty, The most respectful Servant
The Captain of the French frigate "Venus,"
(signed) A. Du Petit Thouars

The Queen was living on the little royal island resort of Motu Uta in the harbor of Papeete. She had very recently had her first child after three miscarriages, a daughter, Ariiaue. [Young Pritchard is mistaken here. Ariiaue was her first son.] *Neither she nor the baby were feeling well that morning so she asked Mr. Barff, the English missionary who acted as doctor for the brethren, and her counsellor George Pritchard to come see her. While they were present a young French Lieutenant arrived with the message, ranted and flung his arms about frightening the Queen and shouted that "France, as a great nation, had sixty grand frigates like the 'Venus' and cared for no other nation in the world."*

The astonished Queen asked Pritchard to read and translate the message. After some discussion she decided she should convene her principle chiefs, consult with them and beg some time of the imperious French commander. They all rowed across the harbor to Pritchard's house and on the way saw that the Venus *had run out her guns. They heard the drums beating the crew to quarters and were left in no doubt that the French were ready to destroy their homes.*

Messengers were sent to the chiefs and Pritchard hurried off with a letter to the Commodore explaining the Queen's need for delay and asking for an inquiry into the charges customary in civilized countries such as his own. She professed herself willing to comply if guilty but she felt a public hearing ought be be held first. But Dupetit refused to read any communication of any sort. He "had made his demands, and if they were not complied with by ten o'clock the next morning he would carry out his threats." He dispatched marines to guard the Motu Uta and to halt all activity in the port. He even invited Pritchard and any other Europeans to come aboard his vessel as a refuge while he bombarded the town. It became apparent that they were dealing with a military madman and they had no resources whatever to protect themselves from complete destruction.

Looking back from today's perspective, the situation seems comparable to a terrorist skyjacking. But this was an unquestionably official naval officer acting avowedly in the name of the King of France. That was perhaps the way of the terrorist in those days, only a hundred and fifty years ago. And we must not forget that English colonels were acting the same sort of way in India and Egypt. The Spaniards had been even more ruthless a couple of hundred years previous and the Germans under Bismarck were to be just as terroristic a few decades later. Those Europeans!

There was no choice but to comply. The spendthrift queen had no money. Her friendly chiefs raised some. The townspeople, perhaps to save their own properties and skins, raised some more, and the missionaries were able to scrape together 1,000 "Spanish dollars" (about $1,000 American). These were turned over to the "cashier of the frigate" and Pritchard was given a written receipt. The banditry was all thus made very legal and circumspect; a "treaty" as later construed between the queen of Tahiti and the king of France. That gun-point treaty rammed through by an impetuous French naval officer, motivated mostly, if not entirely, by his own ambitions for advancement, thereby became the foundation for the French claim to sovereignty over the Tahitian islands; a claim that the Tahitian people are still resenting today, a claim that they are still powerless to resist today.

It is tempting to castigate the French at this time, but one must always bear in mind that their fellow conquerors, the English and the Americans, would almost certainly have turned out to be even more destructive to the Tahitians. The French yoke has been hard for them. Today there is still strong resentment in their hearts against their French masters. But they still speak their own native language and they still own a major portion of their land. Under the American yoke, their fellow Polynesians in Hawaii have virtually disappeared and their precious land (the life sustenance of every Polynesian) has virtually all passed to others. Under the English yoke the New Zealanders have segregated the Maori to pitiful scraps of their ancestral lands. They have almost obliterated their culture by glass-casing it. American Samoa has been "protected" into a living museum—or should we call it a human zoo?

The Tahitians were unfortunate on that fateful day, but not so unfortunate as most of their distant brothers of the Pacific.

So the ransom was paid, but what about the other two demands? The letter of apology was simple enough. The commodore dictated it himself. Pritchard translated it into Tahitian. The queen signed.

But the twenty-one-gun salute to the French flag presented complications. It was found that the royal Tahitian arsenal could produce only one cannon fit to fire out of its whole decrepit battery. And furthermore there was only enough powder for five shots. And still the only choice was a proper salute or war. Pritchard approached Thouars again pointing out that he was the only one on the island who had enough ammunition to fire twenty-one times. Could he loan the powder to the queen? This, the commodore said, was impossible because the French papers would hear of it and he would be guilty of the illegality of supplying powder to the Indians. He understood the predicament however and since a proper salute was essential to the honor of his country (no matter who heard it), he summoned up a bright idea. He told Pritchard he would loan the necessary powder to him as British consul and he could do with it as he pleased. In due course the tricolor was run up on Motu Uta and twenty-one shots were fired, not as briskly as was customary, but fired nevertheless.

The commodore, says young Pritchard, "rested on his laurels" for five days and then presented M. Moerenhout to the queen as the new consul for France. Queen Pomare politely but firmly declined. She had had quite enough of Moerenhout. She would accept a new French consul willingly, but Moerenhout was persona non grata. Whereupon the gallant commodore declared that the rejection would be considered as a declaration of war by Tahiti against France. The queen perforce accepted her foe.

The commodore then raised one more point: a treaty must be signed to formalize the whole proceedings. The queen objected. The commodore insisted. So the document was drawn up in both French and Tahitian and duly signed before witnesses.

Convention between his Majesty Louis Philippe I, King of the French, represented by Captain Abel du Petit Thouars, Officer of the Legion of Honour, commanding the French frigate "Venus" and her Majesty Pomare, Queen of Tahiti.

There shall be perpetual peace and friendship between the French and the Tahitian peoples.

The French, whatsoever may be their profession, shall come and go freely, establish themselves, and trade among all the islands under the Government of Tahiti; they shall be received and protected on the same footing as the most favoured nation.

The subjects of the Queen of Tahiti shall go and come to and from France freely, and they shall be received and treated there as the people of the most favoured nation.

Made and sealed at the palace of the Queen of Tahiti at Papeete, the 5th of September, 1838.

> A. Du Petit Thouars,
> Pomare IV.

The queen pointed out that since all of her subjects were Protestant, it should be understood that none of the French who were to come and go freely should preach Roman Catholicism in her kingdom. But Thouars nodded toward his guns and insisted that as Frenchmen, all priests must receive full protection under her majesty's government. He conceded however that she was free to enact any laws she pleased about teaching religion in her domain.

Young William then writes, *And now, with his two thousand dollars on board, the French flag saluted with twenty-one guns with French powder and the treaty in his pocket, Commodore Du Petit Thouars bethought himself to do the aimable. He presented to Queen Pomare a barrel-organ. And well do I remember that wonderful instrument!*

It was received jubilantly by the populace and played through the streets, for nothing of the kind had ever been seen in Tahiti. But a strange thing happened. As it was being carried across the queen's threshold, mysterious, quake-like, creaking sounds were suddenly heard. The bearers were frozen with fear and the queen told her courtiers to hurry and find out the cause of the strange noises. It was discovered that three of the huge supporting posts of the house had split from top to bottom. *Pomare e, ua riro to tatou hau!* (O Pomare, our kingdom is gone!) said one of the venerable old chiefs. The whole crowd trembled and lamented and the joyous barrel organ suddenly turned into a symbol of doom.

The next morning the queen was invited to dine on the *Venus* and told she would have a royal salute, twenty-one guns. She politely declined, pointing out that she had no powder to return the compliment. The commodore asked Consul Pritchard to try to persuade her to "grace his table," but there were further excuses. She was not well. So Pritchard was invited to breakfast instead, and during the meal the commodore, always solicitous for the welfare of his crew, suggested that Pritchard use his influence with the queen to license a number of Tahitian vahines as prostitutes for his men.

At length Commodore Du Petit Thouars sailed from Tahiti, concludes young William, *and once more Queen Pomare breathed freely, but always remembered the mysterious coincidence of the organ and the rents in the posts of her house.*

A few months later the queen sent her famous letter to Victoria.

Salutations, greetings, and friendship to the mighty Queen of England,

I, Queen Pomare, with chiefs and representatives of my people assembled this day as one body and souls, to manifest to you with the greatest delight our sentiments of obligation under which your constant and Christian sympathy has laid us.

In doing so, we are not only fulfilling a duty transmitted to us by a generation nearly gone by, but accustomed from childhood to cherish the English name, we are obeying the impulse on our own hearts. Since the first Englishman neared our shores in one of your vessels, we have praised you as the only nation which showed us a Christian heart; and now may you lend us a Christian hand!

The blessing of your religion, which, through your pious exertions, you taught us to follow, opened to us two new ways to two new worlds, unknown heretofore to our poor people. With the teachings of Christianity and the paternal care of the missionaries, we may hope to secure one of these worlds; but the other, that into which civilization leads us, begins already to embitter our life, and will ultimately deprive us even of the dominion of the graves of our ancestors, if we are left to our own resources.

The commerce and industry which civilization attracts to our islands, put us into daily relations with the white people, superior to us in mind and body, and to whom our institutions appear foolish and our government feeble. We made our exertion, with the concurrence of what our poor experience and knowledge taught us, to obviate these difficulties; but, if we have succeeded in enacting the laws, we cannot succeed in giving them the strength and force which they require.

Thus, in our utter impossibility to make ourselves strong and respected, we are threatened in what we have dearest to our hearts, our Protestant faith and our nationality.

We have nobody to assist us in our helplessness except you, who implanted in our hearts, through your people, the love to Jehovah, the love of order and industry. Do not let these good seeds perish; do not leave unfinished what you have begun, and what is progressing so well. Lend us your powerful hand, take us under your protection; let your flag cover us, and your lion defend us. Determine the form through which we can shelter ourselves under your wings; cause our children to bless you, and to cherish your Christian feelings, as we do.

May the great Jehovah preserve you, and recompense you for all you do in our behalf!

Peace be with you, the Queen of Great Britain.

No doubt it had been written by Pritchard, but if you read carefully, there will be found in this letter (aside from the missionary palaver) the true basic concerns of the Tahitians: the embitterment of civilization and loss of the dominion of their ancestral graves (meaning, I believe, a loss of their old culture), and, significantly, their realization of their inability to control the present depredations of the white hoodlums.

Pomare received only a secretarial acknowledgment of the arrival of her letter.

This capitulation to sheer naked power was of course a shattering experience for the whole island, but its effect was to take some time

to make itself felt. To the traditional chiefs this must, first of all, have
appeared to be a humiliation of the Pomare clan. That the new
"queen" could stand for the whole society was an unfamiliar and
probably unacceptable concept to them. So they bided their time. Not
so Pomare. She was shaken to her roots. Or, let us say, her chief
counselor Pritchard was shaken to his. Here the dreaded French were,
now officially in power, or about to be. The next blow fell the next year
when Commodore La Place sailed in with his big guns to impose upon
the queen the freedom of the French church to preach what the
English missionaries had told their Tahitian converts were doctrines of
the Devil.

Corruption on the waterfront was bad mostly because the corrupters
were congenitally bad people, all males, misfits, mutinous, even murderous, the sort of unregenerates that even whaling crews rejected. But
at least they were sporadic and few in number. After a brief corrosive
fling ashore, in jail or in the bush, they usually extinguished themselves
in liquor and debauchery. They must have been a succession of fester-
ing sores in the Tahitian social body, but they were obviously of such
low moral character individually that they could not pose a serious
problem to the society as a whole. Even the Polynesians, blessed unspoiled children of Nature, had their misfits and outcasts and always
had had them.

But, what of a mass influx of healthy, hedonistic French sailors?
When the grand frigate *l'Artémise* struck a mass of coral heads off
Tiarei in 1839 and was brought in awash to Papeete harbor, she de-
bouched 465 lusty Frenchmen for six whole weeks while she was
careened, rebottomed and rekeeled. They could not live aboard of
course, so they took themselves to the welcoming shores. If the population of the island was about five thousand, half would have been
women, more than half of them would have been old, matronly or
children; two-thirds of this remaining thousand-odd would have lived
in the south or on the peninsular island, leaving just about every
remaining young vahine a jolly French companion for six weeks of
merrymaking; meat and drink from the man-of-war, fruit, vegetables

and flowers from the shores. Here is how the semi-official chronicler of the expedition, one Louis Reybaud, reported it.

The many Tahitians working at the pumps looked with an envious eye at the bread and wine of France. Then over the mess tins began the adoptions of friends or taio. Soon at mealtime one saw running from all parts of Papeete children and women bringing baskets full of fruits, cocos, oranges, guava, breadfruit and melons. Seated on the shore, these messengers awaited the rolling of the drums that announced the eating hour and the cry of taio, taio echoed in the ship's holds and each one came with her offerings. Then when evening fell the taios came forth arm in arm, French and Tahitians, to the meeting places. All the sailors thus had on shore a house and a woman, a ménage complet. Jealousy being a passion unknown to these naturels, one can imagine what such an arrangement offered the resources and pleasures of our mariners. They were lodged, nourished and blanchis for practically nothing. Their character was in every way congenial to these good islanders who had never found in any other people so much gaiety, expansiveness and good fellowship. The waterfront was continually en fête. To the great scandal of the missionaries it seemed always to echo with joyful songs and bursts of laughter.

Things became even more cordial when, after the careening, the *Artémise became inhabitable. The entire crew, officers and sailors were installed, as best they could be, on shore either in the houses of the natives or in an improvised encampment. The initiation of this French colony into* la vie tahitienne *was as easy and harmonious as could be. One could see how beguiled the sailors were and what friends they found. The officers were no less happily engaged: the island that Bougainville had called the* Nouvelle Cythère *did not belie its name. The sojourn in Tahiti was one long session of fickle and sensual lovemakings. Papeete was nothing but a grand seraglio without constraint. Once darkness came every tree along the shore shielded a passionate couple and the waters of the rivers gave asylum to a swarm of copper niads who came to bathe and play with the young ones of the frigate. No sooner were liaisons formed than they were promptly broken. When attachments became serious, fathers, brothers, husbands intervened for the missionaries had imposed upon them a sort of tithe as a penalty.*

You have perceived by now that Monsieur Reybaud was a freeswinging thinker. Let us see how, as an historian, he assesses the English missionaries.

When they arrived at Tahiti it was still Bougainville's island of pleasures, the isle of graceful dances that charmed even Cook, the isle of love in which Wallis played a personal and almost royal role. The girls crowned themselves with flowers and offered themselves joyously to all comers, without passion and without remorse. Scandalized by such ways the missionaries decided to abolish them at a stroke without transition. To this disordered life, they opposed an inflexible puritanism; against the excessive abandon, they fulminated their absolute interdictions. What was the result? They missed their objective for having overreached it and soon found themselves constrained to deal with vice without the power to extinguish it.

Ridiculous prescriptions for garments, severe chastisement for lesser faults, show today that a secret poison was at work and that fermented drinks had commenced. Hypocrisy weighs heavy on this joyous people, they cannot live in the oppressive atmosphere that is created for them, they suffocate, they die. All was harmonious in their old social organization, everything, their nudity, their freedom, their folly, their license perhaps and it was all taken away in a day. The salvation that was to save the soul had killed the body.

It is on Sunday above all that one can see how the missionaries at Tahiti practice their system of surveillance and constraint. At sunrise the shore is covered with natives who are swathed in their heavy European clothing. Nothing is more curious than this bizarre procession where the dress always contends with the individual. It is very difficult to convey an idea of the monstrous hats and incredible robes that see the light of day on these occasions. Men march gravely without pants and with black long-coats open on all sides, others have boots and no coats. The women packed into their bodices and encumbered in their skirts do not know where to put their feet or how to hold their heads. This European apparel contrasts strikingly with their golden bodies so that all their natural gracefulness is hidden and disappears. One can see only old over-dressed hags. Sometimes one can perceive away in the distance a young girl advancing timidly, her head decorated with flowers and her body enveloped in a large piece of tapa or cloth. But if a missionary spys this graceful child, he bursts out with reproaches and forces the delinquent to hasten out of the church. Such is the tyranny that weighs upon these natives, a tyranny of all the day and all the hours.

But now they possess a place of sure refuge, the French camp at Fare Ute where little by little the ancient habits reappear. Many Tahitians have installed themselves more or less permanently so that everywhere one hears the cry of oui, oui, oui *the only word that the Tahitians have acquired with marvellous facility. It has been very difficult for them to learn how to say* non.

To Reybaud's account Commodore La Place, in his official report, added a high-sounding sales pitch for Catholicism assuring the *naturels* that French priests would let them dance and sing even on Sunday and never impose on them all the onerous rules and regulations of the Protestant missionaries. It is a siren song indeed, but probably one which no Tahitian ever heard. You can imagine however how it was received by the English. Here was Catholicism being introduced by force, officially, legally: the Devil himself authorized to offer his wanton wiles in open competition with the True God.

All this was made even more poignant by the fact that it was an American whaling captain, Tahitian labor and Yankee ingenuity that had saved the French warship and made her seaworthy after six weeks of hard work while the Frenchmen disported themselves with the vahines. Alas, how easy it would have been to let her sink off Tiarei.

The old high chiefs, who had never taken the missionaries or the new religion so very seriously, were probably much less bothered by this new ruckus than they had been by the military one. But the queen was now a devout Protestant and indeed her principal, if not her only, support and refuge was Pritchard and the missionaries. She felt the chills of doom descending. She was evidently quite unnerved, for she fled to her Tamatoa relatives in Raiatea. At first she seemed to bury her head in the sand. She appointed the high chief Paraita, who had been her regent during her royal adolescence, as regent-in-fact representing her now, during her absence and she went into virtual seclusion. Soon afterward Pritchard was to set out for England to plead his case in person to Lord Aberdeen. He was not to return until some twenty months later. It was to be an eventful year.

But life had to go on. Indeed the queen's absence perhaps relieved them of her despondent moods and gave the giddy regent, Paraita, a chance to preen his feathers and sound his proud cock's crow.

CHAPTER SEVEN

Intrusion: Traders, Whalers, Riff-Raff, Settlers

1830s and 1840s

The island was in trouble. Not only because of the maneuverings of the French, the English, and the missionaries, but also because the intrusions of traders, whalers, and beachcombers were reaching a stage of debauchery and violence comparable perhaps to our present-day vandalism. An instance was the midnight attack on the American consul. Moerenhout is a curious member of our dramatis personae. He came primarily as a merchant, trading mostly in pearls and pearl shell (nacre). They were the quickest and surest sources of riches in Oceania. He bought and sold schooner after schooner and toured the islands, bringing food and building supplies and pearl divers; taking back precious cargoes of nacre and of course the inevitable copra —cargoes of pungent smells. He wrote a copious and informative book —one thousand pages in two volumes—about his travels filled with careful observation and reflecting a sympathetic knowledge of the Polynesians. He was not fluent in their language, though he was indeed admiring of their ways. But there was a mysterious streak in him. Why did he bring back a lovely fifteen-year-old bride from Peru and then, after only seven weeks, depart on a year-long cruise whose destination and purpose was never explained? How did he manage to be appointed American consul in Tahiti?

His official status in Tahiti is set forth clearly in two paragraphs of another of those regal letters from Pomare, this time to the king of France. *This is my wish: that the King of the French shall send away the person who has caused all of my troubles. This is the name of that person: J. A. Moerenhout, Consul of France. This man by monetary bribes and other reprehensible collusions, has alienated the hearts of my principal subjects from their Sovereign in such a way that they have become traitors toward their Queen. This man does not observe the laws of my country, but only goes his own way and his conduct in general shows only his evil nature.*

This man is not French, but comes from a certain country near France. He is a very bad man and a causer of troubles, and I can hardly wait until he no longer lives here. I am sure that when the King of the French comes to know his nature, he will send him out immediately.

Historian Léonce Jore says the letter was written by Pritchard and he is probably right. Note that it tries to be delivered in the Polynesian idiom, but its "reprehensible collusions" are certainly not Tahitian.

There are a lot of unanswered questions in the dim background of this very active, aggressive man's career, but like so many others in the South Sea mists, they will probably never be revealed. At any rate, whatever his Machiavellian meddlings in politics and religion, he was always a merchant and at this point in his life he had retired from voyaging and had set up a store in Papeete. He had what was probably considered a rich supply of goods on his shelves to trade mostly to whalers and other passing ships, but also to the English and French residents. One dark, rainy night shrieks and curses were heard. Moerenhout and his young Peruvian wife Petrini were found badly beaten up, unconscious and gravely wounded. So severely was the young beauty mauled that she died a few months later. Moerenhout blamed his arch rival the English missionary George Pritchard for setting a group of Tahitian bullies upon him, but subsequently a black man, "Sambo," a deserter from an American whaler, was apprehended, accused, tried, condemned and hanged. It seems most likely from the hazy records, largely hearsay, that he was a common thief whom Moerenhout heard rummaging about his store. Petrini probably joined the fray with its tragic outcome. It was to be exactly fifty years before Robert Louis

Stevenson visited Papeete, but in the grog shops of that harbor he might easily have recruited a good lot of his cast for *Treasure Island*. And it was to be only four years later that Melville jumped ship to spend some uncomfortable nights in the stocks at that famous "Calabooza Peretani."

Papeete to visiting sailors was indeed one grand, not-so-glorious brothel. Not much law or order restricting foreigners could be enforced except by foreigners. Traditional law and order, that is, respect for chiefs and their ancient *arii* blood line system had by now been undermined, at least as far as the waterfront was concerned. To all in authority it was woefully apparent that some sort of consistent regulation was needed. Tati, the senior chief of the Teva, was the most respected of the Tahitians. He and a few almost co-equal chiefs—Paofai, Utami, and Hitoti in particular—were apparently becoming aware that the Pomare "dynasty" in the person of Aimata and under the aegis of Pritchard could not control the hoodlums who were constantly coming and going in whaling and trading ships and frequently leaving the dregs of their crews as beachcombers. Only European rule could control European infestation. The queen persisted in believing that her sister Victoria would come to her rescue and she was encouraged now and then by a chauvinistic sea captain. One Toup Nicolas of H.M.S. *Vindictive* brought Pritchard back from Sydney in 1842 after his fruitless, year-long trip to England to plead with Lord Aberdeen for intervention. (The foreign secretary did not even give him an audience.) Perhaps fired up by his apocalyptic passenger, Captain Nicolas declared to Pomare that he would sink any French warship that threatened her and he made some grand promises that there would always be a British frigate to follow him. Pomare granted Captain Nicolas a fine piece of land for British naval use and he then sailed away and left her defenseless. The truth of the situation was that the individual sea captains were spoiling for a fight and could not resist the temptations to act like plenipotentiaries when ten thousand miles from home, even though their superiors in the Admiralty in London had no intention of precipitating another war with France. And it was much the same on the French side. The Ministry of Marine had clearly adopted a policy of caution while admirals at sea, such as Du Petit

Thouars and La Place, were boldly flexing their muscles in the name of their king. Alas for Queen Pomare, the British had better control over their seagoing firebrands than did the French over theirs. Not much better to be sure, but enough to make the difference decisive in the end.

As we look back, it is apparent that this uncertainty contributed greatly to the divisions, dissensions, and miseries that were to destroy the independence of the Tahitian people. But before we come to that next phase of action, let us have a look at the day-to-day life of the waterfront. The most engaging character surely is the English doctor Francis Johnstone. He came to Papeete about 1836, established his own private practice, and was evidently loved and respected by all, as is affirmed by the fact that he treated the Moerenhouts to their satisfaction and that when Pritchard was desperately sick in captivity he would have none but Johnstone. The exception is Melville, and it is curious that in *Omoo* he made such an unpleasant, swindling character of this good doctor when all of his other characterizations of islanders ring so true.

Dr. Johnstone was an amateur botanist of considerable repute. He imported and introduced a number of medicinal and other valuable plants and trees. He made exhaustive studies and listings of indigenous flora. Unfortunately his collections and papers were buried with him by his devoted Tahitians who evidently reverted to their ancient custom of interring with a high chief his most precious possessions: adzes, ornaments, fishhooks and such.

One Edward Lucett, a merchant and trader of the times, was a not-so-savory personage, especially in the eyes of the French. He probably did smuggle arms now and then to the rebels and very likely a bit of whiskey went along with them. He was strongly British in sentiment and wrote an anonymous book called *Rovings in the Pacific* which is a venomously prejudiced pro-English, first-hand account of the French conquest, too biased and too vainglorious in my opinion to be given much credence.

*　　*　　*

There were a number of notable visitors who have left a variety of impressions. Commodore Wilkes of the famous American Exploring Expedition stopped by in 1841 and his chronicler gives us his impression of our queen.

On the 7th of May one of the unhappy domestic feuds of the royal family threw the whole of Papieti into a ferment. The Queen followed by all her attendants, with great lamentations, rushed into a foreigner's house, to escape from her royal consort, who was pursuing her, uttering dreadful menaces. The facts of the quarrel, as derived from authentic sources, are as follows. As Pomare was on her way to Papieti from her residence at Papaoa, she was met by Pomaretani riding furiously. Owing to the turn of the road, he did not perceive the queen's party in time to stop, and ran over one of the maids, knocking her down, and bruising her. Pomare, attributing the accident to his being intoxicated, began to abuse him in opprobious terms. Enraged at it, he dismounted, and began not only to abuse, but also strike her. Not content with this, he caught her by the hair, threw her down, and attempted to strangle her, which he was only prevented from doing by the attendants, who held him until Pomare fled for her life. Disappointed in overtaking her, he hurried to her new palace at Papieti, and vented his anger by demolishing the windows, breaking open her boxes and trunks, tearing her wardrobe and finery to pieces—thus doing injury to the amount of some two thousand dollars.

On the perpetration of this outrage, the queen at first declared her intention of summoning the judges and suing for a divorce; but soon changed her mind, and forgave her husband on his promising future good behaviour.

The next year we have Melville's pleasantly contrasting account of his visit to Moorea.

In answer to our earnest requests to see the queen, we were now conducted to an edifice, by far the most spacious, in the enclosure. . . . Pushing aside one of the screens, we entered. The apartment was one immense hall; the long and lofty ridge-pole fluttering with fringed matting and tassels, full forty feet from the ground. Lounges of mats, piled one upon another, extended on either side: while here and there were slight screens, forming as many recesses, where groups of natives —all females—were reclining at their evening meal. . . . The whole scene was a strange one; but what most excited our surprise was the incongruous assemblage of the most costly objects from all quarters of the globe. Cheek by jowl, they lay beside the rudest native articles, without the slightest attempt at order. Superb writing desks of rosewood, inlaid with silver and mother-of-pearl; decanters and goblets of cut glass; embossed volumes of plates; gilded candelabra; sets of globes and mathematical instruments; the finest porcelain; richly-mounted sabres and fowling-pieces; laced hats and sumptuous garments of all sorts, with numerous other matters of European manufacture, were strewn about among greasy calabashes half-filled with "oee," rolls of old tappa and matting, paddles and fish-spears, and the ordinary furniture of a Tahitian dwelling. . . . While we were amusing ourselves in this museum of curiosities, our conductor plucked us by the sleeve, and whispered, "Pomaree! Pomaree! armai kow kow."

"She is coming to sup, then," said the doctor, staring in the direction indicated. "What say you, Paul, suppose we step up?" Just then a curtain near by lifted, and from a private building a few yards distant the queen entered, unattended.

She wore a loose gown of blue silk, with two rich shawls, one red and the other yellow, tied about her neck. Her royal majesty was barefooted.

She was about the ordinary size, rather matronly; her features not very handsome; her mouth, voluptuous; but there was a care-worn expression in her face, probably attributable to her late misfortunes. From her appearance, one would judge her about forty; but she is not so old.

As the queen approached one of the recesses, her attendants hurried up, escorted her in, and smoothed the mats on which she at last reclined. Two girls soon appeared, carrying their mistress' repast; and then, surrounded by cut-glass and porcelain, and jars of sweetmeats and confections, Pomaree Vahinee I, the titular Queen of Tahiti, ate fish and "poee" out of her native calabashes, disdaining either knife or spoon.

"Come on," whispered Long Ghost, "let's have an audience at once"; and he was on the point of introducing himself, when our guide, quite

alarmed, held him back and implored silence. The other natives also interfered and, as he was pressing forward, raised such an outcry that Pomaree lifted her eyes and saw us for the first.

She seemed surprised and offended, and, issuing an order in a commanding tone to several of her women, waved us out of the house. Summary as the dismissal was, court etiquette, no doubt, required our compliance. We withdrew; making a profound inclination as we disappeared behind the tappa arras.

A not so well-known visitor was revealed recently by Bengt Danielsson who translated the original account for inclusion in his splendid *Mémorial Polynésien, Tome I, 1521–1833.* He is Samuel Stutchbury, an English professional botanist who visited Tahiti in 1826 and decided to make a trip across the center of the island, a formidable feat that no European had ever attempted up to that time and one that very few have attempted since, because the island is just as rugged today and the only means of transport is still shank's mare. Unfortunately it would not be as rewarding a trip now because his shy, mysterious settlement high in the mountains has undoubtedly disappeared after one hundred fifty years.

Stutchbury sets out from *Miripeha to the valley of Wyereede . . . a most fertile and magnificent valley,* which must be, in our present-day translation of Tahitian place names, the Vairaharaha River Valley near the border of Mataiea and Papeari.

Our approach to the house of a friendly chief, named Onai, lay through patches of taro, arum, this plant requiring marshy ground for its growth; in these patches are found two species of melania. The vicinity of his house was well marked by the beautiful and ample plantations of native fruits, including many which have been naturalized, such as oranges, custard apples, pine apples, water melons, etc. We were here met by the chief himself, one of the finest specimens of his race, standing at least six feet ten inches high, stout well-proportioned, and active. Upon reaching his house, I was introduced to his wife, a fine handsome young woman, known all over the island as the vahina na na *or "handsome woman," but who at this time had only just been released from*

the heavy task of making forty fathoms of cloth for the state, which she
had been adjudged to do by a jury, for absconding from her husband,
and living with a chief belonging to a neighboring district in Tiarabu.
Shades of Tavi and his Taurua?

He starts out in the usual way up the river bed toward Lake Vahiria
and is soon immersed in the flora, collecting many specimens.

I now noticed with surprise what very excellent naturalists my guides
were, their nomenclature being most extensive and certain; it mattered
not, however insignificant the plant or insect, I had only to ask its name,
when it was immediately given me. Suspecting that Fiope, who was a
clever shrewd fellow, did not like to expose his ignorance, I was afraid
that he gave me names at random, and very soon put him to the test by
asking the guides separately, when I found them to agree in the specific
names, although they carried their distinctions of varieties to such a
nicety, that several, after a short contest, were left referable to a learned
man, whose name I cannot now recollect: in fact, to such minuteness
are these distinctions carried, that the natives generally reckon, and
distinctly name, about seventy varieties of the cocoa nut tree (cocoa
nucifera), above fifty of the bread-fruit tree, of which botanists only name
two species, the artocarpus incisa and integrifolia. It is by a careful
nurture of the different varieties that they manage to have a constant crop
of fruit, each tree often bearing four crops a year. Of the plantain and
banana, the musa paradisaca, and sapientum, they name more than
thirty varieties. Independently of this, they have names for all the differ-
ent stages of growth and approaches to maturity of the fruit.

He climbs that wearisome, watery trail over which so many of us
have sweated and stumbled, crossing the steep river back and forth
until, *after counting its repitition upwards of sixty times, I gave up the*
attempt in despair. Having forced his way up not less than ten miles
he comes to the great cataract *falling from a height of four or five*
hundred feet. At last he comes to that miraculous lake and as usual finds
that the only way to cross it is to swim or make rafts. Two rafts are made
of dead banana trees, one for him and one for his collections and
baggage; his guides will swim alongside and behind for propulsion. Of
course the unfortunate fellow upsets midway across. This would be
expected and would be no great tragedy except that Stutchbury lost all

his precious botanical specimens. But he manages to keep his gun and powder dry and so was able to shoot a few ducks.

The guides took some red bole, which is formed by the decomposition of basalt, and kneading it into a plastic state, cut off the head, legs, and pinion portion of the wings, plastered the whole body over with the clay and then placed it in the midst of an ember fire: when done, which they by practice seemed to know to a nicety, the ball was soused in water, the clay broken off, and the body of the duck produced entirely divested of feathers and skin, full of gravy, and highly palatable.

They built a leaf shelter and, *My bed was formed by two succulent plantain trees, cut down and bruised into machee by large stones. This proved a wet but soft bed; and the principal objection to such a couch was, that when I arose in the morning, it appeared as if I had slept in a tub of indigo, the juice from these plants dying the body of a deep blue colour.*

In the morning they climb arduously over *the highest mountain but one of Tahiti.* (The highest, Orofena, is over 7000 feet) and at noon finally reach the plain at the foot of the mountain. They found traces of a greatly-to-be-feared tribe of *Tutiouries.* Tutiouri he notes *signifies rust of iron;* tuti, *defecated matter;* and ouri *iron, persons of a wild or heedless disposition; Anglice, vagabonds.*

At last, *In the evening we arrived at a very interesting village, distant, as I afterwards found, nearly twenty miles* [which would put him about two-thirds of the way across the island] *from the sea-shore. This village or settlement contained about one hundred and fifty people—I think the healthiest and best looking men I have seen upon that island. They behaved with the greatest kindness, killing a hog and preparing an excellent repast, of which I partook, and at their persuasion remained with them during the night. At dusk these natives assembled in a house adjoining, and kept up a* heiva *or dance until midnight, at which they were very importunate that I should be present, which I declined, rather desiring rest, which however was totally prevented by the myriads of musquitoes.*

At our parting with these kind people, I was surrounded by a groupe of the elder and influential men, who, in the most energetic manner, entreated me not to mention their existence to the missionaries, inform-

ing me that they no longer continued their idolatrous practices, but that they at the same time had separated themselves from their fellow-men upon the shores, rather than subject themselves to the new code of laws, and outwardly follow a persuasion they as yet had felt no conviction in the truth of. It was here that I observed the manners of a people, bearing some resemblance to those described by Wallis, Cook, etc.; the women wearing high headdresses, their own luxuriant raven hair plaited and decorated with wreaths of high-scented native living flowers; their skin much fairer, carrying the bloom of health, and altogether forming a most astonishing contrast with those of the low lands—their clothes were their own manufacture; the men wearing their graceful tibutas, or poncho, as the Peruvians would call it (a sort of mantle, made of the bark of the bread-fruit tree, dyed yellow with turmeric, and painted by impressing fern leaves dipped in a red vegetable dye, and scented with the essential oil obtained from sandal wood); their persons clean and comely, with a bold ingenuous outward bearing, totally unlike the sycophantic, hypo-critical, and degenerate race of the shores.

Here then is first-hand corroboration of the foreign blight. And to emphasize its foreigness: *At eleven, A.M. the ocean opened to our view, and in pushing for the beach, we had to pass through a long grass, called piripiri, which bears a burr covered with prickles of a most annoying kind, penetrating the clothes and scratching the skin, which in tropical climates is readily excited to inflammation. The natives, to avoid this, always on passing through the grass, strip off their clothes, and thus avoid the painful purgatory which the European had to undergo, at whom they always laugh, stating that it justly punishes only the foreign-ers who first introduced it. It was brought from Norfolk Island by Mr. Crook, one of the first missionaries, and is now as completely spread over the whole group of islands as totally to prevent the breeding of sheep, whom it speedily kills by getting into the wool, and worrying them to death by the constant irritation kept up.*

Then after much geological and botanical detail our hero reaches the north coast, the first European to make a Magellanic transverse of the mountainous island of Tahiti.

These mountain people who so charmed the impressionable English botanist were most probably a band of the Mamaia sect or cult, which was in exile at this time. They had been a group of dissidents inspired and led astray by a renegade native preacher named Teao. He began to attract attention in his own parish in 1827, in one of the outlying districts. Another preacher named Hue from Punaauia took up his refrain and almost overnight there was born a personal following that aroused suspicions among the missionaries, then anxiety and fear, and ultimately vigorous opposition.

Such splinter cults or throwbacks seem to be not uncommon when new religions begin to take over old ones and, from an anthropological viewpoint, this would have been a fascinating one if it had been allowed to go far enough. Its tenets are somewhat obscure of course because the missionaries whose accounts have recorded it for us were violently opposed. But it seems to have been a curious mixture of the old religion and the new. Jesus was apparently supplanting Oro, much as Oro had supplanted or was supplanting Tane not many decades before the Europeans arrived. And Jehovah the remote and mystical was supplanting Taaroa, the vague, distant creator of the Pacific world.

A grafting of these new gods onto their old basic religious philosophies made legitimate in Tahitian eyes a return to the old ways of song and dance and sex. An incipient Mamaiaism had been tempting to Aimata before her kingly half-brother's death, and of course any such tendencies in the vivacious teenage wanton had to be swiftly eradicated when she became queen in 1827 at the age of fourteen. This may not have been difficult, for she was quickly isolated when her conversion and instruction was begun. But the cult by that time had been spreading dangerously. Its devotees had been chased into the hills and classed as "rusty feces," but still they persisted and had to be stamped out. This was accomplished mainly through the armed force and moral suasion of the high chief Tati, who was by then an ardent Christian and, in the reports of several visitors, the most Europeanized Tahitian on the island. So the Mamaia movement was annihilated, but the repercussions of its birth and death had severely shaken the religious fabric of the whole society—another, and perhaps the most radical, cause of the unsettlement of the times.

CHAPTER EIGHT

Romantic Interlude
1841

A *tamaraa* was then and still is today a joyous festive occasion. Preparations preceding it sometimes took several months while piglets were segregated, bark cloth of the finest texture was beaten and bleached and impressed with delicate fern patterns. Mats were woven of the finest tissues from pandanus leaves soaked in the fresh mountain streams, cured in the sun, split into strips as wide as a fingernail, then plaited meticulously into large rectangular mats, long enough to extend well beyond the head of the tallest man who would sleep on them and well below his outstretched feet. There had to be plenty of them to serve as gifts at the *tamaraa*. So they must be started months ahead, rolled up and hung from the rafters to await the occasion. Pearl oysters were fetched by plunging to the bottom of deep atoll lagoons and their iridescent shells were polished and ground into gleaming ornaments. Feathers of many birds, black plumes from the giant tropic birds, myriad little yellow tufts from the breasts of golden plovers, bright scarlet curly feathers from the parakeets, all of them stitched into close-woven purau bark nettings to make huge U-shaped gorgets to hang upon the chest; headdresses or long, sweeping pennants to fly from the mast tops of sailing canoes. All these took time, and patience, and all were prepared especially for the particular festival day in prospect, and many of them with the particular recipient in mind, a fussy old aunt perhaps who fancied that only *she* could weave the softest mats or neatest baskets.

As the magic day drew nearer, preparations shifted from furnishings, apparel and ornaments to the most vital feature of all, food. Pigs had been tethered to trees, fed with shoots of greenery and succulent tendrils, fattened on rich coconut meat mixed with breadfruit to prevent what we call scours. Chickens had first foraged about, then were caged and plumped up. Now in the final weeks was the time to gather ripe breadfruit from all over the towering trees; the time to climb into the mountains for *fei*, the wild orange plantain; to dig up swollen taro roots from the artificial swamps and search out the heavy yams. And as the last days approached it became time to fish for bonita, *ahure*, *operu* and *mahimahi*, to lure the *varro* lobsters from their sand holes and the tentacled octopus from their hiding places in the coral niches, to gather shrimps from beneath the stones of the beds of mountain streams, to pry oysters from rocks in shoal waters and lift the sieve-like baskets that had been baited for crabs.

Fruits too had to be assembled: bananas, pineapples, shaddocks, papayas, oranges, the *vi* apple, *ti* roots, soursop, mangoes, bananas and again bananas.

Finally the great day itself approaches. People from the peninsula had started three or four days ago, or even a week ahead to walk the many miles, stopping on their way at nights to visit relatives at convenient intervals. Their produce and many of themselves would go, some ahead, some later, in heavily laden canoes paddled and poled along the lagoon shores. People nearer by set out with pigs on one-legged tethers, chickens upside down in squawking, claw-tied bundles, children scurrying forward and back, to and fro with equally restless dogs; a flowing, weaving entourage around each strolling file of families.

And so the whole populace of the island, except for the sick and the very old, converges on the little settlement of Papeete, most of them squatting in the outskirts, the night before, to arrive at dawn—never before that—on the appointed commencement day to crowd the spacious lawns and tree-shaded glades surrounding the royal (yet-to-be-erected) palace of the queen.

Meantime the wide harbor has filled itself awhile with ships, but mostly with canoes from outlying districts and outlying islands, hundreds upon hundreds of Tahitians, Raiateans, Huahineans, Bora Borans, some Tuamotuans, some Marquesans, their golden brown skins shining with sweat or glistening with *manoi* (the coconut-oil massaging cream), their eyes flashing, their mouths talking-talking; their hands gesticulating; some singing, some crying, some shouting, some laughing, all of it a swelling-subsiding-rising-falling bedlam such as can occur nowhere except in Polynesia on that idyllic little island of Tahiti in the very center of the great Pacific ocean.

In the old days of course, days of our queen's fierce and tyrannical father, a *tamaraa*, or "feast-festival," would have been different: with many human sacrifices clobbered, and skulls stove in to be offered to his patron god, Oro. But those were usually the feasts of war, either for terrorizing the intended victim or for celebrating victories and confirming conquests. In contrast this occasion was one of lighthearted gaiety, a wedding feast for the queen's favorite cousin and best friend.

Although Pomare had sought refuge in Raiatea with her Tamatoa relatives, the *tamaraa* was being spread on the royal grounds of her absent majesty. It is 1841 and the spacious, Victorian-style "palace" is not yet built. European visitors accustomed to great opulence in their monarchs are astonished that Pomare's present houses are not strikingly different from those of other chiefs or even of well-off, upper-class Tahitians. They are only a bit larger and more numerous.

Paraita, the regent, is of course the most important personage present, but the most conspicuous female is that favorite of the queen, granddaughter and heiress presumptive of Tati, high chief of the Teva clan, who is generally recognized as elder statesman or "Supreme Court Justice" of the island. Huruata was her intimate familial name (she had many-syllabled full names also, and some of changes of name) and she was a princess of the isle. Not a princess in the ordinary pattern of the European process, but of the prevailing Tahitian chieftainship, the elected, appointed, hereditary beauty endowed with leadership and bold spirit.

In Polynesia a leading chief was always born of grace, but if he failed to measure up to the responsibilities and challenges, he was very soon deposed or set aside. The people could, and always did, assess and pass judgment on him, keep him in power or throw him out, even though he was born to an advantage and bred for leadership by his blood lines. Still he had to prove himself, and if he proved inadequate, then a brighter one was adopted. It made not much difference where that one's blood came from, so long as he was high born, of the *arii*. Once he was adopted by the "royal" family, he was as good as any blood son.

The queen's large council house in the early days of Pomare's "rule" was a gay, colorful center of social life in Tahiti. Indeed, there was so much social life that very little ruling got done. And, in the eyes of the missionaries at least, the goings-on were highly irresponsible, self-indulgent, and even shockingly licentious. The missionaries had done everything in their power to discourage and suppress the free conduct of morals: the singing, dancing, the instincts of the vahines to dress in flowers and scanty waistcloths instead of the voluminous Mother Hubbards that were the only clothing approved by the church. Indeed they often dropped their dress entirely on impulsive occasions when the singing and dancing reached on orgy pitch.

Now this young beauty of the court, the high born Huruata, had for many years been the closest companion of the queen. She was only a few years younger; the queen was twenty-eight. A combination of things made them close. The queen, like all Pomares, sought the prestige that companionship with the higher born Teva would bring her. The younger girl, being the most marriageable prize in the islands, would inevitably gravitate to the court where she could choose from the handsomest and best-born suitors (or rather, the young "princes" proffered by ambitious parents). Moreover the two girls were cousins, related through many family ties. But most of all they must have been congenial, fun-loving creatures in that glamorous society of the early 1800s when they were growing up together. Aimata's father had been the all-powerful warrior king and Huruata's grandfather was the highest hereditary chief of the island, possessor of the finest and most extensive lands. He controlled huge tracts of Papeari and Papara the rich southern districts that, until Cook and the English came to the northern provinces, were the highest seat of power and prestige. For lack of a direct male descendant, Tati's lands would of course be inherited by this oldest grandchild. And thus for her birth, her beauty and her possessions she was quite naturally the prize catch of the era. Add to this her quick wit and chiefly mind, no wonder she was the best-loved confidante of Queen Pomare, who, although as she matured she became modest and sincere and possessed of commanding dignity, was never comparable intellectually to her cousin. The queen's hereditary position and Huruata's ingrained respect for it precluded jealousy or rivalry; such were the dictates of Tahitian social law.

So the young ladies in their early days had had good times together, uninhibited by the later strictures of power and responsibility. They were fancy free and, to the missionaries, wanton, licentious, libidinous wenches—as was the time-honored way with Tahitian teenage maidens, especially the high born ones.

Huruata had been wooed by many a chief's son, or rather by his relatives, for most marriages were usually contracted at very early ages by parents, especially those from the outer islands, where the chiefs of Raiatea, Bora Bora and Huahine had for many generations been recognized as of even more resplendent ancestry than the chiefs of the larger island who were usually their descendants. But our captious maid would have none of them. Her friend Aimata's early marriage had been a failure from the start. One might guess that the girl had not had time to live her prenuptial experiences and that the boy was just too young for her. A few years later she took a new and older husband, Ariifaaite, son of the chiefess of Huahine. He turned out to be a monster, while her first spouse, Tapoa, became high chief of Bora Bora and one of the most respected of all in the later crucial councils during the French seizure of the Leeward Islands. Meanwhile by all accounts Queen Pomare was to drift gradually from sparkling promise into dignified but selfish mediocrity.

It had been a crazy quilt of a court, newly established for the native new queen after the fashion of English heritage and convention. Her father had assembled his chiefs in the traditional Polynesian ways with *marae* ceremonies and human sacrifices at the open-air "temples" until he had converted himself to Christianity. For his infant son and heir, the missionaries had envisioned a palace to establish the solid, dependa-

ble traditions of good old England, and when the young monarch
suddenly died, the palace became even more important as the school-
house or controlling abode of the irresponsible little savage who was to
succeed him as Queen Pomare IV. The English had always been ardent
believers in the Divine Right of Kings. They could conceive of no
proper order of society and government other than one supreme monarch above all, with his royal family and his layer of nobles isolating him
from the common crowd. And especially in the early years of the 1800s,
those ingrained faiths were very strong. Had not the American colonies
recently rebelled against the sanctity of King George III? And then the
French had taken off on their wild, impious rampage to behead their
divine Louis and Marie Antoinette, and next, horror of horrors of
history, gave birth to that prime villain of all time, the lowborn upstart
Bonaparte, whom the English had only very recently succeeded in
quashing and who had at last died in smoldering exile on Saint Helena
only a few years ago?

So it was perhaps not surprising to find this royal Tahitian court
dressed for formal occasions in scarlet uniform coats with tattered
brocade scattered here and there, or blue naval jackets sometimes worn
as pants with legs thrust through sleeves. But whatever the top sides,
the Body Guard, consisting of many sergeants, a few haughty corporals,
but no privates, were, to a man, barefoot. What firearms they bore were
mostly unshootable and their cutlasses, some shiny still, some speckled
with rust, were more decorative than operable. The queen's regent, her
uncle, Paraita, was more privileged: sporting a French admiral's fore-
and-aft hat and an English general's gleaming epaulettes. He usually
wore boots, though his queen's large brown toes were always peeking
from under the bottom of her voluminous crimson robe. The Ladies
of the Court were also a motley sight to see, Mother Hubbards all at
the start of ceremonies, primly striped cottons of demure blues, greens,
and rose from Manchester and Leeds but with the lavish floral headdresses, neckpieces, and big bright ear flowers of their Polynesian ancestors, with short overskirts of broad green *ti* leaves and sweet-smelling
hinano blooms girdling their waists and hips, but, again, never a slipper
to be seen among them.

"Court" occasions, and the gathering of the chiefs from the many districts, the speeches and counter-speeches, the pronouncements, and judgments and settlements of disputes were as a rule all carried through with a solemn and orderly decorum. But after torrents of endless talk throughout a hot day, all hands seemed to welcome at last the queen's stilted but imperious termination of ceremonies, and then, of course, the fun began.

But enough of past custom, let us get on to the queen's huge bamboo-and-coconut-leaf council house where a fine European-style ball was to take place after the feasting was done. Of course outside on the lawns and in the park, Tahitian wrestling, boxing, dancing and merrymaking were taking place. But inside the spacious "palace," minuets, waltzes and quadrilles were danced with the smart English and French settlers, some of them with white European wives. The visiting military and naval officers glided around, most of them with golden brown Polynesian vahines who, ever adept and adaptable to new ways and styles, were soon learning to caper about as nimbly as any Parisiennes.

In ancient times large feasts of this sort were held with great regularity four times a year at the changes of the seasons; what we call the equinoxes and solstices. Many incidental celebrations took place for special occasions: births, puberty rites, marriages, wars, successions, deaths. None were perhaps as extensive and universal as the seasonal ones, but all were similar and all were frequent, especially those of the Arioi Society, the traveling minstrels and players who journeyed from island to island in great fleets of canoes to entertain the various districts and exhaust their food supplies.

Back at the temporary palace the year is 1841, Pomare has been queen for fourteen years. In her absence her favorite "lady-in-waiting," now about to be twenty, is the most coveted marriage prize of the court. She has had her choice of the handsomest and most high born, but she is still willful, independent and coy. She is determined to pursue her own way—until, as in so many fairy tales, a dazzling stranger enters upon the scene. A young gentleman aged twenty-one, from England, a sparkling conversationalist, a stylish dresser who wears a flashy diamond on his right hand, who dances with consummate grace and flair, whose black hair is oiled and curly, his moustache pert, perhaps insolent above a sly smile, his dark eyes quickly seeking out, and quickly finding the comeliest girl in the ballroom—and as quickly captivating her.

It all seems a classic opening for a typical mid-century melodrama. She of course was a highest of high princesses of "La Nouvelle Cythère," *une fille idéalle* of Rousseau's race of natural innocents and Diderot's popular *philosphie.* He was a black-eyed descendant of a family of Jewish bankers who were émigrés from France to England, escaping of course on the eve of the Revolution. One of three sons, this Alexander Salmon had left his English home, perhaps an outcast, to seek his fortune away from the anti-Semitic prejudices of early Victorian Europe. Well educated, recently a younger partner in his older brother's merchandising adventure in San Francisco in the pre-gold-rush days, he became disillusioned with the rough frontier life. He was by nature a dilettante and was now seeking the romance and gullibility of the glamorous island of Tahiti, a money-maker and wife-seeker in every inch of his ancient ancestry.

This, then, would seem a perfect setup for a tintype tragedy. And sure enough, the pretty little princess of Nature promptly fell in love with the sly slicker from the other side of the globe. She would have none of her local swains. She would have none but him—and maidens of her ilk had ways of getting what they wanted.

Tahitian chiefs by this time were wary of philandering white men: merchants, whalers, traders, beachcombers. Too many of their precious vahines had been lured from their ancestral homes, impregnated, cozened out of their heritages and deserted. Tahitians had of course always been easy going, even promiscuous, where young sex was concerned, but marriage meant family ties and blood lineages meant inheritance of land. In 1837 a universal law had been adopted: marriages between Tahitians and Europeans were now illegal.

What could be done? Here was one of the potentially wealthiest heiresses of the whole island, the equivalent of high aristocracy in European society, with a mind of her own. But of course in all societies exceptions to sweeping laws can usually be arranged if circumstances are compelling enough. No granddaughter of the great Tati could bear a child if she were not married and Huruata would marry no other than the "Peretani" Alexander Salmon.

The French historian Caillot puts the situation neatly. *Des signes de grossesse s'étant manifestés,* the lady-in-waiting's benevolent and understanding queen, Pomare IV, suspends the marriage law of 1837 by royal decree for three days. The couple are joined in holy matrimony by a missionary of the English Protestant Church, official and exclusive religious power in the islands. Several more couples were united during those same three days; presumably to avoid any suspicion of royal favoritism.

It was probably a quiet wedding because of the legal circumstances and because Pomare herself had fled to Raiatea to avoid the French —but more of that later.

What disaster was in store for the young storybook couple? It was too early for Robert Louis Stevenson to paint the villain for us. He did not visit Tahiti until nearly fifty years later, toward the end of his life. Mr. Hyde had not even been created by the time the couple were married. Herman Melville was to desert ship in Papeete the very next year and his Fayaway of *Typee* would have been a close contemporary of Huruata. Pierre Loti was not to arrive until 1869. But even without the great storytellers it was a mis-en-scène of high drama and the years to follow were to be the most dramatic of the little island's history. Alexander Salmon was rechristened, or rather given a Tahitian name, as was the ancient Polynesian custom, of Ariitaimai, which has usually been translated as "Prince from over the sea," though its meanings are subtler and more poetic in Tahitian. Huruata therefore became Ariitaimai Vahine and as such she was best known for the rest of her life. Toward its end when she was a widow, *Vahine* was dropped and Henry Adams, her friend and devoted admirer, was to immortalize her at the end of the century in his *Memoirs of Ariitaimai.*

Tahitian princesses were called indigenously *arii,* which of course meant "chiefs" or "chiefesses," "highest born," "lords of the land," "descendants of the gods." These Polynesian sirens had long traditions reaching back into the most ancient myths through their most ancient ancestors to the demigods. These gods, primary and secondary alike, had a way of yearning for a lovely lady from lands that lay over the seas. Or, as in the famous fable of Oro and Vairaumati, gods or lovers or husbands from out of the sky. There are many such legends and they are rich, varied and colorful; stories of heroes seeking them, wooing them, abducting them, winning them as prizes from chiefly fathers for heroic feats of sport or battle or supernatural wonder-workings. Conversely or symbolically, there are also as many Cinderellas or Brunhilds, rejecting all others to await their prince charmings. They all have the familiar round-the-world melodies of *The Song of Roland*, *The Romance of Lancelot*, *The Tales of Gengi*. So it was not at all unusual for Tahiti's most radiant maiden to wait for, to lure and to capture the dazzling young swain from the world's largest, richest, most powerful and most glamorous European metropolis.

What *is* unusual in this historically true, fairy-tale match is how it all turned out. But let us leave them for the moment to the joys of their nuptial, fine-woven mats, scented and softened by layers of sweet ferns freshly gathered from the mountains each morning. Let us leave them in the flickering evening light of candlenuts strung from the rafters of their bamboo sleeping house, watching, as they make love, the shadows on the serried ranks of pandanus rippling from the low eaves to the high peaks inside their roof. Let us let them listen to waves lapping the shore and booming breakers on the reef and the soft shuffling of the winds through coconut fronds.

Let the merrymaking go on in the background until the sun comes over the mountains in the morning.

CHAPTER NINE

Blast:
Protectorate by Ultimatum
1843

These were fateful years for Tahiti, the turbulent 1840s. England was still standing still—good old England. Some of her naval officers, notably Sir George Seymour in command of the Pacific station, still longed, as in the old days when he was a youngster at Trafalgar, to be beating up Frenchmen wherever and whenever he could. Queen Pomare had adopted a new flag—basically the same one with red stripes top and bottom—but a crown of coconut fronds was now added to the white field between. It was merely a gesture of independence, defiance perhaps, but flying from the little royal atoll, Motu Uta, at the entrance to the harbor of Papeete, it no doubt gave her some consolation for the humiliation she had suffered from Du Petit Thouars in 1838.

The French were in an underdog state of mind those days. Any little incident might have touched off a war. But while England held aloof in the Tahitian islands, the French seemed to sense a change of wind. Thouars had got his twenty-one-gun salute and had later clinched his victory on the streets of Paris. La Place had infiltrated his priests. It was time to follow through. Du Petit sailed in again, now an admiral, on a larger, sixty-gun frigate with another admiral-to-be on board ready to seize opportunity by the forelock. It was not difficult to discover that the queen had violated the earlier "treaty" and the new flag with its

114

crown was of course an intolerable insult to the dignity of the king of France. An immediate conference with Moerenhout revealed that Pomare had not been as obliging to the local French citizenry as had been expected. Her derelictions were not specified, just sensed and summarized, or perhaps dreamed up, by Moerenhout; this was easy enough. The French were feared and detested by the Tahitians. Perhaps they had been egged on by the missionaries, perhaps they smelled the impending military action. So Thouars declared that the king of France was gravely insulted and the only recourse was to depose the queen and install a French governor, one Commandant Bruat who happened, conveniently, to be on board. Du Petit sent a letter to the queen.

Madame—I declare to you, if at the expiration of two hours after this letter this flag [her personal one with the crown] *is not struck, and if, before sunset, you have not written me a letter of apology for your inconceivable conduct, and made a formal declaration that you will renew, in good faith, your treaty with France, I will no longer recognize you as Queen & Sovereign of the lands and dependencies of the Society Islands, & I shall take definitive possession in the name of the King of France.*

A. du Petit Thouars

This seemed a rather radical remedy for a few scattered, injured French feelings, and Pomare saw no reason to take down her flag. So at twelve noon the French landed five hundred troops, tore down the flag and hoisted their own. Pomare wrote a protest to the king pointing out that the treaty said nothing about a flag.

I think that the circumstances of keeping a crown in my personal flag will not be considered a crime on my part, because it was a very little thing that your Admiral demanded should be altered. If I had complied my Sovereign power would have been despised by My high Chiefs. This is my prayer, that the Almighty may soften your heart, that you may perceive the justice of what I ask you, that you may restore to me the Sovereign power and Government of my forefathers.

Pomare was in frightened seclusion on her island, about to give birth to a child. Paraita the regent was easily plied with francs and drinks. So the coup was engineered smoothly enough. Commandant Bruat was installed as *commissaire* with his well-armed, though poorly provisioned marines to back him up.

The French view is summed up by the modern historian Raoul Teissier. *In the absence of the Queen who was in Moorea pour ses couches, the regent Paraita convoked the Assembly of Chiefs and after deliberation, it acknowledged the wrongs of the Queen's administration. In order to put an end to all the grave disorders that were rife in Papeete, the chiefs of Tahiti, followed by the Queen, asked for the protection of the King of France. Du Petit Thouars granted this, subject to ratification by the French government.*

The English view was equally well summed up at the time by the trader-merchant Lucett:

And so inexorably the fatal hour struck and there was no other solution for Dupetit-Thouars—if he did not wish to lose faith—but to depose the Queen and to annex the island. 600 men with 4 howitzers march to the Marseillaise toward the royal palace. "Tabou, tabou!" says the Queen's man. Mare, the Queen's orator, protests. He is drowned out by drums. Captain d'Aubigny makes a proclamation, "Hear ye, hear ye, officers, soldiers and sailors of France, and you inhabitants of these islands! I take possession of this country in the name of His Majesty, Louis-Philippe, King of the French. We are ready to die, if it must be, to make respected our flag of three colors." And so the royal flag with its green crown was lowered and the tricolor was hoisted in its place with cries three times repeated of Vive la France, Vive le Roi!

Pomare's child died soon after birth and she took refuge on the only English ship in the harbor, a small armed ketch named the Basilisk. *As "Governor of the French Possessions of Oceania," Bruat ordered a dance on the* Sabbath *and prohibited Pomare from landing. She was thereby prevented from attending the funeral of her child.*

The Basilisk *eventually took the queen at her request to Raiatea where she was to spend nearly three years with her Tamatoa relatives in a state of vacillation and indecision. However cowed, she seemed unable to give*

*up hope of rescue by the British. She had written to Victoria often
enough without success. Now she tried her hand with Louis Phillipe.*

"*Your well-known benevolence will not allow you to object to the
Petition of a powerless Sovereign, & her weakness will induce you to
compassionate her. This is my Petition, that the treaty of the 9th of Sep.
1842 may be* thoroughly undone *because it was through FEAR that I
wrote my name in said treaty. This is the reason why that treaty should
be thoroughly undone, because the paper of charges out of which grew
the treaty was not written by me. Certain vague reports were circulated.
The money which your Admiral demanded, I could not obtain. If I had
had the money it would have been given, as on a former occasion. This
is another reason why I make this known to you, O King; Mr. Moerenhout, whom you put in office, coaxed & intimidated certain Chiefs who
were not well affected toward me, that they might write their names in
the said treaty. On account of my indisposition and being near my
confinement, great was my trouble. On account of this plain statement
to you, O King of the French, I trust to your benevolence, that you may
thoroughly undo the said treaty, that you may leave me independent in
Tahiti—Pomare.*"

Only four days after this letter Alexander Salmon wrote to Lord
Aberdeen. His views are an interesting contrast to the British. His letter
was translated into French and published in the biography written of
him by his nephew Ernest Salmon, but I believe it has not been
published before in its original language (at least not in its entirety).
His letter gives us an insight into the intimate as well as the official
complexities of the situation. It is so long—and at times tedious—that
I have relegated it to the Appendix. Its purpose is to vindicate the
French and put the blame for all of Pomare's sufferings on the shoulders of Salmon's arch enemy, George Pritchard, who was not only the
ex-missionary English consul, but Salmon's chief adversary as counselor
and confidant of the queen.

Bruat's naming of himself as governor of the French possessions in
Oceania was probably only an impulse in that moment of Gallic glory.
He had been appointed *commissaire* to the Protectorate of the King-
dom of Tahiti, but Pomare was still the legal queen. He was within his

technical rights in forbidding her to land from a British warship, but soon after she took up residence in Raiatea, he let it be known that she would be welcome to Tahiti as queen. Indeed he sailed over to Raiatea and invited her to come back with him. He was evidently sensitive, as the French so often are, to the proprieties of legitimate power. Remember his World War II successors, Darlan, Pétain, and Laval, anxious to have things all spick-and-span in accord with regulations. He needed the queen to decorate his rule, to lend it a European air of legitimacy.

But was not all this a European fabrication? The "queen" of Tahiti, what had she and finicky French protocol to do with the real power of the Polynesian people? Tati of the Teva I Uta, the southland, had been seduced by the French, but the chiefs back in the hills, especially in the lush districts of Punaauia, of Paea and Papenoo had minds of their own. This was their ancestral homeland and they saw little reason why French admirals dealing with an upstart Pomare should take it over from them.

Alas, they were divided, some seeing French rule as a solution to the depredations of the rascals along the waterfront; others standing stoutly for the time-old independence of their land. Few, if any, I would guess, still put much faith in the queen's illusions of salvation by Victoria. Mostly they wanted to settle the issues on their own lands in their own ways. So they commenced gradually to form themselves into an army of resistance. Considering the odds, it was a hopeless task, but they were brave and resolute men. Bruat was a seasoned warrior and the first thing he did was to establish a string of blockhouses along the waterfront stretching east and west from Papeete. The steep ragged mountains protected him from the south and of course he controlled the water approaches from the north with his ships of war. From his stronghold he could make forays along the coast in both directions to break up attacks by the "rebels"—as they were now called since they were defying the newly "legitimate" French government.

These rebels, though they considerably outnumbered the French garrison, were pitifully lacking in muskets and gunpowder. They had to raid at night mostly with clubs and spears to be met not only with gunfire but with cannon. Moreover, they were divided and equivocal in their leadership. Some of the chiefs, notably Tati, believed that French rule was inevitable and resistance suicide. They had best cooperate. Still others of the chiefs were loyal to Queen Pomare, as stubbornly traditional, one might say, as the French were stubbornly legitimate. They kept hoping that Pomare would return from Raiatea, reinstate the Tahitian government under the "protection" of the French, and thus preserve some modicum of independence, at least in internal affairs.

The constant and faithful envoy between these chiefs and the queen was her old friend and closest confidante, Huruata, the bride we left sleeping not long ago with her new husband, Alexander Salmon. The two of them made many trips and long visits over the several years of Pomare's exile. Naturally enough she was being strongly influenced by her Tamatoa relatives and also by Tapoa, her first husband, now "King" —by the grace of the London Missionary Society—of Bora Bora, and also by the strong-willed queen of Huahine, Ariipaea, a close relative of Ariifaaite, husband of Pomare.

These Leeward Island chiefs stood firm for their own independence. They maintained close ties with British ships of war and American traders even though the visits were sporadic. They repulsed to the utmost any French overtures. But one senses that they were willing enough to throw Pomare to the French; a fate they saw as inevitable. There had always been rivalry and warfare between the windward islands and those on the leeward side of the Sea of the Moon. Most of their ways of life were much the same, but their *maraes* were strikingly different: rounded, dressed stone with stepped *ahu*, or "altars," to the east; great, rough coral slabs to the west. And *maraes*, as we have seen, were the enduring evidences of individuality and independence. Moreover and most importantly, their genealogies came down by different lines from different gods.

Only a few years later, this separate status of the two island groups was to be formalized by the Treaty of Jarnac, 1847, when France and England declared the Leeward Islands neutral and independent and agreed to protect them from interference by any other foreign power.

CHAPTER TEN

Resistance: A New Eyewitness
1846

New light has been shed upon these feisty times by the recent discovery of the journal of an English naval captain who spent a year, 1846–47, "spying" (as he himself wryly designated his function) upon the goings-on between French and Tahitians. He characterizes Salmon as a scheming English Jew whose chief motivation was robbing the queen of her money. This can be discounted as normal Victorian prejudice and a bit of vituperative misinformation. Salmon was certainly on the French side, but he was devoted to his wife and his wife was devoted to him and to her cousin the queen.

Now let me introduce this new, on-the-scene reporter whose views have been lying unnoticed, and indeed unknown except perhaps by his family, in the archives of the British Museum for more than 130 years. He is Captain Henry Byam Martin, R.N., with his first command, H.M.S. *Grampus* 50 guns. Not only does he provide us with many revealing glimpses of life in the plush victorious British Navy in that last era of the great sailing ships of war. He also characterizes for us the essential natures of three of the dominant stereotypes of the time —the base, cowardly, scheming French; the pitiful, helpless, happy Polynesians; the haughty, almighty, all-righteous Englishmen.

Captain Martin must have been an extraordinary person, although he thought of himself, and his colleagues probably thought of him, as a typical, well-bred officer of the Royal Navy. He was born in 1804, entered the Royal Naval College at the age of twelve in 1816, rose from

Midshipman in 1818 through Lieutenant and Commander to "Post-rank" or Captain in 1827 and took his first command, H.M.S. *Grampus* 50 guns in 1845, rounded the Horn, and spent the next year or so in the Pacific. He went on later to become Rear Admiral in 1854, Vice Admiral in 1864, and was slated for "Flag Rank" when he died at the age of 61 in 1865. It seems startling that a boy who entered a military school at the age of twelve could be as roundly educated as Henry Byam Martin who was fluent in French, read and quoted Italian, even in the ancient classical language, could assess Samuel Johnson with a critical, perceptive eye, was a brilliant sea captain, an eloquent writer, an accomplished artist, and had a fine sense of humor withal. It does seem incredible, but we must remember that he was one of the three sons of Sir Thomas Byam Martin, GCB, KSS, Admiral of the Red, hero of the Napoleonic wars, and for many years Comptroller of the Royal Navy and Vice Admiral of the United Kingdom. Young Henry must have had unusual educational advantages in his childhood.

The quality of his drawings and water-color paintings is very high, not only as art but as ethnology, satire, and historical record. A British captain's life on such duty in those days must have provided plenty of leisure time. Well over a hundred of his meticulously executed paintings of Polynesia came very recently to light from the attic of the old English manor house of his family. Three other portfolios on other areas also appeared—areas where his subsequent commands took him —Turkey, a fine portfolio on ancient Egypt, and a spirited rendering of ranch life in Mexico and South America.

When Alexander Salmon wrote his letter to Lord Aberdeen, Captain Byam Martin was still nearly three years away from Tahiti. However, shortly after his arrival on September 28, 1846, he wrote a summary in his *Journal* of events during the few preceding years and an abbreviated quotation of this passage gives a good idea of the preliminary military circumstances—a sort of overture to our opera—and also some revelations of the Captain himself. Since the details before his arrival were told him by Dr. Johnstone, the whole gives us the first on-the-scene account from the English point of view and it differs strikingly from the published French accounts. I am of course partial to it because it is so much more sympathetic to the Tahitian.

I am not certain as to dates, but I believe it was about the beginning of 1844, that Q. Pomare took refuge on board the Basilisk—and after being there a complete prisoner for many months, was carried by the cargo boat to Raiatea.

About the same period M. Bruat governor of the Marquesas arrived at Tahiti as "Commissioner from the King of the French to the Queen of the Society Islands."

He immediately set to work to enforce the acknowledgement of the French protectorate. He issued a proclamation calling on all the chiefs to appear before him. Very few obeyed; those of the refractory whom he was able to lay his hands on were put in irons on bd the French ships of war in the port. Those who got out of his reach were outlawed and their property confiscated, as soon as the period for making their submission had expired.

The people began to retire to a distance from Papeete—they were sullen and angry—but I doubt if they would have commenced actual hostilities if the French had not.

He recounts two minor skirmishes and then:

Governor Bruat vowed that the French blood that had been spilt should be avenged; and resolved to attack the natives at Mahaina, where a large body had entrenched themselves. (Mahaina is about 25 miles N.E. of Papeete.)

Accordingly 400 Frenchmen supported by the guns of L'Uranie frigate and Phaeton Steamer, were landed at Mahaina on 28th April. A battle took place without any result, each party losing about 100 men.

The Tahitians then shifted their camp to a better position in the valley of Papenoo with a strong body as an outpost at Pt. Venus. The French attacked the latter place on 30th June—about 4 were killed on each side. On this occasion the Rev. Mr. McLean—the English missionary stationed at Pt. Venus was shot dead, whilst standing in his doorway. Of course a man who looks on at a fight must take his chances, but there is every reason to believe that this unfortunate missionary, who was beloved by the natives, was intentionally shot by a French soldier.

Another body of the Tahitians (about 1600) had taken post at Buna-

roo in the valley of Bunaouia with an outpost at Faa only 4 miles from
Papeete. The post at Faa was attacked about the same time by Capt.
Bonard with 100 men. He was forced to retreat with a loss of 6 killed
and himself and 18 wounded.

During the month of July many other skirmishes took place. (The
circumstances mentioned . . . I had from Dr. Johnstone who was at
Papeete during the whole time.)

One would have supposed that M. Bruat had enough upon his hands
at Tahiti, but finding he could do nothing there, he determined to seek
on another field some indemnity for the checks he had received from the
Tahitians. . . . I believe it was at the beginning of 1845 that reinforcements arrived from the Marquesas. Bruat then placing himself on the
defensive and feeling secure against attack dispatched L'Uranie and
Phaeton, the two harbingers of murder and desolation, to force the other
islands of the Society Group into submission to the French protectorate.

The islanders said "No. You have made a treaty with Pomare for her
island. She cannot dispose of us. We are free and will not receive you
and we will resist you to the last!"

The island of Raiatea where Pomare was residing was blockaded; and
the French protectorate flag was hoisted at the principal settlement on
Bora Bora where some fighting took place.

In the meantime the English government sympathizing with the unfortunate islanders who were firmly English in all their feelings, associations and predilections interceded with the French government on their
behalf and it was agreed that things should remain in status quo till
evidence should be taken whether these (commonly called the Leeward)
islands did or did not come within the limits of Pomare's dominions.

The French troops were soon driven from Bora Bora; and after having
sustained several defeats and lost 200 men retired from the island of
Huahine; not however until they had burnt the settlement, destroyed the
bread fruit and coco nut trees and caused as much sorrow and suffering
as their means permitted.

About the middle of April 1846, M. Bruat finding that he wanted all
his forces on Tahiti, made peace with the Leeward islands.

On 20th March the Tahitians, fancying themselves stronger than they *really were, attacked Papeete; and so complete was the surprize that they were in the middle of the settlement before they were opposed and had burnt some houses before the French soldiers rallied and drove them out. The French had 3 killed and 3 wounded. From that time to the middle of April the natives repeatedly attacked the French outposts, but were always repulsed. On 12th April Bruat resumed the offensive, but was beaten off in an attack on a native outpost at Tapuna with a loss of 7 killed a Lieutenant and 13 wounded and 3 taken prisoners.*

It is believed that about this time Bruat received orders from his government to adopt a more pacific policy; but the only notice he took of them was immediately to prepare an expedition against the principal native camp at Papenoo. He had however a short time before made overtures to Pomare to induce her to return, which were rejected.

On the 9th May, 1000 men supported by the Phaeton steamer started for the attack on Papenoo. Bruat commanded in person and I am told conducted himself with great gallantry. On the 10th and 11th the first entrenchments were taken but the principal position of the natives was found too strong and after vain attempts for several days to force or turn it, the French retired to their fort at Pt. Venus. M. Bruat in speaking to me of this said he was forced to return because the rising of the river in his rear threatened to cut off his retreat and his supply of provisions and ammunition.

In the affairs between the 9th and 15th the French lost about 100 men in killed and wounded—the natives about 20.

On 31st May M. Bruat attacked the native camp at Bunaroo in the valley of Bunaouia—and was repulsed with some loss. Col. de Brea Commandant of the troops and a Lt. of L'Uranie were killed—M. Malmanche chef d'Etat major lost his leg.

M. Bruat now began to find these attacks on the Tahitians a profitless game; he had lost a great many men and had literally accomplished nothing. He therefore contented himself with throwing up a chain of blockhouses from Bunaouia to Pt. Venus—and up to this time no further hostilities had occurred.

On my arrival here, [Sept. 28, 1846] (at Papeete, the headquarters in Tahiti) I find that after a French occupation of 3 years they occupy a straggling village and the ground for ½ a mile in the rear of it; and so much of the sea board as is commanded by their blockhouses and ships.

At each extremity of Papeete there is a work sufficiently strong for its purpose and another by the government house. The village is intersected by barricades of casks filled with earth—the guards many and strong and the troops in a state of constant qui vive. Thus it would seem that up to the present time the protectors have enough to do to protect themselves.

That brings us up to the time when Captain Martin becomes our eye witness of the buildup to the final climax, a matter of some ten weeks ahead. But before we trace this course of events, I would like to flash back to what he had called the "very harsh and summary manner" in which Pritchard was expulsed from the island by D'Aubigny in 1844. The best witness to that important episode, though of course not the most dispassionate one, is Pritchard's son, William, recalling the circumstances some fifteen years later. It is plain that he exaggerates, even perhaps distorts, but again I think we should let him speak his piece.

On the 7th November, 1843—a day memorable in the annals of Tahiti—a proclamation was issued, announcing the deposition of Queen Pomare and the occupation of the island in the name of the King of the French; and for the first time Pomare read the words—"Ex-Queen" of Tahiti.

On the 8th, M. Bruat was duly installed as "Governor of the French Possessions in Oceania," and his Excellency took up his quarters in the Ex-Queen Pomare's residence, her Majesty still taking refuge in my father's house.

M. Bruat admired the carriage and approved the furniture presented by Queen Victoria to Queen Pomare, and was not too fastidious to use them. His first proclamation, as Governor, concluded with these words: "If France is strong enough to pardon much, she knows how to punish. Peace to good citizens, misfortune to disturbers—the sword of the law shall overtake them whatever their rank or under whatever colour they seek to hide their fatal projects!"

It was reported that the Queen would be forcibly taken from the British Consulate; she therefore took refuge on board H.M.S. ketch "Basilisk," a little vessel of two guns only. Half an hour after, ten gendarmes appeared at my father's door, stood there for some minutes and then marched off. Chief after chief was taken prisoner and confined on board the French frigates in the harbour, all for imaginary offences, until at last the excitement of the natives told plainly they could not submit quietly much longer.

The "Basilisk" being anchored opposite the Consulate, two sentinels were always on guard, night and day, close to my father's gate, watching every movement in the house on board the ketch. Scheme after scheme was devised to entrap her Majesty,—and failing her Majesty, to get possession of her children; but all failed. At length Governor Bruat applied privately and personally to Commander Hunt, to send the Queen or one of her children on shore on some pretext or another, just to give his Excellency the opportunity to capture the one or the other. When Commander Hunt replied that he could not possibly think of so abusing the confidence of the Queen, or of sending a little child away from his mother, his Excellency coolly remarked, "Pomare will still have two children with her,—quite enough for any woman's parental affections!" And M. Bruat was a married man, and had his wife with him.

It soon appeared that my father was a marked man. In the afternoon of the 3rd of March, just as he was about to step into the Cormorants' boat, to go on board that vessel on official business, with Captain Gordon—and in presence of my mother, who was standing on the verandah—he was seized by a party of gendarmes and, without cere- mony, led through mud and rain to a "blockhouse," hastily prepared for his reception. No reason whatever was assigned for his capture, no charge alleged, either to my father or to Captain Gordon.
Inter arma silent leges.

The place to which my father was taken, commonly called a "block- house," was a building fifteen feet by ten, and twenty feet high, and in place of doors and windows, had loopholes every two feet apart, just large enough to admit the muzzles of a musket. Ten feet from the ground was a floor, dividing the building into upper and lower compartments. A ladder led up to this floor from the outside, through an opening just wide enough to admit one man at a time. The lower compartment had the bare, wet ground for floor, and as the building was on the side of a hill, the rain, which fell in torrents, drained down the slope, making the place quite a mud-hole. My father ascended the ladder, and when the last soldier had followed, it was drawn up and put down into the lower compartment through a trap-door, and my father ordered to descend to his quarters below. As he stepped off the ladder, he alighted ankle-deep in mud, and found a mattress, blanket, and bolster for his bedding; no other furniture was there in the place. My father asked the officer in command to let my mother know where he was, just to relieve her mind. But nay—martial law knows not the feelings of a wife. And for sixteen hours my father lay in his dungeon without tasting food or water, without changing his clothes, or my mother knowing what had become of him: he might have been hanged or shot for all she knew. At the end of the sixteen hours my mother heard where he was, and at once sent him food and clothes. The guards examined everything, even the plates, to see that there was no secret message written by the wife to her husband, and then gave the prisoner a little cake, a little water, and a change of clothes— at the same time handing him a paper with the Commandant's signature and these words—"A French sentinal was attacked in the night of the 2nd to the 3rd of March. In reprisal I have caused to be seized one Pritchard, the only daily mover and instigator of the disturbance of the natives. His property shall be answerable for all damages occasioned to our establishment by the insurgents; and if French blood is spilt, every drop shall recoil on his head." No sentinel had been attacked; but that did not matter. And instead of moving the natives to attack the French, my father had exerted all his influence to prevent a collision, well knowing that if the Tahitians drove the French into the sea, France would send men enough to sink the island itself.

On the third day after his arrest, my father had a severe attack of dysentery, and begged that the Commandant would allow Dr. Johnstone, who attended our family, to see him. In reply the Commandant stated he was "truly sorry the exigencies of his position did not allow him to comply with the request except under certain restrictions," which were *"as soon as Dr. Johnstone presents himself at the blockhouse, accompanied by the interpreter Latour, he shall be introduced to the upper story; the trap-door shall be opened, and the prisoner shall converse for ten minutes with the doctor, but the doctor shall not be permitted to descend into the chamber of the invalid. Dr. Johnstone shall be admitted to converse in this manner with the prisoner at 8 A.M. and 4 P.M. daily, and the medicines shall also be sent at these hours." As soon as Dr. Johnstone saw the place in which my father was confined, he pronounced it unfit even for the dungeon of a dog, and requested that a French doctor be sent for. M. La Stoique attended, and declared the place very suitable and proper for the prisoner! Nevertheless, Dr. Johnstone represented to the Commander that, to save my father's life, it was absolutely necessary to remove him at once. In the meantime the dysentery increased, and a fever supervened, which brought my father so low that the exertion of clambering up the ladder and standing on the upper step, to let the doctor feel his pulse, induced so great a tremor and excitement throughout his frame, as to make it utterly impossible to ascertain his real condition. In reply, my father was allowed to go into the upper story and to sit there ten minutes for the doctor to examine him. No conversation was allowed on any subject other then the dysentery and the fever; and the medicines were emptied out of the papers in which the doctor wrapped them, the papers minutely scrutinized to detect any writing that might be a secret message, and then the medicines put back. On the 8th the Commandant was convinced by Dr. Johnstone that if my father remained in the blockhouse another three days, it would cost him his life. At night my father was startled from a doze by the opening of the trap-door, and a soldier descending the ladder with a lantern, followed by an officer, who stated that he had orders from the Governor to convey the prisoner on board the French frigate "La Meurte." A guard escorted my father, at dead of night, from the blockhouse to the seashore, where an armed boat was awaiting him. Not a word was spoken above a whisper, and the officer in command never relaxed his tight grasp of my father's arm until the prisoner was safely in the boat between the bayonets of the marines. Arrived on board the frigate, he was put into a compartment on the maindeck, screened off for the occasion from all*

*intercourse with the rest of the ship. As compared with the place from
which he had just passed in a high fever, and through the damp midnight
air, this was a palace.*

*Captain Gordon, of H.M.S. Cormorant, demanded the release of my
father; and after a rather sharp and brisk correspondence, the Governor
agreed to put him on board the "Cormorant," after the vessel was at sea,
if Captain Gordon would give a pledge that there should be no intercourse with the shore. By the firm persistence of Captain Gordon, my
mother was afterwards allowed to meet my father at sea, on condition
that they merely took leave of each other, without making any arrange-
ments as to my father's property or anything else. On the 13th of March,
1844, the "Cormorant" steamed out from Papeete harbour, and when
well out to sea, awaited the French boats. After some little delay—just
to exercise the patience of the British Commander—my father was put
on board, took leave of my mother, and the "Cormorant" steered for
Valparaiso; and thus were the French rid of my father.*

That is young William's version and it is amply supported by the
press of the time—chiefly the *London Illustrated News* which made a
lurid feature of it. But France's most eminent historian of the period,
Léonce Jore, sees it otherwise:

*It must be clearly recognized that G. Pritchard had been the "veritable
instigateur" of the revolt of the natives. Without doubt he had not
preached armed rebellion against us, but nevertheless in arousing difficulties incessantly against our authority and inciting the natives to op-
pose the Protectorate, the British Consul could not help but create
violent incidents.*

*He bears, then from the moment of his return from Europe (Jan 1843)
to the day of the final quenching of the rebels (Jan 1847) . . . the grave
responsibility of all the Tahitian and French blood shed in Oceania
during those four years.* [retombent bien sur lui]

*The departure of Pritchard should have brought out the best feelings
in the rebels. They were indeed only a small minority, the mass of the
population following the example of the great chiefs Tati, Utomi, Hitoti,
and Paraita remained faithful to us. . . .*

This is all nonsense. None of these chiefs were under the influence of Pritchard. Paraita who was the regent of Pomare was only a minor chief, clearly in the pay of the French. The others except for Tati were strongly opposed to the French invaders. How could an historian so delude himself? And how personal he makes it all seem, as if that whole bitter struggle against the rape of their lands by conquerors from Europe was merely the evil doings of one Englishman undermining the "established authority" of the French saviors.

CHAPTER ELEVEN

Counterblast and . . .

1847

Now let us go on to the 6th of October 1846 and the war of resistance of the so-called rebels. I must apologize for skipping about this way, but it seemed a pity not to have a look at Captain Martin's succinct military summary and also a pity to omit young William's impassioned defense of his father.

After Captain Martin's arrival the attacks, repulses, counter-attacks and counter-repulses continued through November when the rains came to discourage the poor Tahitians. They now controlled the whole island except for a narrow strip of some eight or ten miles of coastline along the north, whose center was the port of Papeete. Ordinarily they could have been self-sustaining in this territory, but Bruat was able to send his armed ships periodically along the coast literally blockading the islanders from their chief source of sustenance, the sea. They were thus forced back into the mountains from all their accustomed abodes on the littoral. Most of their taro, breadfruit, and coconuts, and virtually all of their houses were destroyed. Their only substantial foodstuff was the orange mountain banana, the *fei.* But they were deprived of all protein. What arms and ammunition they could scrape together had to be smuggled in by small boats at night. Their suppliers were probably their friends in the Leeward Islands who could still trade with occasional merchant ships and whalers. And yet by Captain Martin's estimates, which must have derived largely from Dr. Johnstone, they mustered a force of some sixteen hundred in Punaauia and Paea, in the southwest, and probably more than five hundred in Papenoo, to the east. Since these are estimates of active fighting men, the "rebels" must have totalled in all well over four thousand. This is of course a very low figure compared with the original populations encountered by the early explorers. But in eighty years, fully three generations, their numbers had probably been literally decimated, reduced to one tenth, by disease and warfare.

So it was a brave stand but a hopeless one. If they had been able to massacre the French in a swift, lucky campaign, Louis Philippe would have soon sent out an overwhelming fleet to lay waste their shores and utterly destroy them at last. But still they fought on and talked on. Captain Martin wanted to negotiate, but his orders forbade him to take any initiative without the consent of the French commandant. Bruat was of course too proud to let an Englishman come to his assistance. He was also probably afraid that an English success might upset the tipsy balance of his regime. Lucett, the English merchant, did go to the principal chiefs in Punaauia with his part-Tahitian wife, but he was scornfully dismissed by them and told they had no illusions about English intervention. Nor did they want Pomare back. They were in control now (or at least they thought they were) and could handle their own affairs.

Meanwhile the negotiations of Huruata and Alexander Salmon with the queen were constantly being stalled. Martin was of course in her confidence, but his conscience would not let him hold out to her hope of English aid and his distrust of the French made him hesitate to recommend that she accept their proposals of a full and legal protectorate. He seems to have trusted Bruat personally and to have respected his avowed intentions. But just at this critical time, Bruat's term of office was to expire. He had sent in his resignation in accordance with the customary military protocol and then had learned, much to his hurt and dismay, that it was accepted. He was to be replaced shortly after the beginning of the new year of 1847 by Admiral Lavaud. Martin had known Lavaud in another naval theater where he had a reputation as a severe, hard-line officer. He was most reluctant to see Pomare turned over to him.

Martin was no admirer of the queen, indeed he personally was repulsed by her, by her corpulence, by her self-indulgence, even by her color—just as you might expect an English, upper-crust gentleman-officer of those days would inevitably be. And yet he had a strong sympathy for her and her people. It might have been warmed of course by his antipathy or, shall we say, his contempt for his ingrained foes the French, but it was *sui generis* also, a sportsman's predilection for the underdog perhaps. One can detect bubbling up here and there throughout his *Journal* a true affection for these people as he saw them, happy, outgoing, carefree and trusting.

These speculations may seem romantic, even sentimental in weighing the motivations and implacable factors of a war; a little war to be sure, a tiny one, but a war that was to decide the fate of the remnants of a unique and beautiful civilization for 135 years ahead—until today. And how many more are the years still to come?

But it seems quite clear in this particular microcosm of warfare that emotional, sentimental, essentially personal factors were critical. The ingredients of the pepperpot were: the ambivalence of Queen Pomare; the greed and venality of her regent; the drive of the vanities and ambitions of Du Petit Thouars and Bruat; the restraint and compassion of Martin as contrasted to the impulsive pickafightness of Toup Nicolas; the Protestant passions of Pritchard vying with the Catholicizing zeal of Moerenhout; the wounded but indomitable pride of the great chiefs Utami, Hitoti, Paofai; the ancient rivalries of the western island chiefs Tamatoa, Tapoa and Ariipaea; and not least the amours propres of the pompous ministers of Louis Philippe and of Victoria, back there in Paris and London.

When you look down upon them all, as if you were standing on the heights of Le Diadème, much as we now stand in the distance of time, it seems that it is those vivid personalities who are making the war and deciding the fate of the few thousands of Tahitians (about to become extinct, they said in those days—ancestors of those who nowadays number nearly a hundred thousand), a people who have at last begun to find themselves as people and who would never tolerate in these days being tossed about by a few fiery alien personalities.

So as Christmas approached, a stalemate seemed to have settled upon the situation. The French in Papeete were in poor shape. Martin notes at the end of November, after his return from a month's visit in the Leeward Islands, that the French soldiers had had no fresh meat for six weeks, that they were eight months in arrears in pay, and that suicides were becoming a serious problem. The Tahitians were half starved and suffering from much debilitating sickness, but they had one impregnable redoubt, the steep, fertile and commodious valley of the Fautaua River, which was protected from assault by a precipitous mountain to the west and a knife-like pinnacle ridge to the east, making a narrow mouth to the valley that could be defended by a tenth or a twentieth of any attacking force. Even cannon could be easily checked by rocks hurled down from the gateway cliffs.

The Tahitians felt completely secure in their stronghold; the French completely frustrated in front of it. And until this impasse could be resolved, there could be no clear-cut Protectorate for France. Bruat's days were numbered and he felt he must make a last desperate attempt. He sent Bonard with some five hundred troops to make a dramatic feint of an all-out frontal attack. But his actual strategy was a flanking assault on that pinnacle, the western guardian post that was so inaccessible that the Tahitians had not thought of guarding it. It was indeed inaccessible to Frenchmen, but, alas, they had found a native collaborator and no pinnacle anywhere is inaccessible to a Polynesian. So Mairoto scaled the peak, let down a line and hauled up a rope ladder. Twenty-five French marines climbed up with muskets on their backs and the war was over.

The Tahitians realized immediately the impossibility of their position. They would just be picked off at leisure. So they surrendered and the great decisive battle was finished—with scarcely a casualty. Probably without a shot fired from a gun, but certainly not without many a shot fired from the gallant mouths of the gloriously victorious French. Byam Martin comments:

This has been a fortunate affair for the French, & of the highest importance to them. I have no doubt that the submission of all the native camps must follow—M. Boussain who had been an eye witness gave me

*a graphic picture of the escalade. He also told me that the native traitor
immediately claimed his reward. . . .*

*Frenchmen understand the act of blowing their own trumpets better
than most people. I do not undervalue their achievement in taking
Faoutaoua, but really to hear them talk one would suppose the storming
of Badajog or Cuidad Rodrigo had been acted over again. . . .*

*Bruat has sent proposals of peace to the camp at Bunaroo and I
concluded they will be accepted after the usual quantity of talk. Utami
the principal chief is disposed to submit, but Maro his second is for
prolonging resistance to the last moment. The Tahitians are suffering
from sickness, & very nearly in a state of famine, and no one can desire
to see them hold out without a prospect or even a chance of success. They
do not, even at this hour, believe that England will leave them in the
lurch. . . .*

*Bruat's star is in the ascendant. The Bunaroo camp surrendered last
night, and this morning came the Ana French armed brig from Callao
with his promotion to the grade of R. Adml. His flag was immediately
hoisted and I saluted it with 13 guns.*

*Bruat tells me 1600 men are on their way from France. He has
changed his title from "Commissaire du Roi pur [sic] la reine des iles
de la Societe" to "Commissaire du roi aux iles de la Societe"—I fear
this bodes ill for poor Pomare. . . .*

*The camp at Bunaroo has surrendered and the people are coming in
gradually from Papenoo; showing how tired they are of the war; which
is now virtually at an end.*

*The submission of the natives has been effected without bloodshed,
and only one thing is wanting to the complete establishment of the
French protectorate—the return of the Queen. This I presume cannot
now be long delayed.*

So goes an account of the Tahitians' Waterloo at Fautaua by an
Englishman on the scene. It should be noted in passing that Martin,
in calling Mairoto a traitor, evidently did not realize that this man was
not a Tahitian but a native of the far south Polynesian island of Rapa.
His ancestors had often considered Tahiti fair game for warlike raids.

Now let us sample a Frenchman's view. Charles Giraud was a young

French painter present in Tahiti at the time, having come out "comme passager a ses frais à la table de l'état major" with Bruat in 1842. Captain Martin mentions him as a dinner guest aboard the *Grampus*. He reviews and admires a portfolio of his paintings. I would say that as artists, the two were of about the same caliber technically, Giraud inclined to be impressionistic and sentimental, Martin realistic and Goyaesque. Here is M. Giraud's estimate of the famous battle. He did not write about it himself but conveyed his impressions to a reporter after he had returned to France.

17 septembre 1846: The assault on the inaccessible fort! One of the highest feats of our national bravery and intrepedity. Search for a narration of it in books about the History of French Colonization: you will find it scarcely mentioned; not a page tells of this incredible achievement. Is it not astonishing that contemporary journals in France have not given more of a spotlight and celebration to this prodigious feat of arms? Fautuhua? Today it is almost completely forgotten. . . . We are therefore all the happier to present a description in the words of an eye-witness, indeed the very man who organized, launched, and supervised this cyclopean assault, Capitaine de Corvette Bonnard [sic].

Bonard, the deep-dyed villain in Tahitian eyes, the man who wantonly laid waste to Huahine, is not so extravagant. Mostly he describes the incredible terrain, the dauntless bravery of his twenty-five volunteers who *went immediately to join the native, Taruru (also known as* Tavana Tariirii, *the most intrepid of the warriors of Oceania).* Since this is Bonard's only mention of any native, one wonders if he is the same man as Byam Martin's "traitor," Mairoto? He tells us his volunteers *left everything at the foot of the mountain, gear and clothing. They climbed up entirely naked having only their cartridge belts and guns. . . . Cords and rope ladders were secured to plants sprouting from the fissures of the rock . . . unheard of suffering . . . hoisting themselves up solely by hand since there were no footholds except bare rock or occasional tufts of brush. . . .*

It is indeed a gallant scene, though one doubts that the famous French battle artist Messioner would have wanted to paint it. The denouement is something of an anticlimax. *Astride the crest of the mountain, as if straddling a roof, with precipices falling off to their sides* [600 meters, he says; that is about 2,000 feet on each side], *and their guns and bandoliers hanging to their sides, they climbed to their position with ardor, in spite of the horrible fatigue. With the wink of an eye the Tahitian flag was reversed, and, an admirable thing, they contented themselves to rest happily seeing the disconcerted enemy, and bidding him lay down his arms to save his life.*

Gallant and great-hearted, these naked fellows must have been; probably by this time looking like lobsters in the scorching sun. Ah well; the painter Giraud came out from Papeete afterward to depict this highest feat of his nation's national bravery and, *à son retour en France, l'artiste est fêté partout. On le considère comme le peintre officiel de l'expédition et il reçoit la Légion d'honneur à vingt-huit ans!*

Yes, the war was over, but it took some time to resolve all resistance. The chiefs in the western districts were slow to turn in their arms in spite of Bruat's insistent demands and threats. We hear of 90 muskets from Papenoo out of 450 promised, and so on from other districts. The chiefs made it quite clear that they considered the surrender to be a bargain. They wanted to know the terms of their future: they wanted especially, or at least many of them did, to be assured about the status and powers of the queen when and if she should return.

This of course was the central problem, and its echoes reach down to the very present day, when the degree of autonomy or internal authority—police, schools, foreign (read French) migration, control of lands and future resources (from the sea mostly) are the vital issues at stake. The Tahitians wanted to keep their land. The French wanted to take it. The Tahitians today, 135 years later, still want that land, but the French still want it also and their's is the power: not cannon these days, but money. How can the Tahitian keep his now indispensable schooling, his motor scooter, TV, and outboard? And have his independence too? His country is the very last now of all the old native imperial colonies—French, English, Dutch, Spanish, Portuguese, or American —that has still not gained its freedom. It seems unfair and unjust that France should still hang on against the whole world's tide simply because the Tahitians are too weak to throw her out, as her other colonies have done. But on the other hand, it must always be recognized that, comparatively, the Tahitians still own a greater proportion of their own land; they are not taxed; they receive more free benefits such as schooling, roads, water than any other subject people has enjoyed, better, much better than their assimilated cousins in Hawaii and New Zealand. What price freedom? It is not easy to see a solution.

A great deal hinged on the return of Queen Pomare in 1847 as a symbol of the ancient traditions and indigenous rights of the Tahitian peoples, a return that was to set a precedent for the dilemmas of today. The event becomes vividly alive in the *Journal* of Captain Byam Martin.

Jan 5th Spy [one of the smaller subsidiary naval vessels under Captain Martin's command] *returned bringing me letters from Raiatea & Bora Bora and from Pomare at Tahaa.*

I told M. Bruat what I had heard from her—namely that she was disposed to return—but knew not how. He said he could make her no new offer, but that he would receive her if she came; that his government had blamed him on a former occasion for having invited the Queen to return & he certainly should not do so again. He does not want her now & is therefore indifferent about her. He says it is a comedy—so it is for him perhaps! But for these poor islanders who have lost their country & their freedom—seen their home invaded, their houses burnt & pillaged —their kindred butchered & all that was most dear & most sacred— polluted by his hated race—there is not much of comedy.

7th. M. Bruat had written me an official letter announcing this as a day of festivity & rejoicing—to be observed as a general jubilee—with a programme of the salutes, ceremonies etc. to take place on this anniversary of the hoisting of the French protectorate flag at Tahiti. It was accompanied by an invitation to dine, which I declined. I made a compromise with my conscience & replied that I had no objection to fire a salute on the restoration of peace & the cessation of part of the sufferings of the people. At 7 A.M. Bruat reviewed his garrison in front of government house, squares were formed, the names of the most meritorious read—and a feeble "vive le roi" was heard. It was as wretched an attempt at a cheer as I ever remember. The soldiers are very dissatisfied—they are hard worked—ill fed & ill paid.

In the course of the day there was running in sacks for the women, & climbing greasy poles for the men; and at 3 P.M. a feast of pigs, bread fruit & other native grub for all hands, amounting to about 2000. There was much discontent at the quantity and quality of the liquor, which was voted rather small for such an occasion—but the Uranie's band played cheerful music & these light hearted music loving people soon recovered their good humor.

16th. Pomare has written to the governor to have the steamer & another vessel sent for her. Poor woman, I am glad she has decided to come, for bad as her case will be when she arrives, it will be made worse by delay. The leeward island chiefs have been invited to accompany her —a little act of conciliation preliminary to coaxing & humbugging them into asking for the French protectorate.

Sunday 24th January. In the evening I had a conversation with Bruat about the Queen. I must say that he speaks of her as an honorable man should speak of an unfortunate woman—with kindness & with consideration for her unhappy condition. He is elated with his success & can afford to be generous. Bruat told me, what I had heard before, that the people of Bora Bora & Raiatea very reluctantly allowed Tapoa to accompany the Queen & had meetings on the subject. He said these meetings had decided that Tapoa should not come, but that Pomare had ordered otherwise—and "therefore," said Bruat, "Tapoa is coming which clearly shows Pomare to be the sovereign chief of all the islands—for Tapoa is obliged to obey her." I could not help smiling at his logical conclusion —The smile was catching & Bruat burst into a laugh at his own reasoning—It was unnecessary to say a word.

29th. I called upon M. Bruat for news of the Queen. He only knew that some of her boats & people had reached Moorea. He again alluded to the Queen having ordered Tapoa to attend her—"a proof," said he, "that she is the sovereign of all the group." He alleges that she has always received a salute—the chiefs of the other islands never; that English, French, Russians, Americans—all considered Pomare the chief *of the Society islands, and then he brought out Ld. Aberdeen's letter to show how often he had mentioned Tahiti as one of the Society group. In my opinion the French have the best of the argument; but they have taken Tahiti contrary to the wish & interest of England, & therefore the English govt. is endeavoring to strip the French possessions of half their value by maintaining that the best part of the group is not an appendage of Tahiti—Diplomacy is a tortuous game.*

1st February. Two of the French blockhouses were washed away by the rain—which has been more constant & of longer duration than for years before. No news of the Queen yet.

6th. The Governor went to Eimeo in the Phaeton to meet the Queen.

Tuesday 9th February. This day the French protectorate at Tahiti was completed & consummated by the return of Queen Pomare after an absence of 2½ years.

At ½ past 11 the Phaeton hove in sight with the Protectorate flag at the fore—indicating that the Queen was aboard. The Grampus & French ships being draped in flags saluted with 21 guns.

Pomare landed at the debarquedere in front of the American Consulate in which I posted myself to see the show. She quitted the steamer under a salute & was escorted on shore by the Governor in his barge.

A vast concourse of natives crowded the beach, the foremost ranks being knee deep in water. Their gaudy colours gave a gay appearance to the scene—which was the only cheerful part of it. There was no sound of joy—no demonstration of pleasure—no expression of satisfaction at her return. A solemn deathlike silence prevailed; not a whisper was uttered—you might have heard a pin fall. Pomare seemed to feel this striking absence of welcome. As she stepped from the pier, she looked as though she were stepping on the scaffold; and the multitude gazed upon her as if she were heading out for execution. As she passed within 10 feet of me I observed she was in tears—but otherwise looking well. She had a native headdress of flowers—a silken skirt & no shoes or stockings—she leant upon Bruat's arm who looked ill pompous & priggish. The Queen's mother, Pomaretani—Tapoa & the Governor's staff completed the melancholy party and they marched off through the troops, who lined the road to government house.

Thus ends the last act of the Tahitian tragedy (Bruat calls it a comedy) and judging by any other standard than that of French morality the seizure of this island would be considered an infamous & unwarrantable act. We have perhaps no right to find fault with France, for Tahiti has been repeatedly offered to England & as often refused. We thought ourselves secure, and that we could take them at any moment. In the mean time France stepped in & on a false & scandalous pretext hoisted her flag. However the deed is done, and it's too late to repine.

A proclamation has been issued that Q. Pomare submits to & acknowledges the protectorate, and that she is reinstated in all her power & authority. Poor woman! Whether for better or worse I believe I have been very instrumental in bringing about her return.

I was amused by a Frenchman in M. Rousseau's store. "Monsieur le Commandant," said he, "nous Français nous sommes cherchés partout; même en Californie avec leurs sucres et leurs cafés on nous à prié de leur donner notre protectorate etc. etc. Ici à Taiti nous sommes assez bien le pays donné des preuves de la civilization et le peuple commence deja manger les truffles." Eating truffles is the best test of civilization I have ever heard!

There is strangely little in the various records about the role of Ariitaimai Vahine and her husband Alexander Salmon. We know of their visits only through Huruata's memoirs as written down by Henry Adams after his visit in 1891. By then of course she was an elderly lady of seventy. Both Pomare and Salmon had died. One might suspect, and also condone, some romanticizing of her role after forty-five years. Only one passage is personally specific.

The *Memoirs of Ariitaimai* were translated, recorded, and inevitably "adamized" by Henry Adams in the 1890s and he had them privately printed in Paris in an edition limited to less than a dozen copies for distribution to his friends. They are referred to reverently by scholars because Ariitaimai as Tati's granddaughter and principal heir was unquestionably one of the highest-born, wealthiest, best-educated, most articulate Tahitians of the time. She has therefore been a prime source of information, and Henry Adams of course was a most prestigious gentleman and scholar. Of the 196 pages, 180 are Tahitian history, almost all of it prehistoric—ancient legends, genealogies, myths and tales. These are the many pages that are of interest to an ethnologist. The last 15 pages are subtitled "The Story of Ariitaimai, 1846," and they are the ones of chief interest to us here, for they tell of her own personal part in the crisis. Unfortunately they are long, rambling, and detailed, a typical literal translation of oblique, idiomatic Tahitian discourse. So a summary will do.

She is inspired to action by an unidentified old woman who says to her *I cry for my land of Tahiti. Our people will soon be at war with the French, and they will soon be opened like a lot of chickens. Don't you know that you are the first of the island, and it remains in your hands to save all this and your land?* So Ariitaimai goes to see Bruat, saying she wants to try to persuade the opposing chiefs to submit peacefully before the French attack. Bruat loans two horses to her and her companion, *my relation Ariipaea.* They set out to the native strongholds beyond Point Venus, encountering much difficulty and danger along the way and again when they arrive in "enemy" territory because her companion had been a deserter to the French. (Why she selected him is a mystery.) They go through much palaver with many minor chiefs until she comes to their headquarters where her Aunt Teriitua *caught me by my legs and began to cry.* She succeeds in assembling the high chiefs, who all seem to be relatives of hers. There is much formal discussion and debate. Finally one of the highest chiefs says, *Ariitaimai, you have flown amongst us, as it were, like the two birds Rua Taa and Teena. . . . You have brought the cooling medicines of vaiure and mahainui-eumu into the hearts of the chiefs that are collected here. . . . You have come forward as a peace-maker for us all. . . . what you have decided, we accept and will carry out.*

So she rides back toward Papeete, though not without interruption from fresh fighting, and gives the glad news to Bruat. *He said, "Is it peace?" I replied that it was peace and that everything was all right. He held my hand, and said "The Tahitians should never forget you; but do not consider your work finished. You must now prepare to leave and go to Raiatea." I told the governor that I would follow out his instructions, and I would certainly go; but that I had to consult my grandfather, Tati. When the old man heard that I was preparing to leave for Raiatea, he came, and with a troubled face said to me: "Are you really going to fetch the queen, and bring her back to this country?" I told him that I was going to do so. This affected him a great deal, but he did not say why. In leaving, however, he simply said these words: "Do your duty!"*

So off she goes with her husband Salmon. There are the usual endless difficulties in landing among the suspicious Raiateans and the usual endless discussions, arguments, persuasions and hesitations expressed by speakers for the queen on the one hand and by Salmon on Huruata's part on the other, with the Tamatoa and Tapoa butting in. The principals say almost nothing. The queen vacillates constantly, but at long length she agrees to go with her friend, but she tells her *not to be in too much of a hurry.*

While the Salmons were in Raiatea a battle had been fought in Punaauia and the French had been badly beaten. It was a matter of starting all over again, but at length Huruata prevails. Pomare goes to Moorea. Bruat comes over to fetch her and to sail her triumphantly all around the island with the queen's flag flying on the French warship to show all the people that she was home and that she had accepted the Protectorate.

The peace of the island was then decided upon. On arriving at the governor's house, we found all the commanders of the troops and vessels there, and before them I was thanked by Bruat for what I had done for my country.

On the whole I think we can accept the assumption that as a confidential, unobtrusive, go-between, Ariitaimai was principally responsible for Pomare's eventual return to Papeete and thus her reinstatement to "queenhood" for the rest of her life. The alternative, for her, would have been oblivion: perhaps it amounted to that in the end. I doubt the Tahitians look back on Queen Pomare today as any great credit to their race. Her chief promoters seem always to have been, as they still are, the French. Whether the transition—thirty years of Her

Highness—was of any real value or not to the Tahitians of that time, it can at least be said to have been a generous gesture on the part of the French.

After all these conflicting passions, and opinions, Père O'Reilly's present-day summary of the events of those times is a comforting one.

This is not the place to trace in detail the ups and downs of a colonial-style conflict during which Pomare and France were opposed for several years. At the instigation of Pritchard, the Queen refused to receive two French missionaries in her lands (affaire Caret et Laval) a refusal which brought to Tahitian waters the frigates of the admiral Du Petit Thouars. France installed herself in Papeete. Upon the bad behavior of the Queen (affaire of the Flag) a French Protectorate was established in the island. Pomare, always under the influence of the London missionaries who assured her of the protection and assistance of England, conducted a policy of resistance and delay. Finally, in March 1844, she took refuge on an English vessel and went into exile in Raiatea.

Excited by their queen, a party of Tahitians revolted. And it took two years for Admiral Bruat to bring to an end the insurgency and to establish peace in December 1846. A regent was appointed. In January, a festival celebrated the reconciliation and the Protectorate.

Amen.

But before concluding this account of that fatal watershed of Tahiti's history, I wonder whether anyone realizes, or will ever realize, how brave, determined, and glorious those Tahitians were who for three long years fought stubbornly for their freedom and their homeland against infinitely superior French firepower and professional militaristics? We have read and sung and orated about the superhuman gallantry of our colonial Americans fighting for their homeland, enduring their Bunker Hills and Valley Forges. We know a lot about South Americans under the gallant Simón Bolívar winning their freedom from Spain against hopeless odds. Russians we honor and praise for thwarting Napoleon; Gandhi for liberating India. These fights for freedom, these defenses of the homelands were all victories. What of the struggles that failed? They are all wrapped in oblivion. However gallant they may have been, however just their cause, they are only "rebels" who were at last "pacified" when the outsiders annihilated them. Only the winners are heroes it seems, no matter how brave the losers.

Someone should tell the Tahitians of today, and I shall try to do it here, how wonderfully courageous and resourceful their ancestors were in those valleys of Papenoo, Punaauia, and Fautaua for the three, long, punishing years that they fought for their land. How they were barricaded by the French frigates that controlled with their cannon the sea shores of the island. They were driven back up into the hills where their sole resource was the wild mountain plaintain, the *fei*—nothing but mush for *three years*. And yet they fought. They had always been shore dwellers since ancient Lapita days in border Melanesia and Samoa-Tonga. Their lagoon flatlands were their living, their dwellings, their cultivated foods, their fishing grounds, their whole sustenance.

What was it like in those camps in the steep mountain valleys? Staunch, desperate men gathered about their chiefs, who traced their linkage to these lands back more than a thousand years. They who knew the turns and twists of every stream, the feel and taste of their waters, the shape of every cliff, the name of every tree. They who knew all the hiding holes of fish, clams and octopus in the labyrinthine corals that were now forbidden them by their enemies' guns. How did they feel about that ancient breadfruit tree under which their grandfather used to argue, laugh, and scold while he told them tales of olden times, of heroes of their family who had discovered far-off islands, who had brought back beautiful princesses to be their great-grandmothers? Under that breadfruit tree which had nourished their family for so long, he had taught them how to haft adzes and hollow out canoes. And their grandmother used to join them to teach their sisters how to strip the thorns from pandanus leaves to part the fibers and weave the soft, sweet-smelling mats on which they slept at night.

Now, as they watched from on high, the trunk of that ancient breadfruit tree, as thick in girth as two grown men could reach around, was chopped down yesterday by a squad of French marines from the frigate; their grandfather's noble *maiore* felled because its fruit would feed them and prolong their unlawful resistance to the white men who were now the "legal" owners of their grandfather's land.

No wonder they fought. They not only fought, but they won again and again whenever there were man-to-man encounters. But of course they could not prevail with slingstones and spears and fists against bullets, swords and cannonballs.

The miracle is that they could keep at it for so long against such unfair odds. But they did. And Bruat kept sending back to France for reinforcements. The admirals and generals in Paris were disgusted. What was supposed to be an easy subjection of the most docile "indians" of the ocean islands was turning out to be a costly, bloody affair. Frenchmen were being killed every day. Malmanche, the gallant *chef d'état majeur*, lost his leg. We are told that he was much embarrassed and hardly dared to return to Paris, because how could he explain the loss of a leg in fighting with simple low-caste indians? A lieutenant of noble blood had his head bashed in. It was ridiculous that these smiling, easy-going people could hang on in the mountains, eating only roots and plaintains, for months and months stretching into years.

There could be no question of the final outcome. It began to seem needlessly costly to the military chiefs in Paris. So they terminated Bruat's governorship and dispatched Lavaud. Then by a sudden stroke of ill luck and treachery the "rebellion" collapsed at Fautaua and the ancient scions of the Tahitian homelands had to hand over their few precious muskets to the newly arrived "legitimate" governors from Europe. Does it not seem strange, even incredible, to us today that those eighteenth- and nineteenth-century white men could sincerely and righteously believe themselves to be legally entitled to all the lands of the world outside of Europe?

What if that agile Polynesian from Rapa whose name was Mairoto had not been on hand to be hired by the clever *Capitaine* Bonard to scale the peak of Fautaua and flip the coin of chance against the defenders? The outcome could not have been different. The French were bound to win in time and a prolongation would only have meant more misery for the people of the land. So we might even tell ourselves that it was perhaps fortunate that Mairoto was such a competent mountaineer and put a period to the resistance. But in resigning ourselves philosophically to the inevitable, we should surely bear in mind the courage and devotion of those Tahitians of old who fought so gallantly to the last for their rights and their homelands.

PART TWO

AFTER THE DELUGE

1850 to 1900

CHAPTER TWELVE

Smoldering Silence
1847 to Today?

The central theme of this book has been the forcible subjection or rape of the old Tahitian civilization by the aggressive colonizers of Europe. We have seen the first tentative overtures take place in Matavai Bay in 1767 when the explorers landed and introduced iron, liquor and gunpowder to the Stone Age inhabitants of the land. The next shock, thirty years later, was the obliterating impact of a new and foreign God on their traditional religion. These corruptions were subsequently augmented by an intermittent stream of traders, whalers, beachcombers and other foreign rascals. And radiating from these intruders to decimate them physically came the alien diseases, principally syphilis. Lastly, the military forces some fifty years later still came to seize their lands, exploit their labor and change their laws.

You might think the establishment of the Protectorate in mid-century, eighty years after first contact, was the totalization of this ravishment, but actually it took another fifty years to reach completion and that ultimate conquest is the subject of this second part of our narrative. At this point the life of the islands divides into two main branches, existing side by side. Yet in many respects they intermingled inevitably in so small a compass. But always they maintained two distinct personalities—the basic indigenous Tahitian on the one hand; the intruding European on the other. It seems best to tell them separately rather than try to mix them into one chronological account. So we shall start with the Polynesian struggling to survive after the cataclysm of his first military defeat and later trace the course of colonial empire through its second and final stage.

After the storm, a time of peace and calm set in. The fighting was over. The chiefs had been cast out: killed or put away, first in captivity, then released and pardoned. Amnesty for all, but an amnesty that was clearly subject to behavior that was satisfactory to the French, an amnesty that must cooperate with the new order. So the true feelings, the hopes and passions of the people, were heard no more. A sullen silence settled on the island. Any echoes of the past or of the fierce passions to hang on to their own lands and to pursue their own ways of life were subtly and quietly subdued. Any leader who stirred in protest was forthwith deprived of his land under the ancient French feudal law of appanage whereby lands reverted to the state "on the failure of male heirs." And male heirs soon learned that it was easy for them to be failed if they were recalcitrant. Thus the new Tahitian administration became a puppet of the French, who had set up the native governing structure in their own European image. Hereditary chieftainships were abolished and elected chiefs replaced them. Such a change, seemingly from feudalism to democracy would bring nods of approval from us of the Western World today. And it was praised in the chancelleries of Europe then as progress from savagery to civilization, just as the conversion by the missionaries from the old pagan deities to the True God was greeted by rejoicing in the religious councils of London. The evangelical sector was not so pleased however when the French confiscated all the Protestant Church lands and even the private houses and plots of the London missionaries.

Yes, it probably all looked circumspect enough to the outside world. Colonization, or "pacification" as it was euphemistically called, was said to have caused only light skirmishes with unruly dissident minorities. As time goes on the views of the historians become more and more bland until you might think there was hardly any resistance at all. To be sure the numbers killed in the Tahitians' fight for their homelands were not great, nothing like the numbers killed in India or Algiers, but when you calculate the losses as percentages of the population, they bespeak a full-scale war. And when you take into account the previous decimation by European diseases, the casualties constitute a veritable massacre.

But however unruffled its appearance to the outsider, the aftermath was an uneasy, baffling change within, a profound uprooting of the old spiritual authority that led to contradictions, paradoxes and dilemmas that persist to this day. The well-known anthropologist Ben Finney tells of an experience of his own on the little island of Maiao a century later in the 1950s. He was living as an adopted son with the chief of the island. It was the rule and custom to devote one day a week to communal labor prescribed by the French government: building and repairing roads, constructing wharfs, water works and public maintenance. Mondays were set aside for such work. But one Saturday it was learned that the boat from Tahiti to collect copra was to arrive the following Tuesday. Come Monday morning all the men of the island filed past the chief's house toward the hills to collect their copra instead of gathering for the customary weekly work assignments. The chief fumed and sat silent. Finney, in astonishment asked him why he did not go out and order them to come back and take up their tools. The chief explained that none of them would obey, that he was only the elected chief whose duty was to carry out the orders of the French government; that only an hereditary chief could command the will of the people. If he insisted, no one would pay attention to him and he would lose *mana*. He was in the employ of the French and such a rebellion would lead only to his replacement.

It must have been much the same, though more acute, in those early years of transition from the high family chiefs to the elected, virtually appointed, paid agents of the new government.

Yes, outwardly it all looked well enough. Strict curfews and military cadres restored order to the waterfront. The people came down from the hills to plant new breadfruit trees to replace the old girdled giants. Sprouting coconuts were arranged anew in straightly spaced files. In seven or eight years they would all bear fruit again, and more efficiently than in the old haphazard days.

Roads were built methodically. Roads had been unknown to the Tahitians before the missionaries first introduced them to gather the people to their churches in local communities—which in turn begat villages also hitherto unknown. Now the roads were pushed from village to village and the Tahitian began to move on wheels, another element new and revolutionary to him. Bridges spanned the streams that used to be waded or crossed on a single coconut log. Houses of sawn plank and coral plaster replaced the woven-bamboo-and-*purau* fare. Flags were run up at dawn and gathered in at nightfall to the sounds of bugles and marching drill. A cannon shot signaled curfew. The clock now divided the day which used to be intervaled by the tides, the cockcrow, the shadows, the heat of the sun. But the night continued to be measured by the moon and the stars, as it still is mostly today.

The Commissioners from France came to rule and to depart, all of them naval captains or admirals, with one exception, a cavalry officer. Most of them were rotating from Algiers, Indo-China, New Caledonia. There were eighteen of them during the thirty-four years of the Protectorate, an average of less than two years apiece until 1880 when the grand charade of the Pomares ended and Tahiti became the colony that she is today.

The Salmon family struggled at first, as we know from a letter of Bruat to Lavaud.

Monsieur Alexandre Salmon, an Englishman of the hebraic cult has married a cousine issue de germains of the Queen. He is a young man of good appearance and of distinction. He is refined, clever, and ambitious. After having tried to become the British Consul at Tahiti for a long time without success, he has contributed exceedingly to the action for and the establishment of the French Protectorate. He is today very much interested in consolidating and making sure of the titles to properties which are held by his wife Ariitaimai and his mother-in-law at their true value. The many voyages that he has made to the Leeward Islands to visit the Queen, the considerable expenses that he has incurred in this regard . . . indeed his desire to be conspicuous have all put his affairs in a bad state and have forced him many times to ask a price for his services. The payments which were granted successively were 500, 1000, and 1500 francs. His experience gave promise for future usefulness;

accordingly the governor with Pomare has named him secretary of ap-
pointments with the Queen at a salary of 3600 francs a year. The
mecurial temperament of Pomare makes it essential that there be an
agent close to her who is devoted to the Protectorate and at the same
time aware of the Queen's own best interests.

But eventually the family prospered. Old Tati had sided with the
French and was allowed to keep most of his rich properties in Papara
and Papeari. His grandson-in-law Alexander planted orange and coffee
trees and raised large numbers of pigs for the new, exploding market
of the California gold rush. Ariitaimai Vahine raised little Salmons.
Her oldest daughter, Titaua, married John Brander, the most successful
and enterprising merchant and trader in the whole south sea. Thus
Brander's father-in-law became his trusted business partner while his
mother-in-law continued to be the constant and closest companion of
the queen. But that did not deter her from bearing child after child,
nine of them, five girls and four boys from 1842 to 1866 the year
Alexander Salmon died, a periodic average about the same as the
Commissaires from Paris. All of these progeny were respected, some
were distinguished, one of them became the next queen. The impetu-
ous marriage of that Tahitian princess whom we knew as Huruata to
the man whom Captain Martin called *a low, swindling bankrupt Jew*
from London turned out to be one of the happiest and constructive
matings of the century in Tahiti. Their descendants are eminent citizens today.

In 1853 Alexander became president of the tribunal of commerce
and vice-president of the Tribunal of Papeete. Tati was elected President of the Legislative Assembly in 1848 and remained its head until
his death in 1854. That was the year of the devastating influenza
epidemic when some eight hundred Tahitians died, one twelfth of the
entire native population. Not a single European fatality occurred. This
ravenous element of disease was one of the tolls of colonializing all over
the world. But the degree of devastation was unique to the Pacific
peoples who had been isolated from the rest of mankind for so many
centuries. Other conquered peoples gave about as good as they got.
Syphilis (the Pox) was bestowed on Europe by the natives of

Mesoamerica. India contributed cholera, Africa and Indonesia malaria, the Middle East the bubonic plague (Black Death). But the Polynesian was literally disease free (except for non-transmutable elephantiasis). How did he achieve this? Pure living in a pure environment? Alas, when his turn came he was as virginally receptive as a germ-free laboratory culture.

The Legislative Assembly had been founded in 1824 when the child-king Pomare III was only four years old. It was a creation of the English missionaries who had reached the height of their power at that time. With a king in the making who was to be shaped in the form of their own limited monarch in London, they very naturally patterned this new body on their own Parliament. But the members were chosen or appointed by the *raatira* or land-owning classes so it was not in any real sense a democratic affair. As we look back on it, it seems to have been patterned on the upper-class English aristocracy, much the same sort of noble, land-owning superstructure, but with Tahitian blood. It was only a toy Parliament for it was strictly controlled by the missionaries, at least at the start. These men, as we have seen, were of the lower-middle and artisan classes, men of God, but men of dissenting sects who in this faraway land were sometimes tempted perhaps to play roles of their counterparts in the aristocratic Anglican Church in relation to the lords, barons, and knights of Polynesia.

But whatever its short comings as a law-making body, the convocations of the Assembly were splendid opportunities to get together and talk, an activity in which all Tahitians rejoice. Here was a chance to exercise their highest powers of oratory. Debates were conducted with great ceremony and courtesy. An interesting example is reported by the missionaries Tyerman and Bennett in 1824 on the subject of capital punishment. The question was whether a murderer should be put to death by hanging or whether he should be banished for life to some outlying island. One must realize that for the Polynesian his thoughts, his inspirations, feelings to be expressed, came always from his heart, not from his head. We know pretty well that our brain is the seat of our scintillating thoughts, the bursts of energy or inspiration that led us to produce relativity, atom bombs and air-conditioning. But we still pay respect to the old French adage, *Le coeur a ses raisons que la tête ne connaît pas.*

The Polynesian did not know his anatomy in the sense that our medical wizards know ours, but he chose the heart as the font of his thoughts and emotions. The head for him was the font of *mana*, of power and magic and influence. It had little to do with the everyday business of action. It was concerned with the higher mystical things. Feeling, impulse, emotion came from the heart.

Since the conventions of Tahitian oratory are filled with circumlocutions, fanciful metaphors involving ancient heroes, intimate relations with sharks, references to the ways of lovers that would shock you, and many other such abstrusities, these speeches have been summarized and simplified here. They are indeed mere outlines of what were probably very long and artistic orations. Nevertheless, even in this pious missionary transcription one can feel the dignity and originality of Tahitian thought, a direct example, expressed in their own words, of the stature of the leaders of these people.

On the question being proposed, Hitoti, the principal chief of Papeete stood up and, bowing to the president and the persons around him, said: "No doubt this is a good law,"—the proposed punishment was exile for life to a desolate island,—"but a thought has been growing in my heart for several days, and when you have heard my little speech you will understand what it is. The laws of England, from which country we have received so much good of every kind—must not they be good? And do not the laws of England punish murderers by death? Now, my thought is, that as England does so, it would be well for us to do so. That is my thought."

Perfect silence followed;—and it may be observed here that, during the whole eight days' meetings of this Parliament, in no instance were two speakers on their legs at the same time; there was not an angry word uttered by one against the other; nor did any assume the possession of more knowledge than the rest. In fact, none controverted the opinion of a preceding speaker, or even remarked upon it, without some respectful commendations of what appeared praiseworthy in it, while, for reasons which he modestly but manfully assigned, he deemed another sentiment better.

After looking round to see whether any body were already up before him, Utami, the principal chief of Buanaauia, rose and thus addressed the president: "The chief of Papeete has said well, that we have received a great many good things from the kind Christian people of England. Indeed, what have we not received from Beretane? Did they not send us (area) the gospel? But does not Hitoti's speech go too far? If we take the laws of England for our guide, then must we not punish with death those who break into a house?—those who write a wrong name?—those who steal a sheep? And will any man in Tahiti say that death should grow for these?—No, No; this goes too far; so I think we should stop. The law, as it is written, I think is good; perhaps I am wrong; but that is my thought."

After a moment or two of stillness, Upuparu, a noble, intelligent, and stately chief stood forth. It was a pleasure to look upon his animated countenance and frank demeanor, without the smallest affectation either of superiority or condescension. He paid several graceful compliments to the former speakers, while, according to his thought, in some things each was right, and each was wrong. "My brother, Hitoti, who proposed that we should punish murder with death, because England does, was wrong, and has been shewn by Utami. For they are not the laws of England which are to guide us, though they are good;—the Bible is our perfect guide. Now, Mitti Trutu (the Missionary Crook) was preaching to us on (naming the day) from the Scripture, 'He that sheddeth man's blood, by man shall his blood be shed'; and he told us that this was the reason of the law of England. My thought, therefore, is not with Utami, but with Hitoti (though not because the law of England, but the Bible orders it), that we ought to punish with death every one found guilty of murder."

There was a lively exchange of looks all through the assembly, as if each had been struck with the sentiments of the speaker, especially when he placed the ground of the punishment of death, not upon English precedent, but Scripture authority. Another chief followed, and "rising, seemed a pillar of state," one whose aspect and presence, and costume of dress (richly native) made the spectators forget even him who had just sat down. His name was Tati and on him all eyes were immediately and intensely fixed, while, with not less simplicity and deference to others than those who had preceded him, he spoke thus: "Perhaps some of you may be surprized that I, who am the first chief here, and next to the royal family, should have held my peace so long. I wished to hear what my brethren would say, that I might gather what thoughts are now growing in my own breast which I did not bring with me. The chiefs, who have spoken before me, have spoken well. But is not the speech of Upuparu like that of his brother, Hitoti—in this way? If we cannot follow the laws of England, in all things, as Hitoti's thoughts would perhaps lead us, because they go too far,—must we not stop short of Upuparu, because his thought goes too far likewise? The Bible, he says, is our perfect guide. It is. But what does that Scripture mean, 'He that sheddeth man's blood, by man shall his blood be shed.' Does not this go so far that we cannot follow it to the end, any more than we can follow the laws of England all the way? I am Tati; I am a judge; a man is convicted before me; he has shed blood; I order him to be put to death; I shed his blood; then who shall shed mine? Here, because I cannot go so far, I must stop. This cannot be the meaning of those words. But, perhaps, since many of the laws of the Old Testament were thrown down by the Lord Jesus Christ, and only some kept upright,—perhaps, I say, this is one of those which were thrown down. However, as I am ignorant, some one else will show me, that in the New Testament, our Saviour, or his apostles, have said the same thing concerning him that sheddeth man's blood as is said in the Old Testament. Shew me this in the New Testament, and then it must be our guide."

Much cordial approbation was evident at the conclusion of Tati's speech, and its evangelical appeal seemed to remove some difficulty and doubt respecting the true Scriptural authority applicable to the case.

Next rose Pati, a chief and a judge of Eimeo, formerly a high-priest of Oro, and the first who, at the hazard of his life, had abjured idolatry. "My breast," he exclaimed, "is full of thought, and surprise, and delight. When I look around at this fare bure ra *(house of God) in which we are assembled, and consider who we are that take sweet counsel together here, it is to me all* mea huru e *(a thing of amazement) and* mea faa oaoa te aau *(a thing that makes glad my heart). Tati has settled the question; for is it not the gospel that is our guide?—and who can find directions for putting to death? I know many passages which forbid, but I know not one which commands to kill. But then another thought is growing in my breast, and, if you will hearken to my little speech, you shall know what it is. Laws, to punish those that commit crime, are good for us. But tell me, why do Christians punish? Is it because we are angry, and have pleasure in causing pain? Is it because we love revenge, as we did when we were heathens? None of these: Christians do not love revenge; Christians must not be angry; they cannot have pleasure in causing pain. Christians do not, therefore, punish for these. Is it not that, by the suffering which is inflicted, we may prevent others from doing as he has done to deserve the like? Well, then, does not every body know that it would be a greater punishment to be banished for ever from Tahiti, to a desolate island than just, in a moment, to be put to death? And could the banished man commit murder again there? And would not others be more frightened by such a sentence than by one to take away his life? So my thought is that Tati is right, and the law had best remain as it has been written."*

One of the taata rii, *or little men, a commoner, or representative of a district, now presented himself, and was listened to with as much attention as had been given to the lordly personages who preceded him. He said: "As no one else stands up, I will make my little speech, because several pleasant thoughts have been growing in my breast, and I wish you to hear them. Perhaps every thing good and necessary has been said already by the chiefs; yet, as we are not met to adopt this law, because one great man recommends it, but as we, the* taata rii, *just the same as the chiefs, are to throw all our thoughts together, that out of the whole heap the meeting may make those to stand upright which are best, whencesoever they come—that is my thought. All that Pati said was good; but he did not mention that one reason for punishing (as a Missionary told us when he was reading the law to us in private) is, to make the offender good again if possible. Now if we kill a murderer, how can we make him better? But if he is sent to a desolate island, where he is all solitary, and compelled to think for himself, it may please God to make the bad things in his heart to die, and good things to grow there. But, if we kill him, where will his soul go?"*

Others spoke to the same purport, and in the result, it was unanimously determined that banishment, not death, should be inflicted on murderers.

The death of Tati was to mark the final passing of the old order. From his obituary in the official local newspaper you would almost classify him as a French hero.

Messager de Tahiti 16 July 1854—80 yrs

The death of Tati is a calamitous event in the history of Tahiti. With Tati there dies one of the last and the most illustrious representatives of the heroic ages. He saw Cook; he remembered human sacrifices, incessant wars which stained the shores of Tahiti with blood. Friend of Pomare II whose elevation he had favored and whom he had supported with all his power, because he believed that only a single and dominating power could assure peace in the island. On the death of that great chief, when he saw that internal battles were beginning to show themselves, he was the first promoter of the foreign protectorate which could control the inner furies of the land. He always showed himself to be the most firm and the most zealous supporter of the French Protectorate; it was his political faith which never wavered and he died satisfied to have contributed powerfully to the founding and to the health of his country.

Tati was of an imposing size and a remarkable muscular strength. His spirit strove mightily to remain in his vigorous body. The agony was long. He was brave in combat, eloquent in assemblies, full of prudence and wise in counsel: a man of good works always. What a loss for Tahiti! She sees today the disappearance of one of the grand figures of her history. He has died taking with him the sorrows of all the inhabitants of the land.

There are many vivid descriptions of Tati's noble bearing and eloquent speech. He was the epitome of the elder statesman, respected and revered by all. He had made enemies in siding with the French, but one senses that he was later recognized as having been wise to embrace the inevitable and to preserve what was possible of the heritage of the past. It was he more than any other who defended the native ownership of the land. Of course he was the island's largest landowner, but his ties to the new French authorities and his prestige gave him leverage to protect his fellow Tahitians as well. While Polynesians in Hawaii and New Zealand were selling for songs their ancient groves and forests, the Tahitians somehow managed to retain their hereditary fiefs and to this day they own a major portion (though not always the choicest) of land in the French colony. This is a phenomenon rare in the history of colonialism. It is, in our present-day eyes, a fine tribute to the French government. But the Tahitian must also be given credit for his persistence. Partly perhaps this was a result of his indifference to money and a realization of what little use it was to him in his isolated ocean world. Partly perhaps it was a result of the Frenchman's lack of acquisitiveness, as contrasted with the Englishman's. He had little taste for settling on these unproductive scraps of terrain so far removed from his beloved motherland in Europe. Unlike his English, and later American, fellow whites, he did not have much stomach for pioneering and establishing a family line abroad. But this was not solely motivated by his sentimental Gallic nature. It was also determined by the nature of the land. The far richer and larger islands of Hawaii and New Zealand were infinitely more tempting to European greed. Many a Frenchman settled tenaciously in mineral-rich New Caledonia, three thousand miles to the westward, to his discomfort and distress today.

CHAPTER THIRTEEN

The Improbable Queen
1827 to 1877

Queen Pomare IV has been too much publicized over the years, either glamorized or besmirched. It may be that she was not nearly as important as popular history has made her. But when you consider the slings and arrows of her fortune, she is an interesting mirror in which to see reflected the even more outrageous misfortunes of the Tahitian people. Perhaps it is hazardous to try to depict a people through impressions of visitors reporting on their queen, but Pomare was certainly the person most noticed and, indeed, she often seems the only one. All reports concentrate on her personality and seem to ignore others except as her background, mostly her attendants. But this is not strange when you realize that visitors were almost invariably transients of a few days. They would naturally seek out the prime curiosity of the land and pay little mind to the multitude whose faces to foreigners always look the same.

So the queen is the best Tahitian type of the time that I can give you in first-hand accounts, manifestly untypical to those who have come to know and appreciate these highly individual people. And yet the very artificiality of this "queen" and this "court" is an important insight into the Tahiti of those postwar days. The real Tahiti retreated or faded into a featureless background nursing its wounds, mourning the loss of its leaders. The Tahitian seems to say to himself: Let the newcomer be dazzled by the spectacle that has been created for him. Pomare will comply. She is not really one of us, but she will play her part well enough and distract prying eyes from our own selves, who prefer to remain in the bush.

We have had some first-hand reports from the early years. Now we begin to see changes. Let me give you a sort of slide show of reports from those who saw her in person, in Tahiti. The French in 1847 started out by strictly regularizing the royal household. There was appointed one "majordomo," one "concierge," and eighteen *teuteuarii*, or "royal retinue." This personnel was engaged by the director of the Caisse de la Reine and operated under his instructions—thirty francs a month for the majordomo, twenty-five francs for the concierge, and variable sums determined by Pomare for the *teuteuarii*. These "courtiers" were chosen from volunteers representing each of the districts and they were changed every year in January. There were others, such as nurses for the children, a scribe, a doctor, etc. The interpreter was Adam John Darling, son of the early missionary who had been principally responsible for the translation of the Bible into Tahitian.

Pomare got 18,684 francs from the "civil list" which provided 1 franc from a married man, 1 franc from a wife, 1 franc per widow with children, 2 francs a widower without children, 2 francs from a boy of marriage age, 1 franc for a girl in the same position, exemption for boys under sixteen and girls under fourteen, infirm people and those unable to work. For the queen it all equaled 18,684 per year plus 18,556 for gifts and expenses. Her total was roughly the same recompense as the governor's. But she got gifts wherever she went and anyone coming to see her had to bring something. Besides all this, she got 40,000 to 50,000 francs a year as rent from her lands; in all about 80,000 francs, or some $18,000. That was the official aspect, but since in actuality the old crowd hung on, she was always broke. We have a note from her written to a Papeete policeman asking for a chicken for her dinner because she had no money to buy one. Always she was in debt. Her huge family milked her all of the time. And she herself, in true Polynesian fashion, overindulged her generous heart.

The palace itself was just an extra-large, typical Tahitian *fare* of bamboo, woven coco fronds, and pandanus thatch, with some sawn-board walls and posts from Australia to give it a half-caste European look. There were many smaller native houses in the royal compound where guests and servants lived; cookhouses, storehouses hung with *fei*, yams and taro; earth ovens; places to string the fish that were brought each day as portions of the catch for the queen, and so on.

We are indebted frequently to Père O'Reilly for a scattering of impressions that spotlight from time to time the behavior and appearance of the queen. At twenty-nine she is described by a French journalist as "tall enough for a woman but markedly stout and massive with beautiful eyes when she glances up." She was dressed just like the common Tahitian girls in a simple chemise, went with the others on board whalers anchored in the harbor and all day long she bathed with them without formality of any sort. She took the customary spells in the shade of Tetiaroa to blanch her skin. She was constantly surrounded with companions. In short, she appeared to everyone as plump, placid, gregarious, a typical *vahine,* and yet she seemed always to inspire a sort of regal reverence. One wonders whether there was really anything special about her or whether this grandeur existed mostly in the eye of the beholder. Personally, I see it frequently even today, flashing from the eyes and smiles that radiate so unexpectedly the faces of naive young girls, flirtatious maidens, amused matrons, and worldly-wise elders. It seems a racial trait born in them, which wells up in *queenly* fashion to startle you and to melt you from time to time.

Captain Martin of H.M.S. *Grampus* gives us some intriguing perceptions into the characters of the principal actors in that drama of the take-over times. His impressions seem to me more reliable than many that have heretofore been recorded. The others are either fleeting encounters by visiting seamen such as Fitzroy, Wilkes, Melville, La Place, Loti, Antione, Souville; or insiders like Moerenhout, Bruat and Bonard, who were distinctly enemies; or relatives like Ariitaimai and Marau, who were family; or like Pritchard and the other missionaries, who had celestial axes to grind.

To be sure Martin had an axe of sorts—a clear prejudice for England against France, but he saw a lot of Pomare, listened frequently to her troubles and constant appeals for advice and support. His first encounter with her was in Raiatea in late October 1846.

Queen Pomare is a thick made, sepia coloured woman, with a profusion of very black hair. Her countenance though perhaps a little dull, is not upon the whole unpleasing; and it betrays more care and anxiety than is often seen among this giddy, light hearted people. Though there may be a certain quantity of romance in Pomare's story when told at a distance of 17,000 miles; a good deal of it vanishes when the reality stands revealed in the form of a fat oily woman without a particle of clothing but a cotton shirt. Little passed beyond common expressions of civility; every allusion to politics being purposely avoided. She said she was well in body but sick at heart; that she had much to talk to me about, and that she would go on board to ask my advice on certain matters—so that our conversation would not be overheard by others—and fixed on Monday—(her Tuesday) for the purpose. After half an hour's visit I took my leave.

26th October—Heavy rain ushered in the day fixed for my banquet to Queen Pomare. At noon, the hour she had fixed for coming on board, it seemed as if the flood gates of heaven were once more opened and another deluge were coming to chastise our iniquities. I found that the disappointment of not coming would be greater than the fear of a ducking—so in spite of a continued pour I sent boats to bring them on board. They seemed to hesitate, for it was past 2 before they made their appearance—a solemn procession of umbrellas walking down the mole to the boats. It was a quaint sight for a lover of the picturesque. Her majesty was received with manned yards, and as she stepped on the deck, she looked every inch a Queen! Her blue cotton skirt was exchanged for one of yellow satin—spotted here and there with punch—on her head was a red velvet bonnet, which, if not an heirloom must have emerged at no recent period from a pawnbroker's shop. Her neck and hands were decorated with flimsy French trinkets—a pair of figured silk stockings and red shoes adorned the feet which hiterto I had only seen naked. Poor woman! She seemed conscious that all this finery was out of character, for she had not been five minutes in the cabin before she pitched her bonnet on the sofa and kicked off her shoes. She brought 4 of her children and 4 attendants—besides her husband Pomare tani—who came intent on a good, deep, heavy drink.

She was accompanied by Tamatoa King of Raiatea, in an old blue coat (with buttons of 39th Regt.) over his shirt—no pantaloons or shoes or stockings—Tapoa King of Bora Bora and his wife—in their shirts— a fat jolly old couple—6 other high chiefs and 3 of their wives and Mr. Charter as interpreter.

After the party had refreshed themselves with some wine—Pomare asked for a private conversation and all but her husband and Mr. Charter were sent out of the cabin. They consoled themselves in their banishment with a few bottles of wine in the gunroom and a few more in the midshipmen's berth—by way of a whet for my dinner.

Pomare then asked me to advise her in her present difficulties; a task to which I really felt myself inadequate.

I reported to her much of what had passed in conversation with Bruat concerning her, and wished her to say what was her own feeling about returning to Tahiti.

She said "Sometimes I think I will go, and before I have time to act I change my mind—I cannot say I have any real desire to return; but my francs are less that they were. If I do go back I know I shall be in reality a prisoner tho' nominally free." She certainly is under the delusion that in arrangement of the leeward island question, something will be done for her. Some one, probably the missionaries, have told her to wait— and it was in vain that I assured her there was no hope of succour from England.

She said she knew it but still she dwelt and harped upon the old friendship of England and Tahiti—in a way that convinced me that she has not yet given up all hope. She asked me if I would take her up in the Grampus. I replied that anticipating her wish I had asked Bruat if he would receive her from an English ship, and that he had positively refused. Upon which the poor creature sighed and said she hated French- men. I told her there would be no peace at Tahiti until the protectorate is acknowledged, and it was folly to hope to suppose the Tahitians were able to cope with the French, and after a long and tedious conversation —most unsatisfactory and totally unproductive of good I rose much disappointed. I confess I saw no evidence of that dignity and intelligence which others have spoken of. At last she said she was hungry—and so we adjourned to the dinner table and sat down 22 in number.

Untill today I never knew what eating *meant—all that I had ever seen was mere child's play to the performance of these people. They ate till they were ready to burst, and pocketed what remained, and would have disposed of twice the quantity if it had been there.*

Most of the men and all of the women got drunk, except Pomare who was sober and well conducted throughout. Two of the maids of honour, *who for lack of room dined by themselves, drank 4 bottles of sherry within the hour and then called for brandy. However as far as I heard or saw most of the party conducted themselves with decency though the men were rather noisy and the women too in their cups.*

Tamatoa's wife not being a chief in her own right was not permitted to dine with those of higher cast—this however did not seem to affect her appetite, nor did she omit to get as tipsy as her neighbors.

The men danced and sang to amuse the Queen and gave her Rule Brittannia in full chorus. When she took her leave at 10 P.M. a royal salute was fired, some blue lights and rockets let off and the ship's Co. gave her three hearty cheers—which pleased her much.

27th. I wrote to the Queen a sort of digest of what passed yesterday, for she is so unintelligent that I fear her misinterpreting what I said.

29th. Mr. Charter came off this morning to say Pomare wished to talk with me. I immediately went to her—and as she feared or pretended to fear listeners, she got into my gig with Mr. Charter and her husband and came on bd.

Pomare had brought Bruat's proposals to her and requested my opinion upon each point. She provokes me by her extreme selfishness and total absence of feeling for her people. The only parts on which she seemed to dwell, were those that related to her income and the native guard. She is sharp enough and cunning enough on matters connected with her own personal comfort or importance—but on all others she seemed dull and unintelligent. I could not keep her attention fixed for 2 minutes. She was thinking of anything but the subject under discussion, so, fearing that she would catch a word here and there without context, and misrepresent what I said, I begged her to leave Bruat's letter that I might consider it and write my opinion.

I do not see much to object to in these proposals which Bruat sent to Pomare in April last; tho it would be better if they were more explicit. Nor could she find fault with them—but she said she disliked all Frenchmen and above all Bruat. She thinks a new governor may do something more for her; but there she is mistaken—the utmost she can expect is a liberal interpretation of the Protectorate Treaty. She seems very indifferent to the opinions of the Tahitian chiefs, believing they will do as she bids. This I doubt and told her so.

I am told she sometimes talks of renouncing Tahiti, as all her children are provided for—one has been adopted by Ariipuia of Huahine as her heir—another by Tapoa and a 3rd by Tamatoa. There is something very generous in the devotion of the chiefs and people of the leeward islands to her cause, even at their own risk. She and her numerous hangers on are supported by voluntary contribution—Tamatoa has given up his house to her, and there is a general idea that if she chooses to remain at Raiatea, the sovereignty of the island will be made over to her. In the days of her Queenhood Pomare was imperious, tyrannical and oppressive, and in her misfortune she is petulant, peevish and capricious.

Her bitterest enemy, Bruat, turned friend now that he had got the best of her, writes a memorandum for his successor Lavaud. *Pomare is for a Tahitian a very distinguished woman. Her associations with representatives of foreign powers and the treatment she has received from them has given her a feeling for her position and her dignity. She has power, over her family and over her people. She gives little and wishes to obtain much. Appearing to care little for honors, she is nevertheless very sensitive and follows closely outward forms that will demonstrate her power and dignity. But in spite of a desire to exercize power herself, she will leave it always in other hands, lacking the ability of regular work, especially if she can find a way to save her face.*

But shortly after Bruat had left for France, she wrote to him.

I have not been able to accommodate myself to the new governor [Lavaud]. He pays no attention to my words. One day he listens to me and the following day he takes no notice of what I had said. The interpreter that you appointed, Darling, does not listen to me either or he does not translate the words I have spoken . . . this letter is for you alone. Don't let the government know any of this for they will be angry with me.

In another letter later on: *Greetings to you by the True God and by Jesus the Messiah! I write you this letter today with a warm feeling for you, for your wife and two daughters. I wish you to know that my new-born son has been named for the son of the King which in Tahitian is Tuavira "Joinville."*

Upon the birth of her last son, Pomare asked Lavaud to suggest a name for him. Lavaud writes about it to the Minister of Foreign Affairs in Paris. *She did not hide from me her desire to take the name of one of the sons of the King of the French which would bestow on her infant the same rights as his father's. . . . I answered immediately with the name of "Joinville" which she gave him this morning. Such childish details would seem to carry high political significance!*

Apparently Lavaud had no appreciation of the anything-but-childish importance of the ancient Polynesian custom of exchanging names.

In 1848 Bonard wrote to his superiors in Paris. *In my opinion, armchairs at 75 francs, a commode at 250 francs, a clock at 600 francs are objects that are much too expensive. In previous years these desires of the Queen were transmitted. In October 8, 1851, the Queen expressed a keen desire for a suite of drawing room furniture, a settee or sofa, a four poster bed and four mahogany armchairs upholstered in red velvet. Add to that a gold ring . . . then a summer outfit for a seven year old boy, such as was seen in the Tuileries in the good old days . . . for the husband of the Queen a box of straight razors called "The Week." One can obtain them chez Gravet, rue Saint-Honoré, at modest prices in a mahogany box. It will contain seven blades, with an ivory handle and a small mirror. See that a little silver plaque is fastened on the box with the name Ariifaite engraved upon it.*

In the same year Pomare let it be known that she would like to have her portrait painted. The "command" was relayed to Giraud on January 27, 1851. (Our gallant reporter of the heroic battle of Fautaua must have returned to Tahiti after receiving his Légion d'Honneur.) On the twenty-ninth of April he advised the minister of foreign affairs that his work was finished and that his fee was 800 francs. But the Minister did not find it comfortable to award him so large a price because "copies of portraits of Louis-Philippe cost 1000 to 1200 francs." It was felt therefore that 600 francs for a Tahitian canvas was adequate.

Père O'Reilly reports one of the most sorrowful times for this queen whose life now seems only a succession of sorrows.

At the age of 16, Arii Aue heir presumptive of the realm died in the night in 1855. His constitution had always been delicate and his dissipations prodigal. His body was kept for ten days in a wooden coffin painted black while the populace visited and mourned extravagantly. At last the "odeur" was "tellemont forte" that the young prince had to be buried.

At 6 in the morning a torrential rain commenced that did not let up till 8 in the evening. The Messager de Tahiti *reported the cortege. "From the first boom of the cannon, the natives were on their feet to take their places in the procession and judging from the constant noise that had reigned throughout the night, many had not slept at all to be ready for the morning. The cortege began to form as cannon thundered. In rags and tatters shot through with bullet holes at the time of the conquest of Tahiti, the flag of the marine infantry had been stored with the government and was now flown again for the first time; on this occasion at the head of the column. Then the missionary Orsmond, chief of the Tahitian Church followed by all of his native ministers; and the children of the schools of the Catholic sisters all dressed in white, one of them bearing a white banner on which was painted the symbols of the dead one.*

Sheltered by a canopy of velvet, richly draped and ornamented with black plumes, the coffin was carried by ten chiefs with others waiting their turn to relieve them.

Queen Pomare kept herself in the rear dressed in a robe of black satin, with a veil that fell to her feet and wearing on her head an imitation royal crown with black plumes. At her side Ariifaite, her husband, dressed in a black suit covered with a Dalmatic ecclesiastical cloak and decorated with large folds of point lace. Then came the regent Paraita in a uniform of gold brocade with a sword and peaked hat, the whole covered with a lace mantel. . . . Messieurs & Mesdames Salmon relatives of the Queen having their heads shaven kept close to Pomare. . . . Then passed the Governor, the Bishops, the Consuls, all the government functionaries, officers, notables, lawyers and merchants of Papeete. . . . Then here at last was the crowd, all the native population of Tahiti, Moorea, and the Leeward Islands. Many parallel columns followed by all those who were not dressed in black. And the troops lined the way.

The cortege arrived at the Fautaua bridge at 7:30. The road was transformed into a swamp of mud through which the crowd stomped splashing our uniforms. Dressed in robes of silk or black satin, coiffed with elegant hats decorated with plumes and floating ribbons, the women were already unrecognizable. They seemed to be rising from the depths, so much driving rain was falling. Their garments clinging to their bodies hardly permitted them to walk. Moreover, many of them had gathered up their clothes so that they had to flounder through. Others keeping on only their blouses trudged along, their lacy robes, which had seemed so elegant only a few hours before, carried in their arms rolled in bundles. Many of them crossed the raging river of Fautaua with the main purpose of washing their clothes and bodies.

The men acted differently; most of them carried their trousers over their arms and wore only top coats. All in all it was a comic spectacle.

At this point the governor P.I. took leave of the Queen and headed back to Papeete accompanied by the Bishop and followed by numerous officers. They had a difficult time bucking the human flood which surged around them blocking the road.

About nine o'clock the religious ceremony took place at Papaoa Point where the coffin was set down between the funeral cave and a pulpit set up for the pastors. A general fusillade of musketry announced the commencement of the ceremony. After much discourse and songs the body of the prince was laid in a fare or native hut painted black. It was just outside of the cave in which the remains of Aimata's other deceased children were laid.

Four natives dressed in ancient Tahitian fashion, guardians of the tomb of Pomare II took up the coffin. These men were not allowed to penetrate it in modern dress. On the occasion of these funerals everyone must remain twenty-four hours without talking, without drinking, without eating.

The return procession then commenced and every soldier passing by the tomb discharged his rifle into the air. The troops did not get back to Papeete till four o'clock.

The frigate La Moselle *discharged a cannon of mourning every five minutes until sundown and all flags were flown at half mast.*

In 1862 Governor La Richerie wrote *Her bearing is full of dignity. She dresses entirely in the European fashion, except for public ceremonies, and then she reverts to garments tailored in the finest fabrics of Lyon. She does not comprehend English at all. She understands a little French, but speaks none.* Had she forgotten by then her trusted London missionaries?

Midshipman Antione, 1864: *I then made my respects conscientiously and was deeply moved. In France one does not dance every day with queens. Pomare IV was giving a ball with her daughter the queen of Bora Bora, and the queen of Raiatea. . . . They danced perfectly. They were a bit heavy, but one should not be surprized since at least one of them weighed as much as two European men. Moreover they had the skill to pirouette with an irresistible flair. Everything depended on the timing. . . . The pleasure left nothing to be desired. Near the salon was a table covered with cakes and refreshments. One escorted the ladies there after each dance, served them and afterward returned them to their places.*

La Roncière in 1866: *The Queen ordered with an open hand all sorts of furniture, large oval mirrors, and at one point a chandelier 6 feet high and 10 feet in diameter. It was to be encased in tin placed in a wooden box and covered with cloth to protect it in the hold of a three-masted sailing ship and when it arrived and was hung from the highest point of the roof beam it was still so large that the Prince Consort could not walk beneath it.*

One wonders whether the shy, modest Pomare really wanted all this civilized splendor or whether she was playing a game with her governors, the sort of game she played with cards and cheated.

As the years pass, Pomare is nearly sixty when Pierre Loti arrives in 1872.

At the end of the salon, the old Queen was seated on her guilded throne draped with red brocade. She held in her arms her dying grand-daughter. . . . The old woman filled the whole width of her chair with the disgraceful mass of her person. She was dressed in a tunic of crimson velvet: a bare lower leg encased more or less in a silk boot. . . . In this old face, lined, bronzed, square, hard, there still was a grandeur: there was above all an immense sadness.

In the massive ugliness one could discern what must have been the characteristics and prestige of her youth, about which the old-time navigators have told us of the original souvenir. He must have been confusing her with Purea. None of the old-time navigators ever saw Pomare.

Marau, third daughter of Ariitaimai Vahine and Salmon, was the wife of the future king, Pomare V, thus the queen's daughter-in-law and herself the last queen of all, is more precise about her dress. *At the beginning of her reign, she was generally dressed as were all Tahitian girls; that is in a pareu, wrap around cotton, knotted at the waist and a sort of camisole with sleeves buttoned at the neck constituting the costume imposed by the missionaries; but for receptions and ceremonies she dressed à l'européenne, as is shown in the portrait of her by Charles Giraud in 1855. Already massive and stout she appeared in white taffeta in the style of the epoch without corset, a flower of red hibiscus behind each ear, and on her head a couronne of artificial flowers. Later on she adopted the grand floating robe and train with a yoke and the sort of Watteau folds that were the mode here from the middle to the end of the last century.*

Like everyone in Tahiti the Queen got up at dawn and commenced her day with a matin prayer by a native pastor. After which came tea, the two other meals taking place at eleven in the morning and six in the evening. Their preparation was quite an affair. First off the foods were distributed. Two earth ovens were prepared, one for the royal family, the other for the members of the household.

Ariitaimai tells us, *The Queen and her children ate on the ground off* mats of fresh leaves, but well apart from the others, following our old customs and whatever European manners had been introduced by the missionaries. She ate alone, as had always been the custom with us; never with her children or granddaughters. I was the only one for which she ever made an exception to this rule, Marau assures us and we owe to her the following details. "She habitually sat on the ground upon mats surrounded by followers who passed her cigarettes and massaged her if she wished. There were always many by her side even at night and when she was awake conversation must be made. To my knowledge the Queen never slept on a bed, but always on mats which were moved to a different place each night after she had escaped being assassinated. This attack was made by a European who was discovered with a revolver, but avoided a lynching and disappeared without a trace. Since then the Queen had always been afraid and, during the night, she had her whole house surrounded, even the native pastors and deacons who had to recite or read the Bible without cessation during all the time she slept, waking herself up if ever they stopped. At her feet were three servants charged with massaging her until the morning. It was only in the Leeward Islands that I saw her sleep without fear.

If her visitors did not measure up the Queen did not welcome them. When a visitor who bored her was announced, she picked up a sprig of aretu, a kind of broad-leafed grass that they used to cover the ground beneath the mats. When she began to roll this into a ball, one knew the meaning. And when she had had enough of the person in question she grasped the blade of aretu, did not raise her head and answered only yes or no. This way of hers did not always indicate ennui or displeasure. Pomare was not expansive. Contrary to Tahitian custom Pomare never kissed anyone. She was indeed very shy. She did not like to look at people directly, but this did not prevent her from being extremely curious and very observant without appearing to be so.

The queen spoke and understood only Tahitian. Visitors who did not know her language had to bring an interpreter. She herself had her daughter-in-law Marau almost always by her side. Did she know how to write? One wonders. Marau is cautious about it. I have never known of a whole letter written by her. I am not sure but I think she could only *sign her name.* Père O'Reilly warns us against the autographs that frequently appear at auctions and in displays: *All those except the most characteristic with her P dangling those triple ringlets should be viewed with strong suspicion.*

Pomare's favorite distraction was cards. She cheated without scruple, but her companions generally were too polite to notice so she triumphed enthusiastically. Pierre Loti tells us *She cheated even at official soirees in the games she played with admirals or with the Governor but the several louis that she was able to win certainly meant nothing to her except the pleasure she got from deceiving her fellow players.*

Other occupations were weaving hats and short skirts or waist wraps from coco fronds or pandanus leaves. She also fashioned *tifaifai,* as patchwork quilts were called, an occupation inherited from wives of New England whaling captains. Soaking, splashing and playing about in the cool, fresh streams whiled away many hours, as they still do with many a Polynesian today. The queen liked to organize expeditions up the valley of the Fautaua River for picnics and bathing in pools under waterfalls. Toward the end of her life, Marau tells us, *the only restful moments for Pomare were those she passed in company with my mother, Ariitaimai, to whose house she went voluntarily to eat and to sleep, and I would hear them laugh together, something that seldom happened to Pomare Vahine, even with her children. . . . She came generally accompanied by two young servants one of whom carried her tobacco. I remember poignantly one time when we saw her arrive, tripping along quickly as usual, her head always lowered and her hand holding the hem of her long robe so that her bare feet showed up to the ankle. We waved to her in passing but she responded only by raising her head without straightening up. When she came to us, she sat next to me and made me a sign to dismiss the servants. She then held out to me two stacks of gold coins amounting to the modest sum of 500 francs which she allowed me every month for my personal expenses.* [Marau at this point was separated from her husband, the crown prince, and living with her mother.] *"I happened to be passing by Maria's shop the novelty merchant who has just received some pretty lengths of silk. I told her you* would pay her a call. Go and choose what may please you, it is I who give you this."

On Sept. 1, 1877 they were going to have a reception on board the frigate-amiral la Magicienne. The Queen was about to go aboard when her son Terii Tapuni came to ask her for money to gamble with at the occasion. Ecarte was then a la mode at Papeete and they were playing with very large sums. The Queen declared that it was impossible for her to give him anything. And she advised him to address himself to Ariitaimai, the second mother to all of them. Upon which Terii Tapuni declared that, if things were so, neither he nor his wife would go aboard, and, furious, made a distressing scene with his mother seated on the ground, even going in a fit of anger to hitting her with a chair. Badly upset by such an outburst, the Queen also, renounced the occasion and from that moment whether because of the blow she received or the humiliating commotion, she was seen to be sad and unnerved.

On the seventeenth Marau wrote in her memoirs that her mother (Ariitaimai) was summoned to the queen very early in the morning, and since we were not in our house, neither she nor I, three messengers were sent to warn us that the Queen was very ill and we were urgently needed. We ran to the palace where we found her slumped on a canape and already unconscious. My mother tried all sorts of resuscitation but she was able to bring out only a sort of inarticulate groan. In tearing open her robe from top to bottom, she found black marks on the left side of her breast and following our customs she began to massage with coconut oil while they sent for a doctor. We learned later that she had gone as usual to her morning bath in a sort of bathing place built above a spring with a stair case over which the water flowed and that in descending she had been taken with a fainting spell. The chief health officer, Dr. Cassanol, her old friend, accompanied by his assistant, arrived at the scene but not being able to reanimate her declared that she had succumbed to a heart attack. She was sixty-four years of age.

Her body rested in state for several days to permit the people of the neighboring archipelagoes to come and attend the funeral.

It was a sign of the times that the official *Messager* felt it was best not to give too much publicity to the passing of the queen. Columns and columns had been lavished the preceding weeks on "The Ball aboard the *Magicienne*," on a "Visit to Lake Vahiria," on the "Distribution of Prizes to Apprentices." But only these few lines on the funeral.

The obsequies took place on the current Saturday the 22nd amidst a large gathering of people. The funeral convoy parted from Papeete to Papaoa at 5:45 in the morning. The traverse was on foot for every one. Customary military honors were rendered by companies of the Naval Division and the troops of our garrison. The weather which had been partly rainy during the night held fair during the course of the ceremony.

Such was the official word (or non-word) delivered out of fear, one suspects, that repressed emotions might burst out. But the actuality was a profound and massive and characteristically Polynesian tidal wave of woe. *Ariitaimai marching at the head of the procession, intoned the* faateni *(supplications) of the Queen with her pathetic plaint. She sat upon the ground, covered her head with a great black veil and commenced her lamentation in the consecrated manner. Her grief was profound and she expressed it magnificently in our language so rich in images, especially as they came from her mouth and were carried by her voice, harmonious and resonant.*

Père O'Reilly believes that *with the passing of Pomare, the Tahitians felt that they had lost not only a queen but a mother, the symbol of their profound personality and the representative of their traditions and their national patrimony.* He believes from personal communication with Marau's child, "la princesse Takau," that old-time Tahitians, *on their ways home at night when they pass over the old Broom road past the place where the old Palace stood, that they still cross themselves out of fear or respect for the tupaupau or spirit of their Queen.*

Perhaps, but casting a cynical twentieth-century eye back over the creation and maintenance of Pomare by the French colonizers, one sees perhaps a showcase queen. They had no public relations specialists in those days but they surely had an inherent instinct for what we now call PR. Real queens had gone out of fashion in France when Marie Antoinette's head had leapt into the guillotine's basket, but queenly nostalgia lingered on. Their rivals the British had an enduring model queen, and the French had even brought Eugénie, a sort of ersatz one, back to decorate Emperor Napoleon III's brief reign. A queen in Tahiti was harmless enough politically, and a romantic attraction for the Pacific show. Her presence even calmed certain sections of the native populace. She was in short useful to the French and amusing enough to be worth her modest keep. It would be a mistake, I think, to consider Pomare of much more consequence than this. And of course she was vain enough and spoiled enough to play her part convincingly to all those who allowed themselves to be bemused.

CHAPTER FOURTEEN

Entr'acte
1862 to 1873

However you wish to interpret the conclusion of the fifty-year presence of Pomare as a personification of Tahitian society as a whole, whether sentimentally or cynically, her death in 1877 is a convenient point at which to switch emphasis from the native islander to the European intruder.

But first let us have a look at a strange episode, a sort of comet from nowhere, that belongs neither to the Tahitians nor to the French and yet had surprising impact on both of them.

During the summer of 1862 a small and unglamorous American schooner, the *Sarah*, sailed into Papeete harbor with an unusually glamorous bit of cargo. She was an ordinary trader, but she had on board seven passengers, all young men, solid, strong, with martial bearings. Their chief was particularly imposing, a tall, bearded and commanding figure, the very archetype of the well-bred English gentleman. He presented himself to the governor, Captain Gaultier de la Richerie, who had been expecting him for some weeks, having been advised by the Ministry of Colonies in Paris that a Portuguese syndicate named Soarès et cie had raised a capital of 855,000 francs (that must have been close to $200,000 in those days) to invest in lands and develop plantations on the faraway, little-known island of Moorea. The French were anxious to improve the financial values of their new Pacific colonies, but apparently there were not many Frenchmen willing to invest such handsome sums. So the governor was encouraged to welcome Mr. William Stewart and to smooth his way. De la Richerie, it so happened, was the first governor in the two decades since the establishment of the Protectorate in 1843 who had succeeded in bringing a modicum of prosperity to the island and he was anxious to go home with a glistening reputation. He welcomed the handsome stranger, custodian of all that money and bade him look about the two islands for suitable tracts of land.

Of course he did not know that his imposing visitor had gone out to the East Indies, perhaps ten years before, as a very young warrant officer in the English army. For some reason he had discarded his uniform there. Possibly he had made friends in Macao, for he is next heard of back in Europe in Portugal, where he married. Then about 1855 with his brother James, he sailed to Australia leaving his wife behind. The brothers ran contraband wine and spirits out of Sydney and built a flourishing trade with assistance that James somehow secured with certain customs officials. Evidently it got a bit too lucrative, for they were betrayed and forced to flee the country.

For several years they shipped as supercargoes in Melanesian waters, selling "calicot," tobacco, alcohol and firearms; buying coconut oil, sandalwood and slaves. There was a brisk demand for cheap labor in Queensland and Fiji. A good deal of traffic of this sort was worked in those days and few questions were asked. Perhaps William was too open and honest to carry on long in this sticky business. Perhaps it got too hot for him. All we really know is that he went back to Portugal and that his brother-in-law, Auguste Soarès, sent a letter dated March 10, 1862, to the French Minister of the Marine and the Colonies saying that he and some Portuguese associates had formed a company to finance a plantation in Papetoai valley to cultivate sugar cane and coffee and that they were sending William Stewart to Moorea to study the situation, look into land titles, costs of operation, etc.

Some very perceptive visitor out of the past must have brought a report to far-off Portugal of the splendid, fertile valley of Papetoai even though it lay on the almost unknown island of Moorea. Could it have happened that Auguste had read Herman Melville's *Omoo* and been intrigued by Mr. Bell's fair acres? Stewart promptly sailed over and began inquiries. But he soon ran into strong opposition from Albert Hort, one of the wealthier merchants of Papeete who was already well entrenched on Moorea. So Stewart turned to the big island and before long found a tract of 385 hectares belonging to the son of the anthropological missionary Orsmond who had only recently died (still puzzled, we might suppose, about the fate of his life's literary work). This thousand acres would seem a good start, but Stewart had cast his ambitious eye on the huge valley of Atimaono between the two rivers that border the districts of Papara and Mataiea. Here was a domain of some 1500 hectares, about 4000 acres of truly regal dimensions, but it was made up of some two hundred parcels of land, each claimed by a different family group, all of them with conflicting genealogies, and each family piece, in typical Polynesian fashion, owned by ten, twenty or thirty individual members of every family.

What a tangle! But French law was clear, and French colonial law, compared to that of other colonizing nations such as Spain, Portugal, England and later America, was amazingly fair and favorable to the natives. (It still is.) But there are always officials who believe they can bend the law and de la Richerie was one of them. Here was a most exceptional newcomer with the best of plans on a scale never before contemplated. And besides, he was a dashing figure very much to the personal taste of de la Richerie and his companions who were by now eager for any fresh company.

When exceptions and easements and slithery interpretations of the law started to crop up, the French settlers and the established merchants began to protest that government favoritism was enabling Stewart to acquire lands and privileges that had never been accorded to them. Brander and Salmon were most strongly opposed. Not only were they confronted with favoritism to a business rival, but Salmon's wife Ariitaimai Vahine was granddaughter of Tati. And Brander's wife was the daughter of Ariitaimai. The traditions of ancient Tahitian ownership of land and of protection from foreign exploitation was of first concern to them. They were the last and the highest-born defenders of the sacred ancestral rights. They were also close relatives of the queen.

De la Richerie cannot have been a very bright or subtle fellow to have sent out this official letter to the governing bodies of the districts of Papara, Atimaono, Mataiea and Papeari.

The Imperial Commissaire Commanding [such was his title in those days of the new Empire under Louis Napoleon] *wishes you to know that Mr. Stewart has come to Tahiti with the intention to found an agricultural establishment and that he intends to settle on lands in your districts.*

You are all advised that on the one hand the government views with great pleasure that a part of the uncultivated lands of this country should be made valuable and give you the prospect of profitable work. On the other hand the government gives you notice that you are completely at liberty to sell or not to sell the lands which belong to you.

However if anyone tells you that the government has ordered you to sell your land you may tell him that he is a liar.

Reflect, that in selling uncultivated land that is useless to you, you are only taking an action permitted to all free and civilized people and besides is it not better to have alongside you a farm rather than worthless land?

I salute you
Richerie

An earlier, more worldly official had once said that all native lands would pass, in one way or another, sooner or later, into the hands of the whites *for a few tons of rum or gin or by any other fraudulent means current at the moment.*

Much land was construed to belong in an overlordship fashion to chiefs who, though they allowed families to live on it and work it, could claim a sort of right of eminent domain. There was also unenclosed land whose fruits were at the disposal of anyone even if an owner claimed the trees. And the governor did not hesitate to tell the chiefs they need not pay attention to the queen. Indeed he made it clear that there would not have been a queen except for the French support.

It was all complex enough and, thanks to the government, fluid enough so that Stewart was soon able to collect sufficient legal titles to become proprietor of the vast Atimaono acreages. First off he had to fence it all against the depredations of cattle, horses, pigs, sheep and goats, most of them domestic but many rapidly going feral. This was done we are told at seventy-five centimes the meter. What he paid for the land is of course a mystery. But we do know that in the general natural enthusiasm he rented 141 hectares for fifty years from Teriifaa-tau, a niece of the famous Ariipaea Vahine, queen of Huahine, for fifty francs the hectare. Stewart was installed with Teriifaatau and it seemed for a while that she was his vahine. Much of the other land must have come by the "rum-and-gin" route with plenty of cash flowing from Portugal for bribes and bargains.

The opposition was steamrollered to all outward appearances, but later on it became evident that it was never quashed.

And now loomed the knottiest problem of all, labor. A work force of well over a thousand men was needed. There were at the time some eight thousand inhabitants of the whole island, of which twenty-five hundred were adult males. Such was the population of Tahiti which had had over fifty thousand by J. C. Beaglehole's reasoned estimate a hundred years before when Wallis found it. And such it continued for another fifty years through the end of the century.

Tahitian volunteers were few and those few were wont to drop their jobs, as was their inborn way, as soon as they had earned enough to pay for cloth for their women and drink for themselves. Stewart had a schooner, named the *Eugénie* of course after France's new queen, which sailed to the Cooks and the Tuamotus for indentured workers. But the pickings were scanty, not much over a couple of hundred, and they, being Polynesian, took to drifting off also.

Stewart's imaginative solution was a radical one: Chinese coolies. Looking back now it seems an impossible one as well, but Stewart managed it. He did so by concocting an agreement of such fabulous legal complexity that it was apparently even welcomed by the French. Perhaps its very intricacy and meticulosity is what won their labyrin-thine legal minds. The historic document provided for everything in its forty-three articles: recruitment, proportions of males, females, children over and under ten years, a blanket age limit of forty years, all strictly voluntary and supervised by French consuls in Chinese ports, clothing to the centimeter per month, food to the exact daily grams, shelter, health, discipline, repatriation—every conceivable detail, except wages. The records show later that in exchange for a twelve-hour workday, twenty-six days a month for seven years, they were paid twenty francs a month! That adds up to about $336 in all for seven years' work. To be sure they were housed, clothed and fed. If they did not squander a bit now and then on tobacco, fireworks or opium, it was all take-home pay, a neat seven-year net.

There were endless difficulties, but by 1864 some twelve hundred Chinese had arrived in three or more shiploads, mostly from Macao and Hong Kong. (Shades of Stewart's past?) Large dormitories were built, kitchens, latrines, slaughter houses, factories for processing sugar cane, carding cotton, and shucking and roasting coffee beans. Bridges spanned the two turbulent rivers; roads ran inland. At the valley's head, guarded by two great gatehouses and a drawbridge, rose the mansion of the master, a spacious three-story, plank-and-plaster colonial with filigreed verandas embracing all four sides. The sawn timber, tin roofing, iron machinery all came from Australia or Europe. Stone for foundations, walls, bridges, towers all came from the magnificent *marae* that Oberea had built for her son Terii at Mahaiatea. Alas, that "most imposing temple of all the Polynesian islands" was almost completely dismantled; its massive old-time glory still lying in ruins today.

This whole enterprise suddenly glimpsed a vision of skyrocketing profits when a world cotton famine resulted from the blockade of the Confederate States soon after the outbreak of the American Civil War. The price of cotton shot up and the long-grained, sea-island variety grown at Atimaono was the choicest of the choice. It all looked to be a magnificent get-rich-quick venture, but the Soarès family was prudent enough to plant half or more of its acreage to coffee and sugar cane.

With prospects bright, officialdom and top society flocked to the feasts, receptions, and gala balls. The new stranger, like the suave

Salmon many years before him, was known as the most brilliant dancer of them all. But the French Protectorate had inconsiderately abolished Tahitian princesses.

There was bound to be a dark cloud in such a bright sky and sure enough it settled upon the over-cooperative governor. Whether the scandalmongers were beginning to take effect back home in Paris or whether there were actual misdoings, de la Richerie was recalled to face disgrace in Paris. And a new governor, Émile comte de La Roncière, moved into the queen's ex-palace in Papeete. One might expect this to have been a set-back for William Stewart, but to the contrary it turned out to be a piece of luck. De La Roncière was a nobleman and a playboy. His philosophy of government was personal. He wanted to encourage private investment and enterprise even more than de La Richerie but without playing favorites. All the merchants found themselves benefiting from import exemptions, loose restrictions, and even a revolving fund to loan government money for development. Now everyone prospered at the top. Although Stewart no longer enjoyed special financial favors, it was not long before the governor's favorite niece was wedded to the young official who had engineered most of the land deals for Stewart, and Stewart himself was presiding and living like a medieval prince in his wooden castle by the sea. The governor's wife was seen with growing frequency at Terre Eugénie and of course there were many who suspected an amorous relationship. But while dreams were rosy, rumors of this sort were to be relished rather than feared.

A disturbing factor to the queen and her staunch Protestant coterie was the increasingly evident fact that Stewart and his six male companions from the *Sarah* were all Irish Catholics and that the Chinese of course were benighted heathens. Atimaono with its own separate church and school was beginning to look like a Catholic fief. Bishop Jaussen, head of the official French Catholic establishment, had not been approving—either of Stewart's enterprise or of Governor de La Richerie and his circle. To old-time Tahitians this religious factor was another sinister aspect of the incredible conclave in their midst.

The introduction of Chinese into Tahiti had of course a significance that was never dreamed of by those responsible. Richerie had said originally that he favored it because he felt there was a good social and racial affinity between the two peoples. Such an assumption should have seemed as preposterous then as it would be today. And yet in spite of fears generated by other examples of imported alien work forces, notably those in Fiji and Mauritius, the blend of Chinese and Tahitian that is everywhere evident today seems a compliment to both of the races. Perhaps that is the happy result of mixing mongoloid genes rather than opposing aryan and polynesian ones. But obviously Richerie never knew what a gene was.

They did not mix at all, however, for a very long time, several generations at least. And on their segregated plantation in those days there even broke out a sort of Chinese civil war. The year 1865 evidently signaled a traditional Chinese celebration of unusual proportions and a splendid display was put on at Atimaono with paper dragons, fireworks, parades, dancing, speeches and rallies. After several days (and perhaps a few whiffs of opium here and there) it got out of hand and the two factions who had been living contently together for three or four years began suddenly and incomprehensibly to fight. Several deaths occurred and the French police had to intervene even though Stewart's own disciplinary forces were supposed to be in control. Later on, the mini-revolution was diagnosed as a conflict between the ancestral tribes of punti and hakka from Macao and Hong Kong.

The end of the big Civil War in America brought an end to the cotton boom, but it took some years to subside and Atimaono continued to appear to prosper. Actually the lush investment was probably about ready to smell a profit when the cotton market collapsed.

Other troubles were brewing. But in spite of personal scandals, things seemed to roll along under their own momentum. Anticipating the cotton disaster, Stewart the Dauntless had acquired new ships and in doing so also acquired new enemies or perhaps refueled his old ones. A newspaper man named William Poole was dispatched to America— presumably in the pay of the Brander interests—where he spread insidious reports of slave labor conditions in the South Sea paradise. Naturally many in the States were eager to assuage their guilt with kettle calling and the tabloids reveled in the crimes of the lawless

Pacific. Then William's brother James who had always been a black sheep began trading on his own in the Tuamotus—trading evidently with his brother's money or his brother's credit, but without his brother's knowledge.

As the old coolie contracts ran out, many, though by no means all, of the Chinese began to be repatriated or to escape the thralldom of Atimaono. Some thirty of them went to Taipi Vai on Nuku Hiva to start up a new plantation for Stewart—a personal hedge of his own no doubt. It failed of course when he failed, but the Chinese attempted to keep on, on their own. They failed too of course, but they are probably the grandparents of the present Chinese in the Marquesas.

As labor in the valley dwindled, it is said that brother James and perhaps others of the schooner *Sarah* began blackbirding where they could, probably for the most part in Melanesia. One shipload of sixty-three from the New Hebrides arrived in Tahiti with an epidemic of dysentery aboard, of which all of them eventually died. A murky side of the glitter and glamor of Atimaono began to show up. But we must realize that William Stewart was by no means alone or unique in these sordid South Sea rumblings. Even the most prosperous and outwardly upright of all, John Brander, dispatched a certain Captain Dutrou-Bornier to recruit on Easter Island for his old enemy. Sixty-seven workers were brought back to the plantation where they lived as a lonely, separate colony and who did nothing in their off-work hours except grieve for their faraway homes on Easter Island. It was from one of these that Bishop Jaussen discovered, and first made known to the world, the famous *rongo rongo* "hieroglyphics." Bornier returned to Easter Island with a cargo of sheep which in a space of five years literally ate the island arid, until the ruthless captain was murdered by his angry neighbors. Today you can feast upon the descendants of those sheep, the only mutton in Polynesia, except of course those other mavericks that the Pakeha introduced into New Zealand.

Troubles now began to roll in remorselessly upon William Stewart. His bankers in Australia impounded his assets to liquidate his brother's debts. Lawsuits were instigated but James vanished, probably to Europe. Stewart's closest partner Atwater, the American consul, was suspected of chicanery. At length Stewart was declared legally bankrupt in 1873 on the twenty-third of September. A recorder entered the famous mansion first but found the master so ill that he left in haste. The judge however was furious and, it was said, so menaced the poor man that he vomited a stream of blood and died a few hours later on September 24—the gallant, cocksure, young, every-inch-a-gentleman who had stepped from the *Sarah* and played such a dazzling part on the Tahitian stage only ten years before—extinguished now like a shooting star at the age of forty-eight. Only one lone vahine named Tiare Gibson stuck with him to the end. He left behind an imposing monument of his swift handiwork, Terre Eugénie, its 4000 hectares, some 10,000 acres, its well-stocked store with twenty-three windows, its roomy hanger and spacious horse barn, its forge, bakery, steam press, fifteen large, half-empty rooming houses for its Chinese and 100 small *fares* for its Polynesian workers, its resplendent three-storied mansion house and, one thousand meters up in the mountains, *une maison de plaisance, hygiénique, avec dépendance.*

The original South Sea Bubble? Today it is a vast, smooth, flat plain of rich green grass—probably the largest and least played-upon golf course in the whole Pacific.

CHAPTER FIFTEEN

Empire: Colony by Guile

1880

Now that the French had their new colony the question was, what to do about it? There had been many in the government in Paris who thought, when Du Petit Thouars took his first impulsive action, that any such colony was a foolish, expensive venture, a tiny island way off there in the ocean with no commercial promise. England had come to that conclusion and therefore had let France have it. But England was hatching out several other substantial colonies and it was prudent policy not to be too greedy. France was becoming more and more nationalistic. Waterloo was fading; envy, pride, and ambition were returning. To the military a new strategic world lay ahead, one that signaled bright prospects for the careers of future generals and admirals. It is surprising to realize that France had many more ships of war in the Pacific than England had at that time, most of them based on the Valparaiso station. There was of course the usual conflict in ministries between expansionists and isolationists. But when Du Petit Thouars delivered his romantic little package, the French populace had welcomed him with rallies in the streets and had raised a fund to present him with a jeweled sword of honor. So Guizot, the most powerful of the ministers, bowed, as you will remember, to public fervor and made Thouars an admiral instead of reprimanding and side-tracking him, as had been his intention.

In Tahiti after the bitter resistance of the natives was quashed, the French set about establishing order, and this of course meant martial law. They evidently had little trouble, as a letter from Lavaud testifies. On leaving the governorship in 1848 he wrote that he *had the satisfaction of leaving to his successor a position free of embarrassment, a country en voi de progres with beautiful roads, an Establishment in perfect state, a population docile to my voice as to my counsels, in the best of financial condition, because, at the 1st of the month the treasury amounted to 1,450,000 francs.* They were indeed docile people now that their leaders had been eliminated. They had for generations been accustomed not only to obeying their hereditary chiefs, but also to looking to them for leadership and any positive action. Now there was no action to be taken, no feelings to be aroused, simply the carrying on of everyday living. The French demanded very little from them. Road building and upkeep was done by prison labor. There was not much incentive for a Tahitian to earn money because he was not taxed. Food was always in adequate supply, especially now that the population had been drastically reduced. The riffraff from visiting ships that had caused so much havoc to the Tahitian *mutoi* (local police) was easily controlled by French gendarmes. Vessels were simply detained and their captains were fined if they abandoned crew members or failed to discipline them. So the early years of foreign rule were stable, orderly and peaceful, a welcome change from the growing chaos of the past two decades. Lavaud was followed by the hated Bonard, the man who had laid waste to Huahine seemingly out of sheer spite and had also brought about the collapse at Fautaua. Now he had the means to enforce an admiral's will, and though they continued to hate and to fear him, there was little they could do but obey his orders—docilely.

So the new little island possession rocked along on its newly calm sea with nothing much happening except a continuing procession of gold-braided *Commissaires,* averaging a little over two years apiece until the time of title change, when they became Governors. From then until the end of the century, their stays in Tahiti averaged not quite a year and a half. These positions were almost invariably rewards for distinguished services elsewhere, or political plums, or kicks upstairs. None of these appointees knew anything about Tahiti before coming, nor did they seem to learn much while there. Two exceptions to this appear in Richerie and Roncière in that they both had long enough terms to furbish up their reputations and do something to show a record, but as we saw in the saga of William Stewart, both men were disasters from a governmental as well as a personal point of view.

The martial law and order imposed from the beginning by the French authorities was effective enough for a while, but of course it was not adequate for widespread civil application. Indigenous Tahitian "law" had been ancient custom and the universal acceptance of judgment handed down by the *arii*, or "high chiefs." This had been modified considerably by the London missionaries to conform to Christian doctrine and English custom, but the high chiefs had remained and their power was considerable until the French arrived and abolished them. Thus the French inherited a strange mixture, not at all to their taste, of English law and tribal customs. It was not until 1866 that they were able to persuade (or compel) the Assembly to adopt the Code Napoléon. It seems doubtful that this was much more than an irritation to the Tahitians, but it gave a deal of satisfaction to the French.

Money became increasingly important to the new masters. One of their first chores was to teach the Tahitians what money was and how to use it. The concept had been wholly new to them and the currencies they had used depended on the nationalities of the traders. Because Valparaiso was the half-way port to and from Europe, the Chilean or Spanish piastre was the commonest "international" money, but it was apparently little used inside the island, serving rather as a medium for trade with traders. The American dollar came along with the New England whalers and the two were considered roughly equivalent in value. The English pound never seemed to count for much, probably because the missionaries never had any money and English ships traded for nails, tools, cloth, trinkets, arms, liquor and the like. But now the franc appeared on the scene to become the official medium of exchange and after a highly erratic period of pricing, gradually came to be recognized.

A visitor from Paris in 1844 writes: *The money which was most appreciated was the Spanish piastre but the inhabitants were so ignorant of the value of silver that it was not rare to see them offer two tarnished piastres for one shiny one and all the objects they possessed, whatever their values, were equated with a* dalla, *or* tara; *a dollar. A coco, a stem of bananas, a batch of clams, a fish spear, a pig were all offered at the same price.*

There were doubloons in halves, quarters and eighths; American eagles; British sovereigns; douros and reals of Spain; Chillean condors, doubloons and ecus; pesos and, expecially from Peru and Bolivia, lots of counterfeit coins. Actually it was not until 1910 that the then French governor reported that he had sent out 35,000 Chilean piastres and felt that the French franc was at last the only currency left in general circulation. This too made little difference to the Tahitian, but was a considerable convenience for the French.

The European's most conspicuous works were the roads along the lagoon shores, with bridges spanning many of the rivers and streams. Slowly and haphazardly this construction worked its way along the west and south coasts to the Taravao peninsula, half way round the island in some fifty years. This was believed to be the greatest of benefits to the native, but actually it was a progressive intrusion on his privacy, bringing more and more foreigners to his most precious lands of the south. It also gradually supplanted his accustomed way of travel by water, substituting for his traditional outrigger canoe, first the horse-drawn coach and then the roaring motor-bus.

French religion made little progress even though it was official and though considerable effort was made to rout out the old English missionaries. The first effort, it will be remembered, was the arrival of those two little French priests Caret and Laval way back in 1836. Very little has been revealed or even speculated about the reasons for that visit, but in retrospect it seems to me to be a repetition of the old colonial strategy of sending out the church as the entering wedge of conquest. The English missionaries had got there first of course, but the English military had not followed up. No collusion there. But the French admirals had been quick to respond to the ousting of the priests and that was their prime, perhaps their only, excuse for armed intervention. Had the Sacred Heart fathers in Paris dispatched these fiery priests for the express purpose of combating the London missionaries? Was the good old Pope in St. Peter's aware? Or had he perhaps instigated the thrust?

Hitherto all proselytizing and converting of heathens all over the world had been strictly Roman Catholic—first the Portuguese, then the Spanish. The Dutch who followed them carried no holy men except for their own shipboard needs.

The same was true of Cook and Bougainville, though not of Boenechea who had landed a few priests in Hitiaa. They attempted to convert but were quickly and rudely dispatched. When Du Petit Thouars followed up the provocation aroused by Caret and Laval, I suspect he may have been all equipped and ready to go when the news arrived in France.

It must be realized that the brethren of the London Missionary Society were the very first Protestants who went forth to collect souls for their True God. They were the first, you might say, to challenge the Roman Church and the competition for souls was perhaps as real and as furious a conflict as the competition between military forces for pieces of strategic land or between commercial interests for colonial wealth, trade and resources—or should we call them plunder?

In this Tahitian instance the respective secular or political powers stood aside, hemmed and hawed and protested peace. Aberdeen restrained his admirals and Guizot admonished his. But weren't they really doing a bit of trading behind the official facades? Bruat came out with ships and soldiers. A bloody four-year war was fought. The Tahitians were crushed, their lands possessed, their spirits quenched.

The Catholics gained their coveted privilege to convert. They sent out Tepano Jaussen in 1849 to become the first Bishop of Polynesia and to build its cathedral. The Protestant missionaries were deprived of power and their lands confiscated. But the strangest result of this long, bitter religio-military contest was that Protestantism prevailed against Catholicism. The Tahitian bowed to military force but not to religious persuasion. The great majority of the people continued to flock to the "temple" and avoid "l'église." After a goodly period which must have been frustrating to Rome, the French Protestants took over from the English in 1863. In many ways they seemed to be even more anti-Catholic than the English. And finally they in turn surrendered to the native Tahitian Protestants, but not until a hundred years later in 1963.

The native pasteurs continue to be in charge today in spite of all the subsequent assaults and temptations, not only of Roman Catholics, but of Anglicans, Methodists, Seventh Day Adventists and, most vigorous and wealthy of all, the Mormons from America, who have built the only competing school system in the islands.

This seems a phenomenon difficult to explain except perhaps that it represents the only way in which the Tahitian can demonstrate his independence from the French. All other colonized cultures and countries of the world have set themselves free by revolutionary force. The Tahitian is powerless to do this so he takes his refuge in a certain amount of freedom of the spirit.

Very recently in the late 1970s the Tahitians decided that they wanted a holiday of their own. They love holidays and had long enjoyed the two-week Bastille Day merrymaking in July when the great canoe races take place. In 1980 many hundreds of canoes turned out in different class lengths with some five thousand paddlers participating. Other holidays, Christmas, New Year's, Armistice Day, the Saints' days are scattered through the year and all are relished. But these occasions are all traditionally French and the Tahitians felt an urge for a holiday of their own. It had to be a calendar holiday to be legal (and thus work-exempt). They had no calendar in ancient Tahiti, so, after much cogitation and consultation, they decided to celebrate the arrival of the *Duff* on May 5, 1797. "Evangelical Day" now has its religious aspects in large prayer meetings which not everyone attends, but it also echos the joyous pagan days of old. Though they dress up in mother hubbards (which they wear over their bikinis) and parade in horse-drawn carriages (when they can find a few), most of them weave their most sumptuous flower crowns and travel about in riotous bus loads, strewing the roadsides with beer cans. So this distinctly Tahitian festival is now their exclusive holiday. The French are obviously not pleased, but they are good natured and indulgent enough toward their wayward, still-half-savage children to put up with it. All this had been predicted with uncanny foresight by Moerenhout back in the 1830s and 1840s when he asserted that the only way to win the religious contest was not with Catholic priests, but with French pasteurs.

Education was to come sometime in the future and it is of prime significance today both to the Tahitian and to the Frenchman. In the early days however it was left to the church. The authorities felt no responsibility and took none. It was not until they realized the vital need to teach their language to their subjects that the state began to build the schools.

And so the little colony rocked along with its small bureaucratic French staff alongside the sprawling but impotent royal court of the queen; both of them paying lip service to the elected Assembly of chiefs and landowners but not giving much attention to it. Even the death of the queen in September of 1877 had little impact on the procession of gold braid through the *Commissaire*'s residence in Papeete. Indeed, there was very little incentive to any action in that particular year. It just happened by pure chance and no conceivable design that Tahiti had five supreme government officials in 1877. After only one year in office, Michaux was to be replaced by Laborde. But when Laborde's wife heard that she was to be sent out to live among the savages, she refused to go. So Amiral Commissaire Général de la Marine Auguste Laborde chose to take an early retirement and a veteran sea captain named Brunet-Miller was found whose wife was ecstatic about the prospect. But she became desperately seasick crossing the Atlantic and had scarcely recovered when they joined the navy frigate *Magicienne* in San Francisco with Admiral Serre, the new commander of the Naval Division of the Pacific, on board. The frigate was a mean sea boat and Madame Brunet-Miller died just as they reached the Marquesas. Whereupon her new governor-husband went mad and soon had to be shipped back to France. The *ordonnateur*, now "second-in-command," at Tahiti was the normal replacement, but he was the officer who had made the inexcusable arrest of the Crown Prince for drunken and disorderly conduct and was thus completely unacceptable to Queen Pomare. She was furious; he asserted his rights. So Admiral Serre declared himself *Commissaire* pro-tem; arrested and demoted the troublemaker La Barbe. The queen died and Serre was relieved in December by the new appointee from Paris, D'Oncieu de la Bathie. He in turn was succeeded the following February by Planche.

Crown Prince Arii Aue was installed, as far as the French administration was concerned, as Pomare V with the same sort of taken-for-granted ceremony and celebration (though on an understandably smaller scale) as any new king in Europe would have enjoyed.

No perceptible change in the routine. It was all very much *la même chose*—until . . .

In April 1879 the imperial German warship *Bismarck* paid a visit to Raiatea in the Leeward Islands.

There had been premonitions back in France. The celebrations for the opening of the Suez Canal in 1876 and 1878 made the chancelleries of Europe suspect new developments of power in the world, of especial significance to the two colonial giants. Then France's foremost hero of the day, the engineer Ferdinand de Lessups, announced that his next project would be the building of a canal through the Isthmus of Panama. Speculation naturally focused on the Pacific and many a strategic study was no doubt set in train. But the *Bismarck!* Here was a jolt from a new and galvanizing quarter. It was only nine years previous that Napoleon III Emperor of the French had begun to feel stirrings of his illustrious uncle and had challenged that new Teutonic upstart who was later to become known as the Iron Chancellor. "Manifest Destiny" was in the air and there were still virgin islands in the Pacific. France had her Protectorate of Tahiti, but it was only a protectorate. The Gambiers to the east and the Leeward Islands to the west were native independencies. The Marquesas, according to the international rules of the game at that time, were indisputably French, but they were occupied only by a handful of gendarmes. Less than half of the Tuamotu Islands, supposedly fiefs of Pomare, had sent representatives to the Legislative Assembly in Tahiti during the decade of 1850–1860. Tahiti must be secured. The obvious first step was to make it a full-fledged colony.

In 1880 a handsome young officer named Isadore Chessé arrived in Tahiti with the exalted title of "Commissaire Civile du Protectorate," an envoy plenipotentiary, in spite of his barely forty years, from higher realms in Paris. Although he was very much his senior, Commandant Planche was summarily dispatched to the south of the island and shipped home forthwith. Chessé then set about wooing the new king of only two years to the idea of relinquishing his crown. He might never have succeeded without a bloody confrontation except for the sudden occurrence of what turned out to be an astonishing piece of luck for him, although it seemed to be very unlucky for the others immediately involved. It arrived, as such things are not unaccustomed to arrive in Tahiti, in the form of a new baby girl, born to the Queen Marau on the ninth of March 1879. Her proud mother, assisted perhaps by her even prouder grandmother, Ariitaimai, promptly named her *Terii nuio o Tahiti te vahine taora terito ma te rai terii ae tua Pomare,* a name with all sorts of connotations of high blood and aspirations to royal power.

The king immediately disowned the child, announcing publicly that it was not his and that he denied it any right to inherit his properties or his title. This was all very well, and he was no doubt stating the truth, but French law, that splendid Code Napoléon, which the Legislative Assembly had adopted only a decade before for the enlightenment and benefit of these ocean "indians," provided categorically and inescapably that no husband could deny parenthood of a child born to his wife while he was still legally married to her. So the royal marriage of convenience became, overnight, very inconvenient to him. It had never been convenient for her, after the first euphoria of expectation, but this announcement made it publicly humiliating to a degree that could never be tolerated by a Teva from a low-caste Pomare, king or no.

But what a splendid mise-en-scène for Chessé! The king's succession was stymied and his estates destined to pass out of the hands of his immediate family: his brothers, sisters, nephews and nieces, who were the only comforts and loyalties in the self-indulgent life of this lonely, dissipated sovereign.

He was not well at the time. His prodigal ways had kept him in an ambivalent state of health for many years past and now he had lapsed into one of his periodic setbacks. Chessé made a point of visiting the patient every day at his home in Papaoa with consolation and advice (and help of course in tending to royal business). At one point it was decided that a visit to Motu Uta, the traditional little harbor island of the Pomares, would be good for his health. He was advised by Chessé to delegate his powers while on a tour of the island. Actually he was gone only for a day. The trip evidently did not suit him and he came back before nightfall. But somehow a return of the delegated powers was not attended to and Chessé was perhaps able to flex his muscles enough to show Pomare how easy and pleasant it could be to be relieved of his tedious royal responsibilities. At length during these sickroom visits a tempting offer was concocted. Pomare was to retain all the regal perquisites: his palace, his flag of the Protectorate, his crown, his yacht, royal salutes, and royal occasions. Not only his own debts but those considerable ones of his mother which had been hanging on (gathering interest no doubt) would all be taken care of. A handsome pension for life would be paid to him and to all of his nearest and dearest. A list of the beneficiaries and their ratings on the French government's payroll is revealing—all annual pensions for life:

Pomare V	*60,000 francs*
Marau Taaroa Salmon	*6,000 "*
Tamatoa and Teriitapunui (brothers)	*12,000 "*
Teriivaetua (adopted daughter of	
Tamatoa) and Teriinavaharoa (adopted	
daughter of Teriitapunui)	*2,400 "*
Isabelle Shaw (widow of Tuavira,	
Joinville, sister-in-law of the King)	*6,000 "*
On the deaths of the two brothers,	
one half of their pensions continue for	
life to their widows and children,	
Isabelle Shaw's full pension on her	
death goes to her son Prince Hinoi and	
Hinoi is to be promoted by the government.	*600 "*
To others of the family	*1,800 "*
	2,400 "
Total	*91,200 francs*

The French government is to be
released from all claims or
obligations to Pomare IV deceased

signed 29 June 1880
Isidore Chessé

Chessé reports that in presenting the list to the king, he remarked with a laugh, "See how I have provided for the queen." He said that Pomare took no notice of this; for him, his wife Marau Salmon did not exist.

In return for all this Pomare V abdicated and handed over to the Republic of France all of his estates—forever. Note the conspicuous absence of any provision for the new-born babe, the legal heir to the throne if subsequent male heirs were lacking. The pension for Marau is obviously a bow to French correctness. Pomare's concerns are reflected in the provisions for his brothers and others of his family. They are especially evident in the generous award to his mistress and sister-in-law, the beauteous Isabelle Shaw. She was the daughter of a Raiatean girl of the common people who had married an Englishman of no distinction. But she was a radiant beauty and that had long been a classical entrée to the upper reaches of Tahitian society. Queen Pomare's youngest son Tuavira (the Tahitian phono-equivalent of Joinville, son of Louis Philippe) had first chosen her as his wife and their son, the charming Prince Hinoi, had been adopted as Pomare V's rightful heir when Tuavira died and Isabelle came to be the consort of the king.

There must have been some sly and subtle bargaining in that sickroom between the wavering monarch and the persuasive *Commissaire.* Everything was arranged covertly in Pomare's residence and when the terms were struck he asked that a representation of the principal Tahitian chiefs be summoned as witnesses. Chessé drew up the formal document in two columns in Tahitian and French. Chessé explained the whole transaction at length. For him it was an occasion of much trepidation. In his subsequent report to his superiors he states that one chief, Porionuu of Hitiaa, launched into a long, tedious harangue that caused him much anxiety. In the end it was claimed officially that all the chiefs signed, but the Danielssons have subsequently cast doubts on this. In any event the chiefs probably neither knew much about what they were doing, or did not care. After all, they were only attesting to the desires of their old fellow chief, Arii Aue. That his name had recently been changed to Pomare V had little significance for them.

It was his family's land, not theirs, that he was in effect selling to the French—the sort of deal they themselves would never have considered, but which, he assured them, was satisfactory to him. They all signed the spacious final page, leaving room at the top for Pomare who signed after them, and for Chessé at the bottom who acknowledged his grateful acceptance of the royal gift and of the royal expressions of faith in France, acknowledging Pomare's indebtedness to that great country for its protection of Tahiti's vital interests when challenged by greedy outside powers.

He must have been very skillful or Pomare an easy dupe.

At first the coup was disapproved vehemently by the three powerful French pasteurs who now constituted the principal religious authority of the island. They had long been opposed to the idea of a colony because they wanted religious independence and they felt that formal French rule would mean Roman Catholic ascendancy. Bishop Jaussen had been working for this and previous governors had usually supported him. But Chessé evidently felt no qualms in guaranteeing them their coveted independence on the spot. So of course they went along.

There was apparently little reaction among the populace. The Protectorate flag, with its three horizontal Tahitian stripes—red-white-red —and the small tricolor ensign in its upper corner, still flew above the royal compound. To all outward appearances Pomare was still king. Internal affairs were left much as usual to Tahitians, external as usual to the French. It seemed that the policy from Paris was to make the transition as inconspicuous locally as possible. After all, the essential purpose was to warn its European neighbors by staking out international claims of colonial sovereignty.

Public apathy? Perhaps—but Marau recounts a stormy family scene when Arii Aue encountered his old familiar aunt, Ariitaimai, sister and life-long best friend of his mother, the revered old queen. He ran to embrace her, his eyes flooding with tears of remorse. She pushed him away and thundered *What have you done? Giving away lands that never really belonged to you? You a Paumotu who never had any right to them! Aue!*

Chessé returned to France to the plaudits of his confreres and

superiors. Tahiti was officially declared a colony and a new procession
of high officials started from Paris. From now on they were called
Governors and they continued to hold that exalted title for nearly a
hundred years until the present-day "autonomists" of Tahiti succeeded
in reverting them to the appellation of *Haut Commissaire* in the late
1970s, a designation that they continue to tolerate today. Their power
remains unchanged.

There is little of significance to report over the next decade. Halfway
along it, a new governor, Lacascade, enjoyed the distinction of the
longest term of office in Tahitian history. He lasted, with a brief
interval, for a full six years. It was under him that the first General
Council was appointed, a vague reincarnation of the old Legislative
Assembly, which gave some representation once again to elected Tahitian chiefs. Otherwise Lacascade, though evidently respected, was not
particularly distinguished.

CHAPTER SIXTEEN

Consolidation:
The Leeward Islands
1880 et seq.

Perhaps before setting forth the climactic events of the last decade, it would be well to go back briefly and review the beginnings of the struggle of the Leeward Islands against the French Protectorate. This indeed is the essence of this second part of our narrative: the aftermath of the capitulation of Tahiti at Fautaua and the establishment of French military rule. Although it was parallel in time during the early years, their struggle had always been a separate and different tale of woe.

It had long been the desire of the military in Paris to annex what they called Les Isles sous le Vent, or Leeward Islands, some one hundred miles to the northwest, on the other side of *Moana Marama*, the Sea of the Moon. These were Raiatea, Tahaa, Huahine, and Bora Bora with their outliers—smaller close neighbors. There was confusion about the name and indeed there still is. France's new colony at this time was called Les Isles de la Société, consisting of Tahiti and Moorea and the smaller nearby islands of Me'etea, Maiau and Tetiaroa. Cook had originally named the leeward group the Society Islands, specifying that the reason for the name was their close geographical proximity. He thus showed that he considered them a "sociable" group, though actually they had been at sporadic wars with each other for many generations. A popular misconception arose, and still persists, that he named them after the Royal Society, which had sponsored his expedition. Perhaps this came about because "the Society Islands" translated into French becomes Les Isles de la Société. But then, many Frenchmen still think that Point Venus was named after Du Petit Thouars's frigate, while every Englishman knows that it was named for Cook's world-famous astronomical observation of the transit of the planet Venus across the sun on May 3rd, 1769.

France had wanted both collections for a long time. Bruat had insisted that they belonged to Queen Pomare and thus to him, but he never succeeded in convincing the English or the islanders themselves. These people had always believed that they were a separate "nation." When the French first arrived the islanders held themselves aloof and felt no internal conflict of interest. They were steadfastly more pro-English than the Tahitians and it was largely because of their influence that Pomare held out against Bruat for nearly three years during her "exile" in Raiatea. Captain Martin's *Journal* sheds new light on the personalities involved. The French, from Bruat onward, had very little intercourse with the Leeward Island chiefs, but Martin sailed his ship to all of the islands several times. They dined with him frequently on the *Grampus* and he attended many of their long discussions ashore especially at the behest of Pomare who was constantly being tugged one way by the missionaries and the island chiefs and the other way by the pro-French Tahitian chiefs, by Ariitaimai and Salmon, by the exigencies of war—most of all by Bruat.

Of all reporters, only Martin gives us an insight into the personal characters of these engaging chiefs. Not the Tahitian ones; for they were either isolated in the "rebellious" camps in the distant valleys while he was there or he saw them (or those few who were left of them) only after the brutal defeat when the remnants who survived had been selected for amnesty. He met Tati only once. *Near this spot (Pappara) we met old Taati, a chief of note, who joined the French early enough to save his property and lose his character.*

Mr. Darling introduced us to Utami—the most influential of the Tahitian chiefs now living. He is a fine old man, of commanding figure and good expression of countenance, with a white head. He was once in affluence and power—being chief of this district (Punaauia) but the French have stripped him of his lands and deprived him of his office, in consequence of his determined hostility to them during the war.

Thus we see that Martin became intimate—as intimate as any white man could—with the kings (as he called them) of Bora Bora, "old" Tapoa; of Raiatea, "old" Tamatoa; and also of the fabulous "Queen of Huahine," Ariipaea vahine.

Amongst these islanders it is difficult to define the distinction of classes. Some are chiefs certainly—others not, that is some have power and possessions—some none. But all wear the same dress—all eat out of the same bowl and smoke the same segar—the daughters of the chiefs are prostitutes for the people; the distinction is in short so small, and the sway of the chiefs so mild that it is difficult to see which is the ruler and which is the ruled. There are judges who seem to be only advisors to the chiefs in settling disputes. The law seems to be public opinion, founded upon custom and tradition.

These three Leeward Island chiefs, especially Tapoa, were key figures in the struggle to preserve the Leeward Islands from French conquest, a struggle that was to continue for more than half a century after the declaration of the Protectorate to the final pursuit when Raiatea's leader surrendered in 1898.

Tapoa was Martin's special friend and was by far the most influential of the four "monarchs." Martin had real affection and respect for him. At one point he contrasts Tapoa and his wife with the new governor Lavaud and his wife, observing that the untutored savages had far more dignity and human depth than the Admiral and his lady, whom he felt was better suited to preside over a gin parlor in back-street Paris than a royal colony in the Pacific. At the same time, he had few illusions. Here is a sampling from his *Journal.*

After the long hassle over the flying of the Leeward Island flags to demonstrate to the world their independence from France: *Old Tamatoa is quite unhappy at being obliged to keep sober so long. He would willingly go home where he might get drunk unobserved—but he is completely under the influence of Tapoa. Tapoa has become a hanger on of the Queen. There is a dash of romance in this connexion. Tapoa was Pomare's first husband. He discarded her for drunkenness. Now that she has amended (tho' another man's wife) his former attachment has revived. He has warmly espoused her cause, and seems to invite the affection of a Father to the respect of a subject. (Tapoa had adopted a daughter of Pomare as his heir. He was childless himself.) As for* independence *except for his private convenience and gain he has not an idea of its value. His avarice has received a stimulant and he looks to being the great monopolist of his island.*

I suppose Tapoa may be put down as the fattest King in the world and his wife almost as fat and quite as jolly. This couple is said to be the most lenient and respectable amongst the chiefs on these islands. Tamatoa is a good natured man but a great drunkard and his wife no better. He has a sufficient share of innate roguery which has been rather refined by his intercourse with runaway convicts and peddling traders. Sir Robert Peel (Pomare's secretary) is a little ugly hunchback, good humoured as all these people are, with an equal thirst for knowledge and for grog. I sat with these worthies, al fresco, for 2 hours this evening. Sir Robert was very anxious to know if his namesake in England was like him and if he always wore pantaloons and a cocked hat and drank much rum.

31st October. Tamatoa sent me a present of bread and bananas—with a message that he had collected pigs and poultry if I would send for them. I declined the gift. It had rained and blown fresh from S.E. all day with a sensible change in the temperature, and when I landed I found Tamatoa wrapt in blankets. I asked if his Majesty were ill. "No only a little drunk and very cold." The thermometer had fallen from 80° to 74°.

Tapoa told me that Bruat offered him the sovereignty of all the North Western group, if he would acknowledge the Protectorate. Some people think he was near accepting the offer but he assured me he hated the French too much to join them. He said the only ground upon which he had opposed the Queen's return to Tahiti was that she could not trust in the promises of the French.

2nd November—At 9 A.M. came aboard Tomatoa with his wife and niece. Wine was immediately called for and in 5 minutes this trio had finished 2 bottles of sherry, when they left the cabin. At noon I found the Queen and Princess had got very drunk in the midshipmen's berth and had gone to the galley to smoke with the men. That did not prevent however their returning to drink another bottle of wine. The niece now became extremely fond of me, but as I was busy and she drunk, I desired the sentry to turn the whole party out of the cabin.

In the evening Mr. Platt accompanied me to Pomare's house. I followed her to Mr. Charter's where it appeared she had been driven by domestic troubles to seek refuge with her children. The circumstances were as follows. Pomare having said something derogatory to her husband, Sir. R. Peel took his part, Pomare tani being absent. A dispute ensued, both waxed wrath, high words followed, and Sir. R. told her Majesty that she was a woman of no value. Upon this she seized him by the hair, boxed his ears and finally dealt the right Honorable Gentleman such a kick on the backside as sent him spinning out of the royal presence. Soon after the enraged husband came to Mr. Charter's with the avowed purpose of killing Pomare on the spot, but being sent about his business he got very drunk with his worthy companion Tamatoa, and so finished the evening. In the evening I called on Sir Robert to condole with him on being dismissed from the office. I found him with his sleeves tucked up embowelling a pig.

12th Feby. A very hot and powerful day. Tapoa the King, Chapman, Collie and Dr. Johnston dined with me. Tapoa came an hour before dinner, as I wanted to talk with him. He told me that Bruat on their first meeting on Eimeo, had made some slight overtures to him. "Don't believe what you have heard of us—judge for yourself how you are treated by the French. In a short time Tahiti will be cultivated and very different from the other islands."

I put him on his guard against these insidious advances. I told him there was no reason why Bora Bora should not flourish more than Tahiti, if there were no Frenchmen to take the lands from the natives and I also cautioned him against Pomare's attempt to get him into the same scrape as herself. He said he was aware of the danger; but I have grave doubts of him if temptation is put in his way. Bruat's object now is to have the protectorate of the Leeward Islands offered to him. By jove he shall not *have them whilst I am here. If he hoists his flag on one I will seize its neighbor.*

I also cautioned Tapoa against the intrigues of the chief Mai of Bora Bora. He assures me there is no truth in the story of the Queen having ordered him to accompany her. He came because he did not like to separate Pomare from her child, whom he has adopted. Tapoa says Pomare is far from happy and sorely feels the restraint she is under. "Well Tapoa," said I, "you see Bruat is King of Tahiti—take care he is not also King of Bora Bora."

21st Being off the island of Huahine, I went into Port Owharre in my boat. I had thought of taking the ship in, but the wind was very baffling and the entrance is very narrow for so large a ship. It is not a cables length from reef to reef. I landed at the dwelling of Ariipuia [sic] the Queen—for a roof resting on posts—without any walls can hardly be called a house. Of this lady I had heard much—as being the most perfect type of an Amazon in the known world. Many good stories are told of her in the island wars, in which she always headed her people, and when their courage flagged she seized a musket, denounced them as cowards, and by her own prowess and personal example retrieved the day.

Ariipuia is certainly no beauty—a tough leathery old woman with a sharp quick eye and a certain look of the devil that fits her character well. She is said to be every inch a griffin—and by Jove she looks it. She seems about 60 years old, but she has not yet renounced the foibles of her sex. She glories in a glass of grog and has lately taken unto herself a good looking husband 25 years of age.

As she smoked her segar, her eyes measured me from head to foot and examined me in every point for 3 minutes—in doubt whether she should trust me or humbug me. At last she seemed to have made up her mind —for she suddenly rose from the ground and abruptly shook my hand. "Yoranha Martin"—then pouring out 2 stiff glasses of sakee, she handed me one and swallowed the other. "Yoranha Martin" and she once more squatted on the ground and resumed her segar.

Each of us determined that the other should speak first; but her patience broke down—"What good news have you brought me, or what bad tidings?" I then told her I had nothing to say but what would be agreeable—that the question of the independence of her island was not yet decided, but that I had reason to know it soon would be settled in her favour. She replied "It is time I was made glad for I have waited long in suspense, but I would resist the French flag to the last." She then asked me what I thought of the change of Sabboth. I explained as well as I could to her that if one day of the week was put aside and kept holy, it mattered little if that day was Saturday or Sunday. "Well," said she, "it is a French change, and it shall not come to Huahine." Whereupon the old lady looked lightning at me—and lighted another segar.

I again advised her to postpone her new code of Port Regulations until the independence question should be settled—which she promised.

She expressed a great wish to come on board—to taste of my cellar.

Her heir, Pomare's 2nd son, was with her—an intelligent child.

At 2 p.m. I made sail for Raiatea.

I sent for Tapoa to give him a lecture. He was very piano and seemed ashamed of himself—feeling he had been foiled in his intrigue. He said he should return to Bora Bora "as soon as Pomare had done crying over her child"—meaning—as soon as Pomare can make up her mind to be separated from the child whom Tapoa has adopted. I fear this will be made a constant excuse for his coming to Tahiti. He told me he had received my declaration to the Bora Borans, and was pleased because he hoped England would watch over them.

He then asked me in a manner which seemed as if he had been prepared by some one for this conversation, "to what extent England would protect the leeward islands." The old fox—but he did not catch me. I replied "Only so far as is consistent with her obligations to other powers." He then made some shrewd observations and inquiries as to the rights which an independent flag would give to the leeward islands.

Tapoa said he had permitted the return of Mai Faita and others to Bora Bora because they had acknowledged his authority, which they did because their pay from the French govt had ceased with the reign of M. Bruat. Untill lately Mai received 80$ per month—Tifaur 60$—Faitu 60$—Hodido 30$ Topa $22 and many other chiefs smaller sums. Tapoa *says the pay to the Tahiti chiefs in the French interest has also ceased.*

June 6th. I sent for Tapoa and Tamatoa to talk to them about their islands—but nothing was to be done with either. Like all Kanakas Tapoa is very fond of money. He therefore objects to any reasons for increasing and opening trade at Bora Bora, because it will interrupt a little project for monopolizing the whole trade in his own hands. He has been put up to this by M. Lucett, who it appears is anxious to share the profits of this bit of roguery.

I told the old fellow that he ought to be ashamed of remaining so long absent from his people, who are becoming dissatisfied and will soon think of setting up a new King in his stead. "Who will set him up" said Tapoa? "The same power that set you up—the voice of the people" replied I. This made him thoughtful for a moment and then he began upon the old story that "Pomare has not yet done with crying over her children." "Well said I, when is this to end, perhaps in 3 months Pomare will want to cry again over her child and you will have to come again to Tahiti." "Very probably" he answered with the greatest sang froid.

I anticipate much future evil from these connections. The 3 children of Pomare are heirs (by adoption) to the 3 barren chiefs of Huahine, Raiatea and Bora Bora and this liaison between the protectorate and the Society group will hereafter be found extremely inconvenient; that is if England desires to limit the extent of the French possessions in these seas. It appears to me that these island Kings only value their independence because they think they will make more money than if dependent on France. I was obliged to speak very plainly to their 2 Majesties and they left in great dudgeon.

Of course you might suppose that Martin, being a Captain in the Royal Navy (and later an Admiral), was perhaps moved more *against* the French than *for* the Tahitians. But he quite evidently cared for them as individuals. Indeed he was England in their time of travail, their only hope, as they thought, against the technologically superior power of the French. He was constrained by orders from his superiors in London, and he always reminded the native chiefs of this, but still for the space of a year he gave them his best counsel when they could no longer turn to the missionaries. He did what he could to ameliorate their plight and, in feeling so, he came to admire them and respect them even though he constantly looked down upon them as inferiors. Was there perhaps always a latent but insistent element of guilt in the white man's worldwide conquest of colored skins?

CHAPTER SEVENTEEN

Stand By

1890s

A long time ago in the so-called Jarnac Treaty of 1847 the independence of the Leeward group was guaranteed by both England
and France. But now that anticipation of the Panama Canal had
greatly increased their strategic potential, the French began to look
into the opportunity of another one of those island-swapping deals with
England. There was an added incentive. As trade had increased in the
islands, revenues from imports into Tahiti became more and more
significant to the administration's budget, since they were, as they still
are today, the main source of revenue for the French government. For
the Tahitians also, whether they realized it or not, these excise taxes
were vital because they took the place of land taxes. For the same
reason the import duties had to be relatively high and high duties are
of course a classical invitation to smugglers. American ships were probably the worst offenders for they brought their cargoes in to Raiatea at
low duties which went to the islanders instead of to the French. And
from there the goods easily found their clandestine ways in native boats
over the Sea of the Moon, usually at night, to Tahiti's many little
harbors hidden along the western and southern coasts. Still another
factor that makes one sympathetic to the French was the increasing
intrusion of German trade. A Godefroy son of the huge Hamburg
trading firm had married a Brander daughter. German commercial
initiative, which was beginning to be felt in the western Pacific, now
had a potential entrée into the Tahitian islands.

New Caledonia was now French; Fiji, English. The next best prize was the New Hebrides, and the French, this time, had a head start. So a trade was in order. The Jarnac Treaty was jettisoned by mutual consent in 1888 and the British stepped into that ridiculous, now infamous, "condominium" with headquarters in Port Vila. The Leeward Islands lay naked. Governor Lacascade first subverted Tamatoa IV, king of Raiatea much as Chessé had managed Pomare V. He then announced the annexation of all four of the key islands. A warship sailed around to each one with French tricolors to replace their native flags, all of which were different variations of the Tahitian red and white stripes. This little exercise was carried out nonchalantly enough. The islanders apparently took it as a sort of game, for as soon as the French ship left port, the old native flags were promptly run up again. Lacascade was understandably incensed at this flouting of his new imperial doctrine, so he selected the largest man-of-war in his command to go from port to port telling each little country who was boss. But when a squadron of marines approached the landing at Huahine they were met with murderous gun fire and quickly retreated, leaving three dead Frenchmen on the beach. (The grandchildren of their famous old warrior queen Ariipaea Vahine evidently had long memories. They were not loath to revenge the cruel devastations in 1845 of the infamous *Capitaine* Bonard.)

Lacascade had a reputation for fairness and calm, but this naturally was going too far. Before taking action, however, he sent off a fiery dispatch to Paris. He must have been puzzled and dismayed to get an answer that cautioned him to try diplomacy instead of force. Parleys were attempted but got nowhere. The islanders saw no more reason to surrender now than they had in the early days of the Protectorate. The *Decrès* was dispatched to Raiatea where Tamatoa in relinquishing his crown had conceded them a beachhead. The "king" of Tahaa, Raiatea's sister island, was a good-natured, somewhat elderly fellow who had long been a friend of the French because he had ambitions to become king of Raiatea as well. This sort of inter-island king swapping had been going on since ancestral days in their sporadic wars and the French thought he would lead them to an easy conquest with little fighting.

But the real key to the situation was a dauntless man of the people named Teraupoo. He would have none of the French. He was carrying the island's old torch of freedom and the great majority of the people were rallied behind him as their new leader.

At this point we are fortunate to have another of our on-the-scene witnesses, a young midshipman named Henri de Menthon who wrote a journal in 1883 that vaguely echoes the sort of frustrations that young Americans might have felt in Vietnam. He introduces us to the first tentative French military action in the Leeward Islands.

26 May Papeete They told us that the Decrès which we were going to board is at Raiatea because of the grave events of the past months. At Raiatea our allies are several hundred natives grouped around a little fort defended by 80 soldiers. The foothold of the King is this few pacified kilometers. All the rest of the island is inhabited by rebels living tranquilly in the bush where it is very difficult to attack them. We in turn have attempted nothing against them, only holding ourselves on an easy defensive. The Vire *and the* Decrès *have been there for two months, frozen in a peaceful blockade, not having enough men to finish off these singular rebels once and for all.*

No one on board much tries to hide his discontent; lamentations, reproaches, unflattering words are all over the place for those who have ordered this drudgery.

29 May Papeete At noon all our preparation is complete. In spite of the charm we shall be leaving behind, we have been diligent. We leave tomorrow with our fill of coal, three months of rations, ten beef cattle and fifteen sheep. In addition we are bringing provisions of all sorts for the soldiers posted at Raiatea and our deck looks like a gathering of caravans, piled deep with merchandize and animals.

The Decrès, *warned of our arrival by a schooner, lies in harbor. The commandant confirms the rumors we have already received; the rebels number about a thousand, well armed, well led. Confident of their capacity for resistance they won't even talk to us. The infantry post is constantly attacked; the houses of our native friends are burned; their plantations devastated; with the orders of the governor permitting noth-*

ing but a little timid defense. To finish things off it will be necessary to make a serious incursion into the interior, to search out the rebels on their home ground. But the countryside is unknown; in the bush our soldiers are at a disadvantage; They are caught time and again in ambush, the attack of invisible enemies, bullets that kill by surprise, all the unforeseeable in a war of thickets that makes the bravest timid.

For the moment then we are going to continue this pacific and ridiculous blockade, awaiting the arrival of the admiral, avoiding as much as possible the introduction of the munitions of war.

Raiatea 1st of June At eight we stopped to await the pilot. We are in the middle of the Leeward Islands, before the pass to Uturoa. To the right of us Tahaa shows its green hillsides and behind, further off, Bora Bora hides its truncated peak and torturous contours in the white morning clouds. At 10 oclock we were anchored alongside the Vire, the transport sloop that has been here for three weeks. The infantry lieutenant of the marines who commands the post confirms for us the reports we have already heard of his situation and of the rebels' attacks, not very dangerous but frequent, which oblige us to be on guard night and day. Yesterday evening again several came prowling about the fort firing ineffective shots that kept every one awake until morning.

The best buildings on the island are two Anglo-German commercial factory warehouses. These are occupied; work and trade continues and the rebels buy their wares. Ultimately it is for these factories, to assure their safety, that we are here.

Raiatea June 23 Here we are completely on a war footing, the cannons mounted, masks ready, projectiles and swabs on deck. Every one here takes his role seriously: it is not permitted to go ashore except to walk scarcely one kilometer. I spent last night in the large armed cutter. The swivel cannon was mounted in the bow; the twenty men who accompanied me had their rifles loaded, pistols at their waists. In this formidable array at seven in the evening I came to anchor before the fort to defend the sea side. The commander before we left had given me the most serious orders. "Every craft that approaches should be hailed. If those who come do not answer with the password at the third challenge, have the men fire."

All the sailors scrutinize the horizon with care. If the enemy comes, he will be well received! "Brrr! the smell of powder" as Tartarin would say. In spite of our temptation to sink a few canoes to pass the time of our watch, we sighted only innocent craft loaded with bananas and oranges. From afar off they came, shouting out the password at the top of their voices so that the rebels could hear it for miles around. These were our partisans who were profiting from the darkness of night to go seek provisions from their plantations in enemy territory.

The rebels had nothing to fear. They knew perfectly well what was going on here and would never risk attack except in our absence. These people are astonishingly superstitious and fearful. They avoid any action during the dark, preferring, on the contrary, to attack during a full moon in a flat calm. Most often when they are at war among themselves they have the kindness to advertize the day which they have chosen to attack.

10 June After inspection, the King of Raiatea invited by the commandant came aboard. He is a chief of the island of Tahaa who has always been on our side and whom we have established here with the title of king and a good round annual pension. Having scarcely any occasions to assert his authority because about three quarters of his subjects are rebels and inaccessible, he quietly plays his role of sovereign, living largely under our protection, in the grand wooden shack that serves him as a palace.

We receive him with all the royal honors and he survives without turning a hair, the avalanche of cannon fire that salutes his entry. He is a big handsome man, almost white, with a soft and affable manner, not knowing a word of French but speaking English perfectly. He is dressed in white linen with large epaulets of gold braid. The commandant invites us to the royal banquet, and luncheon passed agreeably, the king talking very little and we making many protestations of friendship. The wine, which he much appreciated as do all the kanakas, reminded him of the native orange drink whose qualities he expounded to us. It is the only fermented drink known to the inhabitants of these islands and the enormous quantities they consume prove how much they like alcoholic beverages. Our guest today loosened his royal mien little by little and owing to his libations he soon became rather tiresomely familiar. At three oclock in spite of his reiterated cries for champagne! champagne! we had him brought back to land to safeguard his sovereign dignity.

11 June After a bright fresh morning full of sun and gaiety we are awakened from the false security of these last days by a burst of gunfire. It is midday and we are lunching tranquilly; here we all are on deck. Through the binoculars we see that in the post they are taking up arms, everyone is bustling about, soldiers go out one gate while the female populace enters at the other to take shelter. On the signal mast of the fort flies the red pennant that announces the approach of the enemy.

Quickly we are the sloop of war; the clarion sounds; the officer of the deck calls the men, one by one they embark in haste, buckling on their ammunition belts, wiping the grease from their guns and cursing the armorer. We are thirty; the steam cutter takes us in tow and heads us toward a small beach where the action seems to be taking place. At four hundred meters from the water's edge among scattered trunks of coconuts a hundred blacks, disbanded and in disorder are firing upon an invisible enemy. I fire a salvo over them; the swivel cannon sends several bursting shells. I hear howling. In the midst of the confusion the surprized ones save themselves pell mell. I see wounded being carried off; useless to continue firing; the place is deserted!

My sailors are desolate by such a rapid result; I and they, we hoped for some resistance; we wanted something better. For the one time that we see these invisible rebels who resemble soldiers in an operetta we are thwarted by their flight. But the order of the governor is firm, which forbids any offensive. After an hour's waiting we survey in vain the neighboring beaches; the birds have flown, we calmly take our way back to the Volta.

21 June Two long days aboard under a torrential rain. In a chaos of greys without shape or form the water falls without cessation, seeping everywhere. As soon as the watch ends everyone descends to the wardroom a sort of smokey cavern, weathertight against the rain where one helps to pass the slow hours with interminable games of whist.

The admiral has held up his departure to attend the submission of Teraupoo, the military chief of the rebels. Since yesterday between the Duquesne and the enemy camp there have been exchanges of letters, *comings and goings, continual talk. We follow this movement with passion, watching with impatience for every sigh, praying with all our souls for a good move on the part of this poor dispossessed King that will give him back his kingdom and give us our freedom.*

But after a last secret conference we learn sadly that things have not reached this point. We are chained to our unpleasant task. Obedience and resignation! We well need these two virtues so that we will not show our misery too blatantly.

8 July The commander in view of the tranquil attitude of the rebels authorized us to go ashore to walk a bit outside our coop and we took prompt advantage. To understand the joy we felt in touching the ground and moving our legs about, you must realize the oldest of us was thirty and that for fifteen days our only walking space had been half a deck ten meters long!

Today along paths where one strolls under a blazing sun I encounter only inoffensive natives carrying on their shoulders at both ends of a pole bunches of bananas and long strings of coconuts. The women also, without hurrying return to the village chattering away. With their indian dresses over their arms they glide, supple and graceful over the greensward with their carriage like young queens, saluting us in passing with a smile of their white teeth and the fresh music of their voices; a temptation to caress their young bodies. Along the Path of War they go singing, carrying round their heads their wreaths of orange blossoms, swinging their supple forms to the amorous rhythm of their songs. Before us the golden sun sinks slowly in the midst of the tangled foliage strewn with scarlet flowers that blaze in its last rays. Here is the night, the clear night when the rebels come by the warpath with guns loaded and daggers drawn. The gates of the fort close on the last comers, near the shore our whaleboat awaits, its red lantern alight, riding on the evening swell.

Let's get back quick and never forget that we are at war!

Papeete 1 Dec. After long days of boredom at Raiatea, at Huahine, comings and goings devoid of interest, bombardments that make more noise than damage, interminable talk talk talk with rebel chiefs, here we are at last indefinitely stalled in these islands. The flag of the rebels always flies in the bush, not far from our own banner. As easy-going neighbors they are little by little getting used to each other, and are even commencing to render services to one another. Because the admiral and the governor seem content, we are also. We rejoice above all in having finished with that monotony and too long drudgery.

Our friends of many months made us their farewell visits, the "fetii" brought last loads of bananas and oranges in their canoes, taking in exchange several liters of tafia.

Leaving without regret this marvellous realm bathed in sunlight, the Volta gained the pass at the slow pace which her age still permits and here we are since this morning securely moored to the quai in Papeete.

The governor who so exasperated our young midshipman was, of course, Lacascade acting (or perhaps non-acting) under orders from Paris.

CHAPTER EIGHTEEN

Fire!—and Finis

1899

Early in June 1891, Pomare was taken with another of his periodic illnesses. This caused little immediate concern; it was assumed to be an extra severe hangover or perhaps a spell of grippe. Since he was only fifty-two years old and of a basically strong constitution in spite of his excesses, the sudden death that followed came as a surprise. His nephew Prince Hinoi, recently adopted as his son and heir to the family line, was away on a visit to Moorea. The governor had to dispatch a warship to fetch him back.

The flag of the Protectorate was lowered to half-mast. The Palace was hung inside and out with huge black drapes. The coffin was set in state in the central ballroom, with the old family crown on top, the Pomare crown, which this deposed king had never worn. A long line of mourners filed into the palace, passed through and out again—a long, somber occasion, as was the Tahitian way. The following Monday the ceremonies began with the Protestant pasteurs in charge and all the high chiefs and officials present. Everything went off much as usual until, toward the end, the chief of Mahaena, Teriinohorai, rose unexpectedly. On his own initiative and authority he launched into a long speech that had everyone puzzled until in a vague and roundabout way it seemed to turn into a proposal that Pomare be succeeded by his son Hinoi and that the old monarchy be, in effect, reestablished.

Bengt Danielsson writes in his *Mémorial*, volume III, that no mention of this appeared in the report published in the *Messager de Tahiti*, the official and only voice of the state. So, historically it has either been forgotten or has never happened. But Danielsson went to the records in the Ministry of Colonies in Paris and found a detailed report from Governor Lacascade that sets forth plainly the dangers that he perceived at the time in this rousing speech by such an influential chief.

There was a huge crowd present and rumors began to fly about. The formal end of the dynasty and last vestige of the Protectorate was to take place officially on the morning after Pomare was buried. His flag was to be hauled down in a large public military ceremony and the French tri-color was to take its place as the symbol of the final transfer of power. Lacascade's fear was that there would be an uprising before the body could be interred, which might delay or perhaps even prevent the final exchange of flags so crucial to his career. According to protocol nothing could go forward until the actual burial took place. Of course the state of the corpse in this tropical climate was another urgent consideration. The governor reports that he drew up orders for the police and the military to be prepared to dig a ditch on the palace grounds and bury the body there if the funeral cortege did not proceed as planned.

As it turned out his fears were excessive. A moderator was called upon. In Adolphe Poroi do we see a dim reincarnation of the great Tati? He was the head of a Tahitian family firmly loyal to the French yet highly respected by his own people. He was sent for in his garden at Tipuerui on the outskirts of Papeete.

Meanwhile the crowds from the outlying districts were becoming restless. Echoes of the far-off days of Du Petit-Thouars's first imposition seemed to reverberate. That was when the high chiefs gathered their forces to wage the bitter three-year war that ended in the sudden fillip of Fautaua. The high chiefs were no longer. More than fifty years, a full two generations, had passed since Bruat and Lavaud had succeeded in buying off some, neutralizing others and quietly eliminating the proudest and fiercest. But if the chiefs were gone, their spirits were perhaps still flying about. The situation was tense.

Poroi came back to his home in Papeete that afternoon and gathered the chiefs about him. By morning all was calm. It was arranged that the governor would appoint Prince Hinoi to the presidency of the High Court and grant him a handsome addition to his pension. Pomare's royal body was spared the humiliation of being ditched in its own backyard.

The funeral procession started out headed by the traditional groups of somber dignitaries. It wound up eventually at the royal mausoleum of the Pomares in Taonoa with the usual old-time ceremonies of Maohi entombment. We have an interim report on it from a participant named Paul Gauguin.

Along the way in the confusion, the indifference of the French set the example and all these people, so solemn for several days, commence to laugh, the vahines taking the arms of their tanes, wagging their behinds while their broad feet shuffle the dust of the road. On arrival at the river at Fautaua, everything falls apart. Here and there many of them, hiding among the rocks, crouching in the water with their skirts lifted above their waists, purify their haunches soiled by the dust of the route, refresh the joints that the march and the heat has irritated. And so in that state they took up again the road to Papeete, bosoms thrown forward, the two "coquillages pointus qui terminent le sein" pressing through the muslin of their dresses with all the suppleness and grace of a well built animal. Hovering about them a mixture of body odor and the perfumes of sandalwood and tiare. Teine merahi Noa Noa—See how very fragrant, they tell us.

That was all. Everything fell into the habitual order. There was one king less, and with him disappeared the last vestiges of custom . . . Maori. It was finished; nothing left but the Civilized.

The next morning the flag of the Protectorate was hauled down for the last time since it had been flown in 1841. And even Poroi, who received on this occasion "La croix de chevalier de la Légion d'Honneur" for his devotion and services, stated that "It was not possible to see, without an aching heart, this vestment of our history disappear after fifty years."

You may be sure that the old "rebel" chiefs would have preferred to see it disappear forever and the French tricolor along with it; to be supplanted by their own old red-white-red three-striper alone.

But of course it was the Tricolor alone that attained the masthead, and there of course it still flies today, the symbol of the supremacy of the civilized French over the two-thousand-year-old "savagery" of the original human inhabitants of the Tahitian islands.

After this period of monotonous, boring and inactive "war," the French high command seems to have taken a several-year-long siesta. Lacascade was succeeded in 1893 by a new rosary of governors from Paris—Cassaignac from June 1893 to October 1893, Bouvier to December 1893, Oars to April 1894, Papinaud to April 1896, Gallet to January 1897, Gabri to February 1898, Gallet again to March 1899, De Pons to July 1899, Rey to November 1899, and Gallet still again. For the six and one-half years until the end of the century, eight different governors filled ten terms of office, since Gallet jumped in and out three times. That is an average of less than eight months per governor. Small wonder that nothing much happened. And yet toward the end it did.

To a reader of today the most notable events of these last years before the final conquest are the visits of Robert Louis Stevenson in 1888 and of Paul Gauguin and Henry Adams in 1891, but no one in the islands at that time took any notice of them. The big local events were the great Papeete fire in 1884 and the death of Ariitaimai in 1897 at the age of seventy-six, the very last of the glorious *arii* of old. The economy, we are told, was stagnant but generally satisfying. The vahines young and old, mischievous and dignified, still dressed in the voluminous mother hubbards that the English missionaries had wrapped them in a hundred years before. Lacascade had pushed vigorously for a railroad from Papeete to Taravao, but horses and stagecoaches were still the only competitors of the outrigger canoes.

Across the Sea of the Moon to the west, where the spirits of the ancestors used to fly from Mount Rotui on Moorea to Mount Temehani on Raiatea, French troops continued to man their little outpost at Uturoa. This seemed to have little impact, but at least it limited somewhat the smuggling of foreign imports because Uturoa was the only harbor large enough to handle cargoes from trading ships.

At Bora Bora Queen Teriimaevarua, wife of Prince Hinoi, had come back to her natal island and was encouraging and legalizing all the bad habits and debaucheries of her race. At least that is the way the French pasteurs saw it, a revival of paganism and especially of the old-time licentious dancing, which was worst of all. Perhaps she came because she wanted to dance and could not do so in Tahiti. At any rate she was friendly to the French and thus they considered themselves officially in control of Bora Bora. To be sure the tricolor flew at Vaitape, the "capital," but around the harbor and over the hill at Faatai they were still flaunting the old flag of independence.

At Huahine Queen Tehaapapa II, aged sixteen, was married to a young cousin of Hinoi, so the French felt themselves secure there also. Actually the queen's father, Marama, controlled the "court" as regent and he was happy to welcome the French expansively whenever they came with gifts and drinks. He did not tell them that his dominion was limited to the small district and port of Pare and that all the other chiefs on the island were his enemies.

All of this time the rebel Teraupoo continued as undisputed leader of the peoples of all of these islands. He continued also to refuse to talk to the French.

One gets the impression that the Europeans in the colony of Tahiti, government officials, colons, or plantation owners, and most of the business and professional community were living in a gay little world of their own, isolated or insulated from the people at large. They had their constant comings and goings of governors with parties of welcome and parties of farewell, inspections, receptions, salutes, parades, dances, and banquets, all of this small, select society quite confident that their toy kings and queens were as representative of the general populace as they would have been in Europe. It seems indeed that they were playing an entertaining game of self-illusion. Were the officials more interested in their medals and ranks and pensions than in the actual acquisition of power or building of empire? But no doubt this was just another example, in miniature, of the normal state of affairs in any colony anywhere during those last glorious Victorian decades.

Then in Tahiti the new governor, Cassaignac, in 1893 made the rash decision to invalidate the election of five chiefs to the General Council on the grounds that they were anti-French. The council objected, even its leader Tati Salmon, grandson of the original Alexander, who was usually loyally French, agreed to appeal to the Conseil d'État in Paris. That remote body delayed its decision for two years before rejecting the appeal. Things began to seethe.

Who should arrive upon the scene but our old peacemaker and kingbreaker, Isidore Chessé, again with overriding powers, to integrate the Society Islands into the Colony of Tahiti? This time he brought his son with him, who turned out to be an old friend and schoolmate in France of Prince Hinoi. They all set out together, a gay company in the smart flagship *Aube*, to Huahine, where Marama the regent welcomed them in Pare. Hinoi and his Parisian school friend joined his royal cousin married to the hedonistic young queen of the island. They must have had a fine *tamaraa*. The old flag of Queen Ariipaea was hauled down before they came and the Tricolor hoisted high when the empire builders sailed on for Raiatea, no doubt in a jubilant mood.

Marama had neglected to tell Chessé that all the other chiefs on his island were hostile. Huahine had already been solemnly annexed three times, so it was an old story to them. The small district of Pare, though it contains the best harbor, was actually no more the ruling center of Huahine than was Uturoa on Raiatea. The other chiefs were flying the old flag of independence, biding their time, awaiting word from Teraupoo who had told them not to attack at this time.

Chessé found a very different welcome at the main island of Raiatea. The situation at Uturoa must have been much the same as we left it in company with Midshipman Menthon some ten years ago. The other principal harbors around the island were; firstly Avera, on the east coast directly south of Uturoa. There a more or less independent queen, Tuarii, was supposedly in power. She inclined to side with the French because Uturoa was the only port where the comfortable provisions that most appealed to her were available. She was evidently an energetic and politically conscious lady, for she had voyaged to Rarotonga in April of 1895 to ask protection of the British. But the English Resident there had said no, referring to the Treaty of London of 1888, which gave France a free hand in the Leeward Islands. Chessé wooed the queen of Avera and it is said that his charm elicited many fine agreements by day, but each new morning he found they had been undone during the night.

Teraupoo whose main base was south of Avera at Opoa, the ancient religious seat of the island and in pre-European days the religious center of the whole of eastern Polynesia, was perhaps just playing his cat-and-mouse game. Teraupoo himself would not speak with Chessé, but here again charm was extended and extended, and force withheld. At length Teraupoo agreed to accept the Protectorate subject to four conditions: (1) Exile of the local French partisans; (2) Suppression of the French flag at Uturoa, to be replaced by the Protectorate banner; (3) Indemnities for damages inflicted in 1887–88; (4) Signatures of all the foreign consuls at Tahiti to guarantee these terms.

This was the best concession that Chessé could obtain and it was of course no concession at all. He continued to attempt to negotiate, but at length he must have realized that his wily opponent was not trying to reach any middle ground by refusing to fight and refusing to surrender. In contrast to the old "rebel" chiefs of Tahiti in 1843, this rebel was suffering few hardships. His houses were intact; his food supply was normal. Clandestine trading brought him some revenues. Indeed he could only gain strength as time went on by acquiring more and more of what he needed most—muskets and gunpowder.

And then a change in the Ministry in Paris put an end to one more fine French ego. Chessé was recalled in disgrace. It was now up to the current governor, Papinaud, whose two-year lease of office was soon to run out. He took the most unusual step of asking the English Consul, one Robert Simons, to go tell the rebels that they would never be able to fly the English flag. Oddly enough Simons consented to go and sailed over on the *Aube* to Opoa. There followed the usual overtures, persuasions, threats. Always the English consul was invited ashore—providing no Frenchman landed with him. But no results were achieved. So the mighty warship shot down the flagpole at Opoa and sailed out the famous pass of the ancient chiefs, past the sacred motu, Iriru.

They had better luck at Tahaa because the main chiefs there had had no word from Teraupoo. Their next objective was Tevaitoa, the northernmost port on Raiatea. There they landed, but the consul came back an hour later saying that he could get nowhere and that they were the most arrogant and obstinate people he had ever encountered. So again they squared away to shoot down the flagpole. But this time it was farther inland on a hill and was partially protected by those great slabs of the ancient *marae* on the point. It took fifty shots of cannon to hit the mark. This was a bit expensive since the only result was a broken tree trunk which was easily replaced. The natives took it all as a good show and did not even shoot back. They just waited until the flag fell, then gathered it up and hoisted it on a new pole as soon as their thundering naval opponents had left.

But in March of 1896 another governor arrived from France and this one meant business. He was an old campaigner and soon after his arrival he wrote the Minister of Colonies that with 1000 soldiers from Tahiti, 150 marines from New Caledonia, and 150 auxiliaries from the Marquesas he would achieve *the complete submission of the rebels of Raiatea and Tahaa and their disarming within 18 hours without it being necessary to fire a single gun shot.*

Before commencing these efficient hostilities he sent for Tati Salmon to persuade Teraupoo to listen to reason. Tati was not even allowed to land. The next step was an ultimatum to be delivered by messengers to each of the rebel outposts at Avera, Opoa, Tevaitoa.

Your repeated affronts to the French flag have exhausted the patience of the Government of the Republic.

I am therefore sending soldiers and ships of war to force you to lay down your arms and to obey.

I give you one new chance and a last delay of 4 days to listen to the voice of reason and make your complete submission.

If, at the end of this delay, my appeal has not been accepted, my troops will march against you and you will be chastized as you deserve. Moreover I warn you that if you oblige me to use armed force, I will confiscate the territories you occupy and will subject you to the most severe measures.

*I now summon you to evacuate your districts without delay and to
betake yourselves with your chiefs, your families, your arms and munitions by Friday Jan 1 before 7 in the morning to the following places.*

1. *The rebels of Opoa to the islet of Iriru*
2. *The rebels of Tahaa with their women and children to the islet of
   Toahatu*
3. *And those of Tevaitoa to the islets of Tahunave and Torea.*

*A white flag should be hoisted at the fixed hour on each of these points
to indicate that you have complied with the present summons.*

> *Done at Uturoa, the 27th Dec 1896*
> *The Governor*
> *Gustave Gallet*

The messengers tried their utmost to deliver copies of this formidable document wherever they could, but no one would accept them. In
some cases they nailed copies to trees, in others they anchored them
with stones in the middle of the meeting place, in some they cast them
through open doorways.

Two days later Gallet ordered the captain of the warship to land 700
soldiers and 200 native auxiliaries to parade at Uturoa. He was confident that such a show of force would do the trick without actual
fighting. He later reported that 900 people of Tahaa complied, "a
certain number" from Tevaitoa, 746 from Avera.

*On the first of January I had detached more than 2400 inhabitants
from a population estimated to be 3000 but who might more likely be
3500. . . .*

But a certain Lieutenant Deman who had been present on the
schooner *Papeete* wrote a different version in his book published the
same year in Paris. *A few chiefs in Tahaa gave themselves up . . . in
Raiatea at Opoa and Tevaitoa the ultimatum was refused.* He goes on
to say that a goodly number of women and children went to the motus
in order to leave the men folk free to fight in the bush.

Danielsson's estimates on the contending "armies" are: Teraupoo,
500 men with only 235 guns and only ten shots per gun. The Queen
of Avera, 250 men with 65 guns. The French on the other hand had
a well-equipped expeditionary force of 600 men.

It all went off methodically and probably without many casualties on either side. How could it be otherwise? Two columns of French regulars worked down the east and west coasts accompanied by 180 Tahitian auxiliaries plus 90 porters and 20 guides. It must have been very slow, rugged, and wet, for both coasts are deeply indented with river valleys; precipices often descend to the lagoon's edge and thick jungle is present everywhere. The villages of Avera and Opoa were bombarded from the sea. Tevaitoa was invested with bayonets. The two columns proceeding south burned all rebel houses, canoes and plantations along the way until they joined together at Fetuna on the southern tip of the island. Teraupoo decided that he could not defend Opoa, so he and his men took to the bush, sniping and harassing as best they could.

At Fetuna the French forces embarked and sailed back to Tahaa where they divided the island in two and soon cleared out any last resistance.

Their main objective was to take prisoners and deport them. A first shipment of 116 men was collected mostly from Tahaa, many of them with women and children. These were sent off to the Marquesas to be stranded on the barren rock island of Eiau to the north. But when they arrived at Nuku Hiva to pick up a garrison that was to guard these dangerous criminals, the soldiers assigned to that thankless duty refused to leave their comfortable quarters in Nuku Hiva, so the band was sent to nearby Uahuka. There they became fiercely religious and set about vigorously to convert the Catholics of the Marquesas to their Protestant faith. Evidently they were quite successful, for the Picpus Catholic priests, who had never before had competition, soon began to complain of serious disruptions to their holy work. And thus you might say they fought their way religiously back to freedom, for they were repatriated after some two or three years.

Meantime the redoubtable Gallet, who had been only acting governor, was replaced by a kinder-hearted regular appointee named Gabrie. He immediately restrained the vindictive field commander Bayle, who by now had collected another five hundred prisoners and wanted to deport them. This did not make much sense to Gabrie, who told him instead to go after Teraupoo.

According to a contemporary writer and reporter René La Bruyère, who visited the island a year or so after the final capitulation, the potential exiles were reduced by a third because "the governor perceived that this measure would be very costly to the Government of the Republic since the Marquesas islands could not support them."

He goes on to explain to us in a delightfully French fashion the dilemma that harassed the gallant campaigners. *How to explain the tolerance of the French govt toward Teraupoo? Why don't we force him by main strength of arms to give up? It is because the officers of the Naval Division are repugnant to shed the blood of a race as sympathetic as the Malayo-Polynesian. For a long time, in accord with the custom described by Loti, the officers have contracted unions with the women of the country to which Loti has given the name of marriages. These ephemeral fusions are often based on profound sentiments. Nothing is more charming than this sensual and sentimental idyll between these young officers of the west and these exotic maidens, so fetching in their primitive ways.*

One had to know the ocean race, one had to have appreciated the sweetness of their customs to understand how painful it would be for an officer of the marine to fire upon an unfortunate native who in the evening had treated him as a fetii *[relative] and had offered his daughter. It was evident that the resistance reposed uniquely in one man, in Teraupoo! The commander of the* Durance *said of him in July 1892:*

"This man is ambitious, audacious, persevering, intelligent and with foresight, who having imposed his will on the majority of the population of Raiatea had to take care lest he compromise himself. Under the conditions the only choice was the death of Teraupoo or an expedition against him."

An artillery officer who fell into the water from a canoe was saved by the rebels. He then made prisoners of his saviors who were only waiting for a good occasion to give themselves up.

Little Moe of fifteen years, the lovely niece of the queen of Avera, en fille sauvage, heritor of the ancient kings of the island, was a fervant Teraupiste, she called in her prayers for his victory, but her complicated spirit desired at the same time to know the love of Europeans who had stained with blood their marae of Tevaitoa.

*   *   *

The patriot leader was hidden away in a cave in the mountains, where a large rock was rolled across the opening to hide him by day. It kept him safe for a long time and was all very romantic, but of course an astute French lieutenant discovered a mysterious light one night and the jig was up. The orders were to capture him alive, so he was led out with a pistol at his head, sad and dejected. His wife and daughter followed, both still proud and defiant. He was then sent to prison in New Caledonia and we do not hear of him again until he was sent back seven years later to end his days as a silent, unreconstructed recluse.

The annexation was ratified by the Chamber of Deputies in Paris on November 19, 1897, *the victorious end of the last military campaign in our islands . . . Les Isles Sous-le-Vent de Tahiti sont partie integrante du domaine colonial de la France.*

One hundred years to the dot after the arrival of the *Duff* in Matavai Bay.

Paul Gauguin wrote a letter to his friend Charles Morice, a journalist in Paris.

Mon cher Morice,

Here is some news that I send so that you may use it: no one will have it before you, considering that the same mail will bring all such news. An article in a newspaper will bring you some money. Perhaps!

France has sent a warship here, the Dugay-Trouin, *plus 160 men from Noumea sent on the* Aube, *warship of that station. All this to take by force the Leeward Islands said to be in revolt. At the time of the annexation of Tahiti, these islands refused to be part of the annexation. Then one fine day that devil Lacascade, governor of Tahiti, wished to do his stuff and cover himself with glory. He sent an envoy supposedly supplied with all power who, having embarked at Raiatea, went to find the chief and promised him mountains and marvels. This chief being reasonable came to the beach accompanied by others to be taken aboard the man of war. Forthwith the warship, under orders from governor Lacascade to capture natives, sent ashore longboats armed secretly with leveled cannons.*

The natives who were very astute and of a defiant spirit became suspicious of the plot and retired in good order. The troops upon landing were met with gunshot and obliged to hurry back aboard. Several sailors and an ensign lay dead on the beach. Afterwards the natives went about their business tranquilly refusing to let the French circulate about the island, restricting them to a limited area.

Last year, August 95, the delegate Chessé came to Tahiti having promised the French government that he would bring an end to the revolts by simple persuasion. That has cost a hundred thousand francs to the colony which was charged for the expenses. That goose Chessé flexing his wings sent messenger after messenger to make presents to the native women of red balloons, little music boxes and other toys, (this is the truth I am inventing nothing) recited a lot of foolishness from the Bible. Nothing tempted them in spite of all the lies. Chessé retired completely defeated by the diplomacy of the savages.

Actually everything soldierly, plus the volunteer Tahitians enrolled here, is now at Raiatea. After an ultimatum sent the 25 December, the firing commenced the 1st of January 1897. For 15 days there were no results, the mountains long being able to hide the inhabitants.

You should be able to concoct a jolly informational piece (the idea seems to me original) with an interview between P. Gauguin and a native, before the action.

————Why don't you wish, like Tahiti, to be governed by French laws?

————Because we are not minions or stooges, besides we are very happy just as we are, governed by laws conforming to our natures and our land. As soon as you install yourselves in one respect, everything belongs to you, the land and the women whom you leave after a couple of years with a child for whom you no longer have any concern. Everywhere functionaries, gendarmes who must be given little gifts to mitigate innumerable vexations. And for the least conduct of our ordinary affairs, we must lose many days searching for a piece of incomprehensible paper; formalities without number. And because all of this is very costly, we are burdened with taxes which we natives cannot pay. For a long time we have known your lies, your petty promises. Fines, prison when we sing and drink, all that to teach us the alleged virtues which you do not

practice yourselves. Who does not know the devil servant of Governor of Tahiti Papinaud, entering our house at night to force the young girls. Impossible to bring action against him because he is the servant of the Governor!!! We are happy to obey a chief but not all those functionaries.

————But hold on now. If you won't give in willingly, the cannon will teach you reason. What hope have you?

————None. We know that if we give up the principal chiefs will go to prison in Noumea, and for a Maohi death in another land is an ignominy. We prefer to die here. Now I will tell you one thing which will simplify everything. As long as we are side by side, you French and we Maohi, there will always be trouble and we do not want trouble. Therefore you must kill us all, then you can dispute amongst yourselves alone. And that you will find easy with your cannons and your rifles. We have for our defense only flight every day into the mountains.

(This last answer is the one that was made to the ultimatum.)

You see my dear Morice what to do and do well, all of it in the very simple language of the native.

And if you succeed in placing the article in a magazine, send me a few copies. I will be quite satisfied to show here that when I make funny faces, I can also show a few teeth. Of course it must be understood that my name should have some importance.

> *Let's go to work*
> *Cordially yours*
> *P. Gauguin*

Not much is known about this minor example of resistance or its leaders, writes Colin Newbury who is the most reliable and up-to-date historian/scholar of French Polynesia. Minor, indeed! Perhaps in the sense that the numbers are small, but how minor if you were one of that minority? By his estimates there were 359 Raiateans "under arms" (counting clubs, spears and slingshots as equivalent to rifles?) out of a total population estimated at 3000. That is about 12 percent of the island's people. When hostilities ended and resistance collapsed, he says that about 200 prisoners were sent to the Marquesas. That is certainly no minor proportion to be exiled, and think what it must have meant to the Raiatean families.

This was a small island, but we must remember that during her earlier war Tahiti was small also, with a population of about nine thousand, one thousand of whom were fighters. Theirs therefore was proportionally not quite as large a resistance as the Raiateans. There is also the question of duration. The Raiateans had spurned the very first attempts at annexation in 1843, but of course they had some protection from the Anglo-French treaty of 1847. Chessé made his first efforts in 1880. Then in 1888 Tamatoa was both bought out by the French and thrown out by his fellow chiefs for his own dissolute and weak character. He was, after all, a Pomare, the sixth child and fifth son of the queen—another despicable Paumotu in the eyes of Ariitai-mai.

The French had put one of the higher chiefs of Tahaa in his place, the one we were introduced to by midshipman Menthon. But no one paid any attention to him except the French.

The real power was the patriot leader Teraupoo, a man of the people who had developed a dedicated following that demanded extraordinary loyalty and sacrifice for long years until Gallet finally overpowered them all in 1898. It is a pity we know so little of this man because to his fellows he must have been an inspiring commander in chief. When Tamatoa was dethroned the London Missionary Society missionary Richards wrote, *the whole of the Raiatean Government (save one governor Teraupoo) were enrolled as Frenchmen and nearly the whole of the people banded together as one man to resist them.* Newbury could discover only a few letters written by him which, he says, reveal little except that he never failed to believe that the English would come to their rescue. This seems a naive illusion that contrasts strangely with his shrewdness as a guerrilla leader. He knew he could not compete with the French on any field of battle, so he practiced restraint, hit and run, sabotage and ambush; tactics that have now become so familiar to us in Vietnam, but which are so difficult for a commander in the bush to carry out, especially over a long period of years.

Altogether, considering the relative sizes and resources of the two main opponents to the French military forces—Tahiti, 1843–47; and

Raiatea, 1888–98—this "minor example of resistance" should be given credit for its gallantry, bravery, resolution, and sacrifice. These last gasps of the broken heroes in Raiatea deserve to be honored as much as the earlier ones in Tahiti.

The victors always write the history books and of course they write them their own way, so it is not surprising that we find little or nothing on the record concerning our chief interest, the Polynesian islanders. After wars between civilized peoples there are usually a few of the conquered who set down the feelings of the other side, as the writers of France have glorified Napoleon and those of the Confederacy have built their heroes after Appomattox, as Anne Frank recorded in her diary in occupied Holland. But here the losers could not even write, so the feelings are obscured forever in the tales of tribulation and humiliation they must have passed down through their families and friends. What those feelings were can only be guessed at or deduced from traits and emotions that have somehow slumbered through the generations and that still show up today. However long suppressed and secretly guarded, they do seem to be surfacing now. That same rugged, dauntless, proud independence of spirit, that same abiding love for their land, that same insouciant laughter in the face of calamity show clearly enough that the essence of these people was never quenched. It faltered. It held its breath and, during one or two decades after the turn of the century, it was generally thought to be surely on its way to extinction. But somehow it has lived on and the push for independence gathers strength every decade now as the population increases and the twenty-first century approaches.

But of course we see the same spirit emerging in all of the former colonies of the world, each with its own individual peculiarities: in India, in Asia, in Africa and even in the most helpless of all, the American Indians, it still stirs faintly.

Will the home-grown peoples of this world, on their own true lands, ever be able to be truly free?

It is tempting to conclude with a plea for the universal freedom of man from the arrogant injustices of colonialism. Especially in this instance to vilify the French and deify the Tahitian. But that would be a simplification and an ingenuous one. The evils of colonialism were many and they linger on today. But they also may be seen, indeed I believe they must be seen, as an extensive wave in one of the great tides of the social evolution of man. Inevitable it is that civilization must come. We see now, after the many heart-rending Fautauas of the world, that the innocent, unspoiled people of nature actually want to be spoiled once the agonies of spoilation have passed. The Tahitian of today will never now surrender his motor scooter or outboard or television. His mind, even in those early days of the explorers and missionaries—well before the conquistadors—was ready and eager for new reaches into the realms of acculturation that the white man opened up for him. Today he is striding forward powerfully. The shock almost killed him, as it has killed other indigenous people elsewhere. But he has not only survived; he flourishes. I would like to believe that this can be said of all of the Polynesians. Yet one despairs at present when considering the Easter Islander, the Marquesan and the American Samoan. One has grave doubts about the Hawaiian and many fears about the New Zealand Maori. The Tongan looks solid and strong. But of all the branches of this closely related, yet widely segmented ocean race, none is so sturdy and his genes so prevalent as the Tahitian.

A very good friend of mine, an American lady who has lived for over fifty years in the islands, declared recently when the talk was on the subject of the scourge of the white man, that she liked the French. She believed that no other Pacific people had been so lucky.

Everyone hates masters—outsiders who make the rules. But in colonial days everyone had to have a master. It was the destiny of the times and, villains though the French may often seem today, no colonizer has hit a fairer balance of good and evil than the countrymen of their romantic first Pacific hero, Louis Antoine de Bougainville.

Would a wise Tahitian chief of today—one such as those who debated the death penalty in the old Assembly—rise up now and say,

"E . . . Haere outou i teinei fenua tahiti?"

Meaning: *I am aware of what you say. . . . But is it not time for you to leave my land of Tahiti?*

Chronology

1750   *The High Chiefs:* Vehiatua of the Teva I Tai, whose district was Tiarapu; Amo of the Teva I Uta whose districts were Papara and Vaiare (with his wife, Purea, and his son Teriiterai); Hitoti and Paofai of the Te Aharoa, whose district was Tiarei; Utami of Punaauia; Potatu of the Te Atehuru; Mahine of Moorea; Tu of the Porionuu (who was to become Pomare I)

         The Kings: George III of England, Louis XV of France, Carlos III of Spain

1767	Wallis in the *Dolphin*
1768	Bougainville
1769	Cook I
1772	Boenechea
1773	Cook II
1774	Tati born, death of Louis XV, Louis XVI king
1776	American Revolution
1777	Cook III
1779	Pomare II born
1783	Defeat of Pomare I at Pare
1788	Bligh I
1791	Vancouver, victorious return of Pomare
1792	Bligh II
1793	French Revolution until 1804
1797	Arrival of the *Duff*
1803	Death of Pomare I, Pomare II "king" of Tahiti
1804	French Empire, Napoleon I
1808	Paofai defeats Pomare II

1811   George III retired, George IV Regent
1812   Pomare asks for baptism
1813   Birth of Aimata (future Queen Pomare IV)
1814   Restoration, Louis XVII, Napoleon exiled
1815   Pomare II conquers Teva and is baptized
1816   William Ellis arrives
1817   Orsmond and Williams arrive
1819   Code of Pomare enacted
1820   Teriitaria born (future Pomare III), George III dies, George IV
        king
1821   Death of Pomare II, Pomare III (Teriiteria) king
1822   First Tahitian flag
1824   Pritchard arrives. Legislative Assembly started. Louis XVII dies,
        Charles X king of France
1826   Treaty with U.S.A.
1827   Death of Pomare III, Aimata becomes Queen Pomare IV
1829   Moerenhout arrives
1830   French Monarchy, Louis Phillipe king. George IV dies, William
        IV king
1830s   Massive arrivals of whalers
1835   Darwin in the *Beagle*. Truro affair in the Tuamotus
1836   Caret and Laval. Dr. Johnstone arrives
1837   Pritchard becomes British Consul
1838   Du Petit Thouars's first visit. Moerenhout becomes French Con-
        sul. Victoria becomes Queen of England
1839   La Place in *L'Artemise*. Arii Aue born (future Pomare V)
1840   Queen Pomare flees to Raiatea
1841   Pritchard goes to England. Salmon arrives. Wilkes visits.
1842   Protectorate declared, Bruat Commissaire. Melville visits. Death
        of Paofai
1843   Pritchard returns. Thouars returns, Pomare deposed and Tahiti
        annexed to France
1845   Moerenhout departs
1846   Byam Martin arrives. Fautaua and surrender
1847   Treaty of Jarnac. Return of Queen Pomare
1848   Louis Napoleon ousts Monarchy and founds Second Republic.
        New laws abolish hereditary Chiefs

1849	Bonard succeeds Lavaud
1851	Tahitian Dictionary published
1852	Second Empire replaces Second Republic, Napoleon III Emperor
1854	Death of Tati. Great flu epidemic
1857	Tamatoa V, son of Queen, becomes king of Raiatea
1860s	Development and moderate prosperity under Governors de la Richerie and de la Ronciere
1861–65	American Civil War
1862	Stewart arrives
1863	French Protestant Mission ousts LMS
1864	Importation of Chinese to Atimaono
1865	Paraita dies
1866	Death of Alexander Salmon. Assembly switches to French law
1869	Pierre Loti visits
1870	Franco-Prussian war. End of Napoleon III. Third Republic begins
1872	Death of Pomare's second son, Arii Aue becomes Crown Prince
1873	Bankruptcy and death of Stewart. Ariifaite dies
1875	Marau daughter of Ariitaimai marries Crown Prince
1877	Queen Pomare IV dies, Pomare V becomes last "king" of Tahiti
1879–80	Abdication of Pomare V. Tahiti becomes full French colony
1881	Chessé makes unsuccessful overtures to Teraupoo. French buy off Tamatoa V and commence campaign to conquer Leeward Islands
1885	General Council established
1887	Treaty of Jarnac revoked
1888	Robert Louis Stevenson visits
1891	Henry Adams visits. Gauguin arrives. Pomare V dies
1897	Ariitaimai dies. French launch final attack on Raiatea
1898–99	Teraupoo captured and exiled. Resistance ends. Leeward Islands incorporated into the Colony of French Polynesia

Glossary

You should be warned first-off about place names. Every visitor spelled them as he heard them and the results are often wildly divergent. Expect not consistency.

The Tahitian language is a fascinating one, but it is very difficult to appreciate it through written words. It should rather be approached as music is—for its tones and inflections. A word that can be spelled with only one set of letters can have a dozen different meanings depending on how it is pronounced musically. And to complicate things further, this same written word can have different meanings when it has different associations or contexts. Further still, the expression on the speaker's face or the gesture of his hand or the shrug of his shoulders can, in some cases, change that word from black to white. The Tahitian language from its inception many, many millennia past has been a means of communication ear to ear and eye to eye. It is difficult for us writing people to grasp the wonderful range of its sights and sounds.

Throughout this book I have been purposely parsimonious with native words to avoid confusing an already complex culture. So most of those listed here are common, utilitarian terms. Among them are included, however, some non-Polynesian words such as *Lapita* (pottery) because they may not be familiar to readers unacquainted with the Pacific Ocean cultures.

ao   Light. *See* page 54 for a good explanation of this meaning of the word. But it is also, by happy chance for me, an excellent example of the difficulty of trying to spell in our written English the meaning of a Polynesian expression. The splendid Tahitian dictionary compiled by the missionaries lists no fewer than twenty-three meanings for the term they spell *ao!*

arii   High chief or chiefs, high born. *See* page 28 for arii raha and tahi

Arioi	The Arioi Society was a selective, hierarchical group of players who traveled about the islands in fleets of canoes, presenting lavish entertainments, mostly dancing and theatrical skits that were, in European eyes at least, so daring and exuberantly erotic that they were considered degenerate and even unspeakable. Sometimes the Arioi descended in troupes of several hundred for weeks at a time, exhausting the bountiful provisions of their hosts. But they were always honored and welcomed wherever they went. The highest ranks in the Society were usually attained only by the hui arii after years of dedication and experience. All members while active were pledged to remain childless and thus were rigid practitioners of infanticide. Membership was considered a great honor aspired to by all the upper classes.
breadfruit	*Artocarpus incisa*, the main staple of the Polynesian diet, an oblong fruit, nearly the size of a rugby football, that is starchy, not sweet, growing abundantly on a large handsome tree
copra	The dried meat of the coconut out of which is expressed the oil that makes the sweet-smelling base of their massaging unguent, *monoi*. Europeans greatly expanded the use of copra for commercial purposes.
Eimeo	The ancient name of the island of Moorea
fara	The pandanus. Probably the only tree that is truly indigenous, all others with the possible exception of the coconut having been brought by the Polynesians from Southeast Asia. The fruit is a compact of keys outwardly resembling a small pineapple, edible but not comestible. The long leaf is the prize material for fine mats and roof thatch.
fei	The mountain plantain, an orange, bananalike fruit, but larger and thicker and growing upward. Another favorite staple. It must be cooked.
fetii	Family relatives, parents, uncles, aunts, cousins, in-laws, etc.
haere	The common verb of motion—come, go, move, do, etc.
hinano	The handsome male flower of the pandanus, a favorite for decoration
hui arii	The high born
indians	Natives. The early colonial European's demeaning term for all non-Europeans
kanakas	Same as indians

Lapita   The newly discovered (1970s) pottery, which is now recognized by modern anthropologists as the hallmark of the race or culture that was ancestral to the Polynesians. Its unique decorative motifs enable us to trace the migrations of its makers from New Guinea through various Melanesian islands to the three island clusters—Fiji, Tonga, Samoa— where the so-called "Polynesians" developed their distinctive racial traits. Over the centuries the elaborate ornamentation of Lapita pottery gradually fades from its flourishing designs of 2000–1000 B.C. to plain ware at about 500 B.C. and disappears altogether soon after the birth of Christ. Presumably the pottery makers gave up boiling their foods and took to cooking with hot stones in earth ovens—as they still do today.

maiore   The old-time word for the breadfruit tree, still used in the Marquesas, but largely replaced nowadays by *uru* in the Tahitian islands

mana   A whole book could be written about the meaning of *mana*. A very brief description is on page 28. It is one of the three famous Polynesian "originals"—mana, tapu (taboo), and tatu or tatau (tattoo).

manahune   Lower-class people in the old days, mostly workers for the *raatira*

Maohi (Maori)   Today the indigenous Polynesians of New Zealand are called the Maori, but the term in old days was used to denote the race as a whole throughout all the islands of the oceanic triangle (*see* page 35). Gauguin uses it in this sense. A more acceptable pan-Polynesian term, advocated by Douglas Oliver, is Maohi, obviously an alternate variation due to European ears.

marae   The outdoor temple or tapu (sacred) area where what we call religious ceremonies were held. Its importance is noted on page 12. Marae construction differed markedly in the Leeward (Raiatea, etc.) and Windward (Tahiti, etc.) islands, being all rough coral or basalt slabs in the former and walled enclosures with carefully dressed stone altars or ahu in the latter.

marama   The moon

maro   The girdle or loin cloth. The *maro ura,* or red feather girdle, was the highest symbol of birth and authority, reserved for the *hui arii* of Raiatea and their descendants in Tahiti. The *maro rea*, or yellow feather girdle, was worn by the next highest rank.

monoi — Coconut oil massaging cream, usually scented with jasmine, gardenia, pua, etc. *See* copra

mutoi — Native police to whom the gendarmes allot the more menial tasks

nacre — The European term for pearl shell or "mother-of-pearl." In early times a precious trading commodity

niau — The commonest term for the coconut tree, frond, etc. There were and are a hundred names for all the different parts, uses, ages, etc. of the coconut.

oromatua — Spirits of the dead who ate you if you were not careful

pandanus — *See* fara

po — Darkness, realm of the spirits. *See* ao

poi — A sort of gelatinous pudding dipped in coco cream and always eaten from the fingers with a deft and graceful twist. *Poi* of all sorts is made of mashed fruit, *taro, uru,* etc. wrapped in leaf bundles and baked in the *umu.* It is the Tahitians' favorite way of preparing their favorite foods.

purau (burau) — One of the most useful of trees—leaves for plates, bark for ropes, the light wood for outriggers, small saplings for palisado walls, large ones for rafters, etc.

raatira — A sort of squire who managed land and lived on it as his own, although it was owned by his chief. *See* Peter Bellwood's comment on page 23

rea — Egg yolk, i.e., yellow as for the maro of the chief of second rank. The feathers usually came from the golden plover.

rii — Little, small. Iti is more common.

rongo rongo — The famous so-called hieroglyphs from Easter Island. Kenneth Emory is skeptical of their purported and much publicized importance and so am I.

Rotui — The mountain on Moorea between the two great bays. In olden days the spirits of the dead always landed here for a brief spell before going on to their crucial sorting of the ways on the Temehani in Raiatea.

Taaroa — The original god who created the world and afterward the lesser gods and all other existing things, last of all man

taata — Men, people

taio — Friend, companion, namesake

tamaraa	A feast, a festival. *See* page 104
tane	A male, a husband, boyfriend
tapa	Bark cloth made from the paper mulberry tree, which was extensively cultivated for this purpose. Also made from breadfruit bark
tapu	Freud took this indigenous Polynesian word and made it famous as "taboo." The Polynesians had no "b," but their "p" sounded like one to us and the corruption is widespread, *viz.* Bora Bora for Pora Pora.
taro	The favorite root vegetable of the Tahitians. Taro has to be cultivated in level, irrigated swamps. It was and is about the only foodstuff that demanded hard work.
Temehani	The sacred central mountain of Raiatea where the souls of the dead went for "final" assessment on the way to Havaiki. It is also the home of the famous *tiare apetahi*, a botanical wonder flower that grows only here in all the world and has never been successfully transplanted.
teuteu	Little or little people, lowest classes
ti	A fine plant whose leaves were used for dancing skirts and whose root is a much-prized sweet food, also distilled into an intoxicating drink
tiare	Flower. Any flower but especially the *tiare tahiti*, a gardenia —favorite for wreaths and leis
tupa	The much-despised land crab, eaten only when one is starving
tupaupau	A ghost or spirit of the dead—fearsome
umu	The Polynesian hot stone oven
ura	Red, especially the *mara ura* or red feather girdle of the highest of high chiefs. The feathers came from the parakeet of Rarotonga.
uru	Breadfruit. Alternate name is maiore
vahine	Female, woman, girl, wife
vi	The Tahitian apple or peach, a favorite fruit growing on a huge, handsome tree

Appendix

Tahiti, Society Islands
8 November 1843

My Lord

As a near relation (by marriage) to Her Majesty Queen Pomare, I feel myself compelled to write you concerning what I conceive the unjustifiable conduct of Mr. Pritchard the British Consul in these islands, regarding the advice that he has from time to time given to that unfortunate woman, and the fatal influence that such counsels have had over herself and government; and in explaining myself more fully I must go back to the time when Admiral duPetit Thouars made his first visit to this island to demand satisfaction for the cruel conduct shewn to two French missionaries—I need not inform your Lordship that the result was that a demand was made of 2000 dollars for such behaviour —But, my Lord, whose was the fault that such sum was demanded? Whose advice was followed by which the Queen was led into error? Mr. Pritchards. It was he so utterly ignorant of all respectful feeling that is due from one independent nation to another; it was he so filled with bigotry and unchristian feeling that advised the forcible expulsion of two unfortunate men— Such was the British Counsul's first attempt at foreign diplomacy— And now I must leave him for a little to fully relate to your Lordship the events that subsequently took place— In the month of August 1842, the French Admiral came to Tahiti, with the best feelings towards Queen Pomare, her chiefs and government, expecting to find that all difficulties that previously existed (but which had been amicably arranged by a treaty signed with M duBoucet commanding the French corvette "L'Aube") were fully at an end; he learnt with astonishment that such was not the case, but that the chief clauses of the treaty that had been signed, neither were fulfilled, nor was there any intention of there being so— It was on this occasion that he published the declaration which no doubt your Lordship has already seen, and in the end the treaty placing the exterior relations of Tahiti under the protection of the King of the French was signed, after which the Admiral departed expecting as every reasonable man would have done that the treaty was to be held inviolable— For three months or so, the Queen stopped quietly at Moorea, an island about 20 miles from Tahiti, and gave proof of her acquiescence to the treaty by writing to the French Provisional Govt established at Tahiti— When the "Talbot" arrived the Queen was sent for by the Captain Sir Thos. Thompson; on her arrival she was saluted under her old flag; meetings were held, and every thing possible was done, that could impress the natives with the idea that England right or wrong would force the French Govt to undo all that the Admiral had done— A day or two before the departure of the "Talbot" the Queen at the instigation of Sir Thos Thompson retired to Punaauea where she remained till the arrival of the "Vindictive," when on the very night of Mr. Pritchard's landing which he did at Punaauea (the "Vindictive" not anchoring at Papeete till the next day) he informed the Queen in my hearing that the "Vindictive" had come to protect her, that they would haul down the French Protectorate flag, and various other things all calculated to induce the Queen to break the treaty that she had formally signed with the French Admiral. The Queen then came to Papeete, when Commodore Nicolas saluted her old flag, and gave her in a spirit of opposition to the French a new one for herself (vis, the old Tahitian flag with the addition of a crown in it)— After this all things were carried on under the influence of Commodore Nicolas, and Mr. Pritchard, meetings were held, laws were made, & every thing was done to prejudice the Queen & her people against the French, and Commodore Nicolas at a public meeting states thru the Queen's speaker that he would stay with the "Vindictive" till she sank, or rotted away to protect the Queen from her enemies (?), thereby encouraging her and her people to do what they chose against the French, feeling assured from the Commodore's words, that he would protect them— A short time after, the "Vindictive" left, thus falsifying the declaration of the Commodore, and not long after the "Dublin" arrived, when the same proceedings were gone thru the flag was saluted etc. etc.

On the 1st November the French Admiral arrived here bringing with him the treaty signed and accepted by the King! and altho fully aware of the many hostile acts that the Queen had done during his absence, he fully forgave all, knowing that she had been influenced by bad advisers, all that he requested was, that the flag that had been given her in a spirit of opposition by Commodore Nicolas and Mr. Pritchard might be hauled down, and whatever private flag she wished should be allowed her— Was such demand extravagant? No, but it could not be agreed to by the Queen, because Mr. Pritchard advised to the contrary— The Admiral requested of her by writing repeatedly to haul down the flag, he waited on her twice personally to relate to her what would follow if she refused but Mr. Pritchard's influence being compounded of counsular and Missionary advice was paramount, and the end is that the Queen is no longer recognized by the French Govt.— Such are the facts— Your Lordship will see that Mr. Pritchard has exercised here an influence fatal to the interests of the Queen, that his ignorance has been her ruin— I standing in the position that I do in regard to her tried all I could do to induce her to comply with the moderate demands of the Admiral, but any efforts were unsuccessful; she has been grossly deceived by Mr. Pritchard, and all the mechanisms and machinery of superstition and hypocrisy has been set to work by many of the Missionaries to poison the Queen's mind against the fulfill-ment of a treaty formally signed by her, and agreed to by H.M. the King of the French— For the last few days she has been advised by Mr. Pritchard to go to his house to live, as the French wished to seize her to take her to France, and every childish report has been spread to frighten her to stay with him in order that other advice might not reach her— Oh, my Lord, I call on you, justice calls on you, to censure in your strongest language the unwarrantable interference of the Commodore of H.R.M. ships of war and Mr. Pritchard in the affairs of this island an interference that has for its intention the embroiling of the two greatest nations of the world in war for the benefit of Missionary ignorance, superstitution and intolerance— We are contented to live under the French Govt. satisfied of its justice and protection, it is only Missionaries who fear the destruction of their hierarchy and despotism that are discontented and envious— What could have been given more to the Queen, her people, and foreigners than was given by the terms of the treaty — The most solemn declarations were given by the French that the Missionar-ies should receive every protection and equal favor, but equality on any scale is not what they want, they want overwhelming influence & power, and like priesthood in all times & ages of the world are not content either with equality of privileges or protection— I say I will always defend my opinion that the Queen, by agreeing with the French Govt. would have been happy, indepen-dent & respected; but her Consular and ghostly adviser Mr. Pritchard would not let her receive the benefit of either happiness, independence, or respect, but by counsuelling her to stand in opposition to the French Govt. has caused her to forfeit all that could render her what her true friends wish her to be — The only cause why Mr. Pritchard has so advised her is in my opinion this: that by giving the Queen the appearance of a martyr for the sake of religion, he wishes to enlist in her, or more properly speaking, his favor, the whole religious population of England— Mr. Pritchard has been playing a deep game, but as is usual in some cases, the cards have turned against him— For the sake of the maintenance of religious depotism he has staked what he ought not to have done, the happiness of the Queen; he has lost what he staked, but unfortunately the loss here to be sustained by another. But he is only another example how priesthood cares not, heeds not, how she squanders away the happiness or good of others so long as her own insatiable ambition is satisfied — In conclusion I have to beg your Lordship's attention to the above written account

And remain
Your Lordship's most obt servt
Alex Salmon

Bibliography

This book is not an academic history with its customary specific references to back up all of its key arguments. My most important witnesses have been credited in the text when quoted. A recent list of my more valuable sources, even though prudently winnowed, added up to ninety-three authors, and if the "various works" of such prolific authorities as Kenneth Emory or Elsdon Best were counted, it would run well over three hundred entries. What is the purpose of this sort of compilation except to give the author a chance to show off?

During some twenty-five or thirty years of immersion in the subject of Polynesian culture, with its pertinent affinities, one absorbs a lot of useful insight without knowing precisely where every jot of it comes from. Indeed, if the source of each thought were pinpointed the result would be only a compilation of related items, the sort of stuff that we feed into computers in order to store it, sort it one way or the other, and feed it back. The conclusions one distills, the enlightenment one is able to put forth, the feelings one can arouse, are, it seems to me, the more important contributions that an author may make. So to anyone wishing to draw different conclusions from the same reading matter, I refer him to C. R. H. Taylor's *Pacific Bibliography*. Everything I have read is almost certainly listed there and easy to find under the pertinent headings.

The places I have been in Polynesia and the people I have known there are a different matter and, I believe, a more significant one. Not many readers will have the good fortune, as I have had, to set foot on some thirty-four of the various Polynesian islands; on many of them several times and on some of them for periods that add up to years. The people of course are quantitatively uncountable and qualitatively unassessable.

However, for readers who have not yet made an acquaintance with these most fascinating people (except perhaps to have seen the movie *Kon Tiki*) here is a brief list of what seem to me the best introductory books. Read them at your peril: they are likely to lead you into a wonderland that has no bounds.

For those who want easy reading to get their feet wet:
1. THE ISLAND CIVILIZATIONS OF POLYNESIA by Robert C. Suggs
2. VIKINGS OF THE SUNRISE by Peter Buck (Te Rangi Hiroa)
3. TYPEE and OMOO by Herman Melville
4. NOA NOA by Paul Gauguin
5. MARRIAGE DE LOTI by Pierre Loti
6. NO MORE GAS by Nordoff and Hall

For those who want to swim out a bit further:
1. MAN'S CONQUEST OF THE PACIFIC by Peter Bellwood
2. POLYNESIAN RESEARCHES by William Ellis
3. NARRATIVE OF A WHALING VOYAGE by Frederick Bennett
4. ACCOUNT OF THE TONGA ISLANDS by William Mariner
5. WE THE TIKOPIA by Raymond Firth
6. THE JOURNAL OF JAMES MORRISON
7. MEMOIRS OF ARIITAIMAI by Henry Adams
8. OF ISLANDS AND MEN by H. E. Maude
9. ANCIENT TAHITI by Teuira Henry
10. JOURNALS OF JAMES COOK, edited by J. C. Beaglehole
11. JOURNALS OF JOSEPH BANKS, edited by J. C. Beaglehole
12. ANCIENT TAHITIAN SOCIETY by Douglas Oliver

Index

In most cases page numbers refer to first mention. Numbers with asterisk are the more important references.

253